THE ART OF BYZANTIUM

I VISION OF EZEKIEL. Detail from the Homilies of Gregory Nazianzus. 867–86. *Paris. Bibliothèque Nationale*; Ms. gr. 510. f438. v.

THE ART OF
BYZANTIUM

TEXT AND NOTES BY DAVID TALBOT RICE

PHOTOGRAPHS BY MAX HIRMER

44 COLOUR PLATES
196 MONOCHROME PLATES

HARRY N. ABRAMS INC · NEW YORK

CONTENTS

PREFACE

The idea of a book on the art of Byzantium was originally inspired by the theme of the exhibition of Byzantine art held at Edinburgh in August and September and in London in October and early November 1958. But on reflection it seemed that a more comprehensive volume, which would take into account the larger works which could not be moved as well as others of the small ones, which were too fragile or too precious to be transported, would be both more complete and more useful. The scope of the book is, however, limited, for it is concerned with the art of Constantinople only, and not with work done elsewhere within the Byzantine area. But both works on a large scale which are preserved in the city to this day, and small ones which there is, for one reason or another, good evidence to assign to Constantinople, are dealt with. There are, of course, vast numbers of works falling into both categories which it has not been possible to consider here, but an attempt has been made to include all the more important monuments of the city and the majority of the essentially typical ones from among the small things that are now to be found elsewhere. Thus nearly every work that can be definitely dated, with the exception of manuscripts, has been noted, as well as examples of each of the groups into which the various arts can be most satisfactorily divided for purposes of classification. The text constitutes an abridged version of the author's Rhind Lectures delivered at Edinburgh in the spring of 1959, and at the Courtauld Institute in London the same summer.

The plates have been arranged as nearly as possible in chronological order, though exact sequence has sometimes been broken in order to effect stylistic comparisons or for technical reasons. The descriptions of the plates are fairly full, and arguments as to dating or attribution to Constantinople rather than to some other centre have been included in the descriptions. The actual text is of a more general character, intended primarily as an introduction. No attempt has been made to give complete bibliographies for each object illustrated, but in each description the most up-to-date or essential writings have been noted, and the reader who desires further information will be able to find it by turning to these. A key to the titles cited in brief will be found before the descriptions of the plates.

Some of the descriptions have been drawn from the catalogue of the exhibition, in the preparation of which Mr John Beckwith of the Victoria and Albert Museum in London was associated with me. In particular the discussions of the objects illustrated in Plates IV, 36, 44-5, 72-3, 74-5, 78, and 152-3 reflect his views, and I take this opportunity of expressing my thanks to him for allowing me to make use of them. I would also like to express my thanks to Dr Paul Underwood and the Byzantine Institute of America for allowing me to use some of their photographs of mosaics in Sancta Sophia at Constantinople, and to them and Feridun Bey Diremtekin for allowing photographs to be taken in Sancta Sophia, St Eirene, Kariye Cami, and Fetiye Cami. Every help was given for photographing in the Archaeological Museum at Istanbul, thanks to the kindness of the Director General of Antiquities at Ankara and the Director of the Museum, Rüstem Duyuran. Help was also accorded in numerous museums and treasuries all over Europe, and Professor Hirmer joins me in expressing his thanks to the authorities of these museums, especially those of the British Museum, the Bodleian Library, and the Victoria and Albert Museum in Britain, the Bibliothèque Nationale and the Louvre in France, the Museo Nazionale at Florence, and the Treasury of San Marco and the Marcian Library in Venice. We would also like to thank the Hungarian Cultural Attaché in London for procuring photographs of the crown of Constantine Monomachos at Budapest and of the Esztergom reliquary.

Edinburgh, 1959   D. TALBOT RICE

BYZANTINE ART

A SURVEY

It was in 312 that the Emperor Constantine gave his official support to Christianity, and eighteen years later the capital of the Roman Empire was formally transferred from the old and powerful city of Rome in Italy to the comparatively insignificant town of Byzantium on the shores of the Sea of Marmara, on the very confines of Europe. The new city took the name of its founder Constantine, for it was established as Constantinople, but the old name lived on, and was, in subsequent times, adopted as the normal designation for the civilization that developed under the inspiration of the new faith. Today it is used in the form Byzantine to describe the East Christian Empire which existed, except for a brief interval in the thirteenth century, until its final overthrow by the Turks in 1453. The same word is also used to designate the art that was nurtured by this new civilization, though it is often used very widely, to include any objects or works of art produced in the East Christian world as a whole. But the name Byzantium has a rather narrower connotation, in that it refers to the city itself—and it is in that sense that it is used for the title of this book.

The adoption of Christianity as the official faith of the empire may to some extent have been responsible for the decision to move the capital from Rome, so that the criticism and opposition of the conservative pagan aristocracy might be avoided; the East was also, no doubt, a more advantageous centre for the new Church, since the Christian faith had already been widely adopted there. But the main causes were political and economic; for on the one hand, the East was proving itself to be the most important section of the vast

Roman Empire from the point of view of defence, owing to the threat from the greatest rival of Greece and Rome, namely Persia, while on the other it was vital as a source of supply, not only of luxuries like spice, silk, and ivory, but also of the most urgent necessities, more especially metal and foods. Indeed, other emperors before Constantine had been exploring the possibilities of the area, and Diocletian had already thought of Nicomedia, some sixty miles distant on the Asiatic side of the straits. Had his choice been followed, a great opportunity would have been lost, for few sites in the world could boast the same geographical advantages as Byzantium; indeed, the inhabitants of Cyzicus on the Asiatic shore were mocked as blind men for their lack of foresight in not selecting the other situation.

The choice was made in 324, and the enlargement and reconstruction of the old city was set in hand at once. Work forged ahead rapidly and the new capital was officially inaugurated on May 11, 330.

The city of Constantine was a good deal smaller than that which was to emerge in the course of the next two centuries. Its basic character, however, was to remain unchanged, for the site was the triangular spit of land with the Marmara to the south-east and the Golden Horn to the north, and this permitted of expansion only in one direction, unless the natural protection of the water was sacrificed. The two natural lines of defence were joined by a single connecting wall. The line of this wall was only once extended, by Theodosios II between 413 and 447, when the defences that survive to this day were built 12, 13 parallel to those erected by Constantine, but a mile or more farther to the west. It is only within the last few years that any houses at all have come to be built outside their limits, though in the Middle Ages a new suburb, inhabited exclusively by western colonists—Venetians, Pisans, and Genoese—grew up on the opposite side of the Golden Horn; it is the suburb we know today as Galata.

Though emperors were to reign in the West conjointly with those in the East for another century and a half, the old Rome ceded its importance rapidly to the new, and

II THE ENTRY INTO JERUSALEM. Illumination from the Rossano Gospels. Sixth century. *Rossano. The Cathedral.*

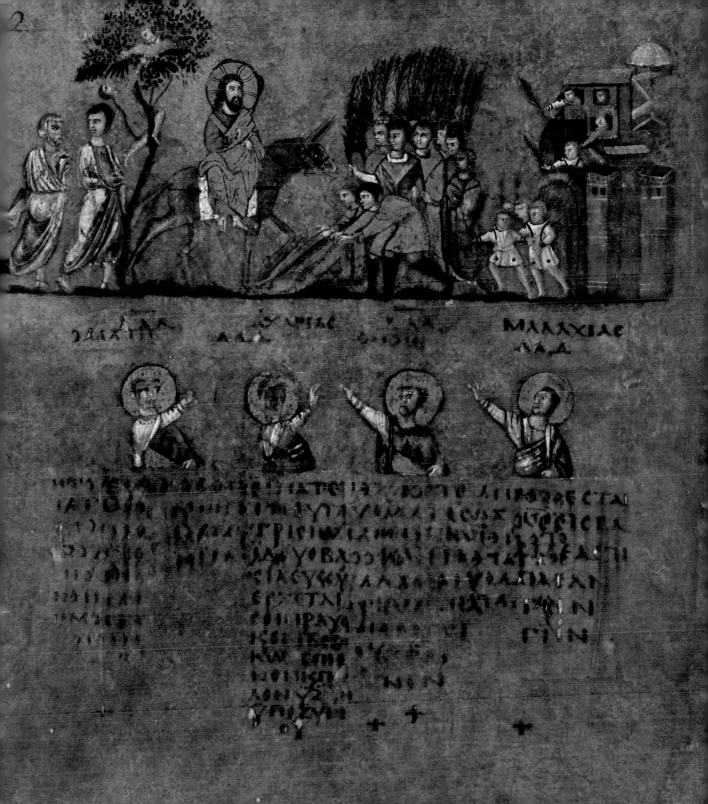

within a generation there was no disputing the fact as to which was the more significant city of the empire. And the position of Constantinople when once established was never really lost. For nearly five hundred years it was indeed to remain the chief city of the civilized world, the seat of the most powerful and stable government that was then known, the residence of the greatest emperor, the home of the primacy, and the first centre of culture and learning. For almost another four hundred years, till its conquest by the Latins in 1204, it remained the capital of what was still the most developed and highly civilized state, even if by then new rulers had sprung up in the West, who established their independence and set up empires of their own, more often than not founded on the Byzantine model. Throughout these years the city of Constantinople was the main bulwark of Christendom against the advances of Islam, given new impetus by the arrival of the Seljuk Turks on the confines of Asia Minor in the middle of the eleventh century. Throughout these years the workshops of Constantinople remained supreme in the production of the sumptuous arts—ivory carvings, textiles, or works in enamel and metal —while Byzantine artists produced for the churches decorations in mosaic and paint which have never since been equalled. It was indeed at this time that the city asserted its great artistic pre-eminence, even if the empire it controlled was much reduced in size, and it was during these very centuries that it assumed the position with regard to art that Paris held in the later nineteenth century; it was, as Diehl once stated, the Paris of the Middle Ages. As he wrote, from the tenth to the thirteenth century, Byzantium was for the West the great source of inspiration, and the whole world of the Middle Ages looked towards Constantinople as the queen of cities, considering it a town of miraculous wonders reflected against a cloud of gold.

For fifty-seven years after 1204, Latin emperors ruled at Constantinople, but new Byzantine states grew up in Greece, at Nicaea and at Trebizond, and Byzantine culture survived. Though, when the Greek emperors returned to Constantinople about 1261, their realm was small in size and greatly impoverished, art nevertheless flourished once

---

III THE COMMUNION OF THE APOSTLES. Illumination from the Rossano Gospels. Sixth century. *Rossano. The Cathedral.*

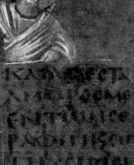

more, and it was indeed around the year 1300 that some of the most glorious of all Byzantine works in painting and mosaic were produced. And it was at this time, or shortly before, that the influence of Constantinople became greatly extended, to inspire the development of new schools of painting in Greece, the Balkans and Russia, and even to exercise an influence on developments in Italy itself.

The Turkish conquest of 1453 put an end to the story of Constantinople as a great centre of production of Christian art. But the style that had been created and developed there continued to live, and much that was good, even if it was not great, was yet to come out of Greece and the Balkans. And within the old walls, set up more than a thousand years before by Theodosius II, creation began again, for it was really in the city of Constantinople, named anew by the Turks as Istanbul, that Ottoman art saw its fullest and most complete development. The buildings, textiles and ceramics favoured by the new rulers owed much to what had gone before. Constantinople stamped them with its hallmark and, though their story falls outside the scope of this book, they are things of real beauty which deserve close attention, even if they were made for Moslem and no longer for Christian rulers.

When Constantine founded his new city, the texts tell us that he assembled there builders, technicians, artisans and artists from numerous other centres, in order to accomplish the works that he had in mind. These men inevitably brought with them the techniques, styles, or building systems that they had learnt in their native lands, so that the first works to be produced were not so very different from those that were being set up or executed elsewhere in the Roman world. Constantine's churches were basilicas, no doubt closely similar to those which survive from the fourth century in Rome, though the evidence of archaeology shows that in the East these buildings tended to be wider in comparison to their length than in the West. The oldest surviving church in Constantinople, 14, 15 that of St John of Studion, is of this type. It was built about 463, and is indeed

IV SILK TEXTILE. A LION STRANGLER. Eighth century. *London. The Victoria and Albert Museum.*
V SILK TEXTILE. THE ANNUNCIATION. *c. 800. Rome. Museo Sacro Vaticano*

conservative even for the period, for the aisles are separated by columns supporting an entablature of classical form, whereas in many basilicas this essentially conservative system had already given place to the more 'medieval' arcade. But the sculptures that decorate the western façade of the Studion show the embryo of a change, for the straightforward naturalism of the classical style has already begun to give place to a more abstract, more formal treatment. The development that we see here was indeed heralded in the previous century in the works of Theodosios I. It was carried further in the next century, as the

50, 51 cornices of SS. Sergius and Bacchus, built between 527 and 536, or the capitals of Jus-
57 tinian's age serve to show. In architectural ornament the new style saw its culmination
54, 56 in the great church of the Holy Wisdom (Sancta Sophia), built between 532 and 537. The capitals and cornices there are clearly enough in a new and distinct manner; they are in fact Byzantine in the narrower sense of the term, and they illustrate the way in which the new art developed out of the old in this particular sphere. Old elements, like the Ionic volutes or the acanthus leaf ornament, survive, but they have been formalized and stylized till they are now almost abstract. The changes that took place here were paralleled in figural work, though they were less definite and more complex in character. They too took more than a century to develop.

It was natural that for a century or so after the adoption of Christianity the old Roman art of portrait sculpture should remain important. Busts and statues of individuals, members of the imperial family, consuls or notables, were thus produced, and many examples are to be found in the galleries of the Archaeological Museum at Istanbul;

4 recently a head, for long disregarded, has been identified as that of Constantine him-self. There was at first little to distinguish most of these works from sculpture done in other cities of the Roman Empire. But by the end of the fourth century a change had set in, and the nature of the sculptures on the base of the Egyptian obelisk in the Hippodrome

5 at Constantinople shows this quite definitely. The base was set up by Theodosios I about 395. The frontal poses of the figures, the serried ranks in which they are grouped, and the

---

VI THE RAISING OF LAZARUS AND THE ENTRY INTO JERUSALEM. From the Homilies of Gregory Nazianzus. 867–86. *Paris. Bibliothèque Nationale*; Ms. gr. 510. f196. v.

rather large accentuated heads are characteristic. All these features were the result of oriental influence; they were developed in works done in the Parthian world at a rather earlier date, and they probably came to Constantinople by way of Syria and southern Asia Minor, where there were important schools of sculpture in the third and fourth centuries.

But not all the sculpture of the Theodosian period was of this character; some of it
8 indeed was much more classical in style, like a fragmentary relief found at Bakirkoy just outside the city, while other work boasted an elegance and polish that was distinctly
9 Greek, for example the carving on a child's sarcophagus to be dated to about 400 from the city itself. It is usually known as the Sarigüzel sarcophagus. Its reliefs are more re-strained in style than those on the Theodosios base, and we see here for the first time hints of that balanced, clear-cut, precise, even exquisite manner which was later to be developed as the most outstanding characteristic of the art of Byzantium. The style is paralleled in
35 the acanthus leaf ornament which decorates a statue base, dug up near the Hippodrome in 1927. It is to be seen again in the carvings that adorn part of a ciborium or altar
63 canopy now preserved in the Archaeological Museum, which must date from the time of Justinian or slightly later; the clear-cut, precise style, the combination of stylization and naturalism, of straightforward representation and of spiritual feeling, is already charac-teristic of developed Byzantine art. It may be compared to a very lovely little head in the
61 Castello at Milan, which is in all probability to be identified as that of Theodora, Justinian's consort. Certain features, such as the type of hairdressing, make this rather easier to date than the canopy, for such worldly details are absent in the more conven-tionalized heads of the apostles on the arch.

It is, however, in the mosaic floor that decorated a portion of the Great Palace of the Byzantine emperors, and which has recently been unearthed by an expedition sponsored by the Walker Trust of St Andrews, that the developing art of the capital during the period of formation can be seen at its finest. This pavement originally occupied a cloister-like colonnade on four sides of a great square court; each side was about seventy metres

---

VII THE VISION OF EZEKIEL. From the Homilies of Gregory Nazianzus. 867–86. *Paris. Bibliothèque Nationale*; Ms. gr. 510. f438. v.

long by ten metres deep. On it were depicted a series of individual figures, buildings, or scenes, all unconnected with one another, and each shown separately against a plain white background. Many of the compositions were conceived in an essentially natura-

38–41 listic manner; there was a great feeling for the picturesque; grandeur and elegance were hallmarks of the work. In many ways, indeed, the figures are close to classical models, and much of the work has a distinctly Greek flavour. But it is not wholly naturalistic; only on very few occasions is the ground on which the figures stand indicated at all; there are no cast shadows, and there is a curious abstract feeling about the work which is medieval rather than antique. In fact, in spite of the conservative nature of its elements, the composition is experimental, and attests the birth of a new style in just the same way as do the architectural sculptures of the Studion or SS. Sergius and Bacchus, or figural work in marble, as in the Sarigüzel sarcophagus.

Apart from their interest as illustrating the birth of a new artistic outlook, these mosaics are extremely important in themselves. Their technique is of the finest and is extraordinarily delicate, the palette is extremely rich, drawing upon practically every conceivable shade of natural stone, in addition to blues, greens, and yellow in glass, and the scenes are astonishingly varied. One of the most exciting is a portrait—or so it would seem: a great moustached head which forms part of the border. The hair is intermingled with the scrolls of which the principal part of the border is made up; the colours do not follow nature, for the moustache is blue and the hair in places green; yet the general effect is extraordinarily expressive and natural. We see here that combination of stylization and vividness which later became a hallmark of Byzantine art.

Thus, in brief, the centuries between the reigns of Constantine and Justinian saw in general a decline of the truly classical style and the substitution of a new, more abstract outlook, which is admirably illustrated in silver work by a vessel in the Hermitage at

28, 29 Leningrad called the dish of Paternus. But developments were far from uniform, for much was also done that was surprisingly antique in character, and there exist in various

---

VIII THE PRAYER OF HANNAH. From the Paris Psalter. Ninth century. *Paris. Bibliothèque Nationale*; Ms. gr. 139.

+ Η ΠΡΟΦΗΤΙΟ ΆΝΝΑ
ΗΜΗΡ ΟΑΜΟΥ ΗΛ
Ἀ ΝΘΟΜΟΛΟΓΟΥΜΕΝΗ
ΤΩ ΙΘΩ ΚΑΙ ΛΕΓΟΥΟΑ ⁘

42, 74, 75 museums, but more especially in the Hermitage, numerous silver plates with classical subjects upon them, which would at first glance pass for products of workshops in Rome or Alexandria of the third century, did they not bear 'hallmarks' or control stamps in the names of emperors from Anastasius (491–518) to Heraclius (610–641). A technical study shows that these stamps were usually put on before the designs were finished, so there can be no question of their being later additions. Finds of such silver vessels have been very widely spread, from Syria and Cyprus in the south to Central Russia in the north, and it would seem that they were not only used and treasured in the late Roman and early Christian worlds, but were also exported outside the confines of the empire, where they were probably exchanged for luxuries such as furs. But, although they have been found so far afield, there is reason to believe that all the vessels bearing 'hallmarks' were made in the royal workshops at Constantinople.

Apart from this classicizing silver, a good deal of other metal work was produced, much of it of very fine quality. Stylistic evidence suggests that some of it was made in places other than the capital. But such works as the series of silver plates from Cyprus, bearing scenes from the life of David, and now divided between the Island, New York 72, 73 and the British Museum, are in all probability to be assigned to Constantinople. The designs are in low relief. The style is still classical, akin to that of the finest sculpture of 5 the age, and the oriental rigidity and frontality of the Theodosius base has given place to something more elegant and refined. But even more typical of all that Constantinople stood for is the lovely dish in the Archaeological Museum in the city itself bearing as its decoration a seated female figure, the 'Personification of India', surrounded by beasts 43 regarded as characteristic of her realm. It was found at Lampsacus in north-western Anatolia. The way in which the figures are, as it were, silhouetted against an open-work background is close to that of the mosaic floor of the Great Palace.

All these vessels, in the accomplishment and elegance of their style, are typical of Constantinople, and one or two other pieces of silver may be noted by way of contrast.

IX THE PRAYER OF ISAIAH. From the Paris Psalter. Ninth century. *Paris. Bibliothèque Nationale*; Ms. gr. 139.

ΝΥΞ

ΗСΑΙΑС

ὄρθρος

400 there must have been enough trained artisans in the former city to preclude the likelihood of work being commissioned elsewhere. But there is always the possibility that
the carver working in Rome or Constantinople might have been trained in another
centre, notably Alexandria or Antioch, where there were also important workshops, as
was the case with the silversmith who made the plates depicting the Communion of the
Apostles referred to above.

The earliest in date of these diptychs, and also the most characteristically Roman, is
that of Probus, who was appointed Consul at Rome in 408; it is now at Aosta. The
consul wears Roman military uniform; he stands frontally, a solid, matter-of-fact figure,
and the whole ivory is redolent of that interest in recording fact as it was which characterized so much Roman art. The diptychs done for consuls at Constantinople did not
20, 22 begin till nearly a century later with that of Areobindus, Consul in 506. He must have
been a rich man with numerous friends, or a very vain one, for no less than seven ivories
in his name have survived to this day, and there were perhaps originally others. All of
these are different one from another, but there are two main types; on one, the consul is
seated on a throne, while circus games take place below—or rather in front of—him, for
the perspective is that known as vertical, where the scene farther away is placed vertically
above that nearer to the spectator. On the other type the ornament is of a formal character,
consisting of cornucopias or acanthus leaves; in an example in the Louvre a bust of the
consul appears in a medallion at the centre. The figure is disposed in a severely frontal
position, but the face is well modelled and the features are full. This is the most Constantinopolitan of the ivories in Areobindus' name. The floral work is characterized by a
hard, rather metallic style, which is not far removed from that of the stone sculptures done
in the city or in the neighbouring quarries on the Marmara Islands.

23 The next consuls of Constantinople whose ivories survive are Clementinus (513),
Anthemius (515) and Anastasius (517), the first two represented by one ivory each, the
26 last by as many as six. One of these, in the Bibliothèque Nationale at Paris, may be

---

XI PORTRAIT OF THE EMPEROR BASIL II BULGAROCTONOS. From the Psalter of Basil II.
976–1025. *Venice. The Marcian Library*; Cod. Gr. 17.

26

69 Two patens, one in the Istanbul Museum and one in the Dumbarton Oaks Collection at Washington are most important; both bear the scene of the Communion of the Apostles, where Christ officiates as priest. The heads are large, the treatment rather crude, and the style forceful rather than refined. This is the manner characteristic of Syria, and, though both plates bear hallmarks, they are Syrian in style; perhaps they were made by a man trained at Antioch, who was working in Constantinople. Both belong to the sixth century. Another work which is also probably to be regarded as Syrian is a famous piece now in an American collection, the Antioch chalice. It has a plain silver core, over which there is an open scroll design in which occasional small figures disport them-selves. The scroll is closely similar to those that appear in Syrian architectural sculpture of the fourth and fifth centuries, and there is every reason to attribute the chalice to the same date. Certainly a claim once put forward that this was to be identified with the chalice used at the Last Supper cannot be taken seriously.

By far the most complicated problems of attribution arise with regard to the ivories, of which there are a good many examples dating from the period between about 400 and the age of Justinian; there are, indeed, more important ivories than there are works in all other materials put together. Happily a firm basis on which to establish a system of classification is furnished by the consular diptychs, tall ivory leaves which were carved to celebrate the assumption of office by the Consuls until the office was abolished in 541. They were apparently distributed by the consuls to their friends, like wedding invitations today; the wedding invitations, indeed, retain the same two-leaved form. Two consuls were appointed, one in the West at Rome, and one in the East, at Constantinople; their identity is in most cases recorded, so that it is certain in which place the consul held office—and that serves as a useful guide as to where his diptych was carved, though the evidence does suggest that the diptychs were sometimes made 'in series' and that the name of the consul who ordered them was added subsequently. It is, however, probable that these diptychs were all carved respectively in Constantinople and in Rome; by around

X RELIQUARY FOR THE TRUE CROSS. Enamels at centre of the outer container. *c. 955. Limburg on the Lahn. Cathedral Treasury.*

24

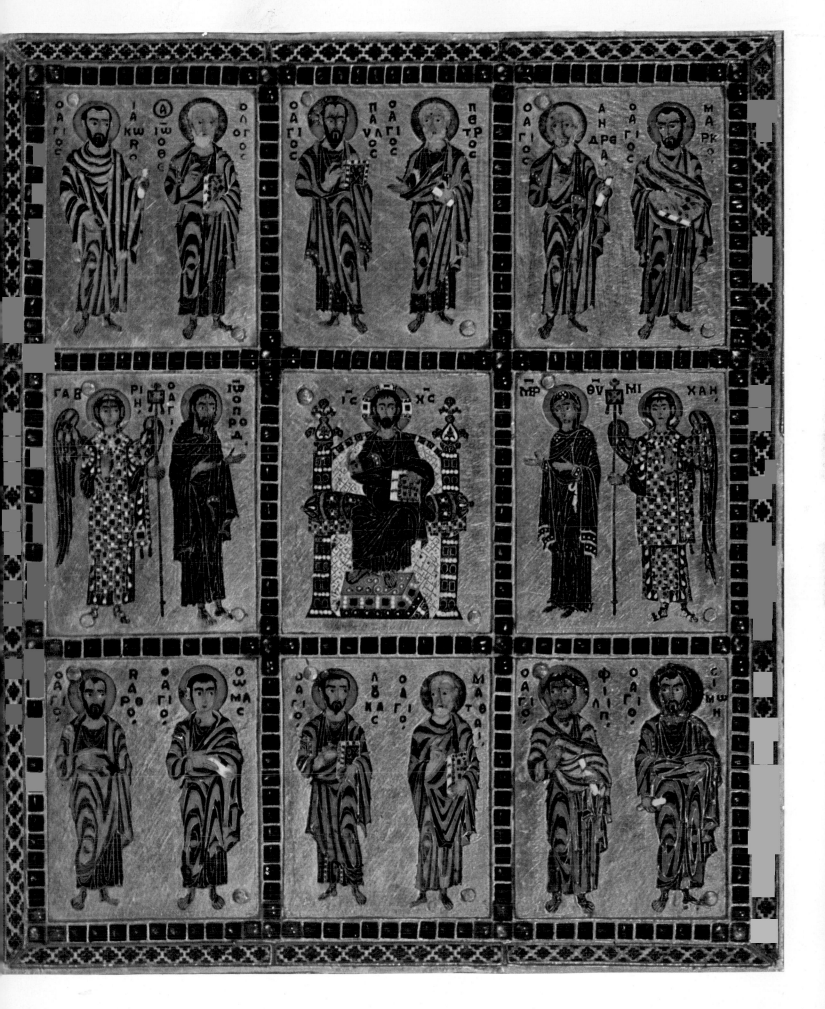

400 there must have been enough trained artisans in the former city to preclude the likelihood of work being commissioned elsewhere. But there is always the possibility that the carver working in Rome or Constantinople might have been trained in another centre, notably Alexandria or Antioch, where there were also important workshops, as was the case with the silversmith who made the plates depicting the Communion of the Apostles referred to above.

The earliest in date of these diptychs, and also the most characteristically Roman, is that of Probus, who was appointed Consul at Rome in 408; it is now at Aosta. The consul wears Roman military uniform; he stands frontally, a solid, matter-of-fact figure, and the whole ivory is redolent of that interest in recording fact as it was which characterized so much Roman art. The diptychs done for consuls at Constantinople did not begin till nearly a century later with that of Areobindus, Consul in 506. He must have been a rich man with numerous friends, or a very vain one, for no less than seven ivories in his name have survived to this day, and there were perhaps originally others. All of these are different one from another, but there are two main types; on one, the consul is seated on a throne, while circus games take place below—or rather in front of—him, for the perspective is that known as vertical, where the scene farther away is placed vertically above that nearer to the spectator. On the other type the ornament is of a formal character, consisting of cornucopias or acanthus leaves; in an example in the Louvre a bust of the consul appears in a medallion at the centre. The figure is disposed in a severely frontal position, but the face is well modelled and the features are full. This is the most Constantinopolitan of the ivories in Areobindus' name. The floral work is characterized by a hard, rather metallic style, which is not far removed from that of the stone sculptures done in the city or in the neighbouring quarries on the Marmara Islands.

The next consuls of Constantinople whose ivories survive are Clementinus (513), Anthemius (515) and Anastasius (517), the first two represented by one ivory each, the last by as many as six. One of these, in the Bibliothèque Nationale at Paris, may be

XI PORTRAIT OF THE EMPEROR BASIL II BULGAROCTONOS. From the Psalter of Basil II. 976–1025. *Venice. The Marcian Library*; Cod. Gr. 17.

26

noted, for here the clear-cut, precise manner, which is to be regarded as characteristic of the capital, is to be seen very clearly indeed. The victories above, and the vivid hunting scene below, are both typical; details of the latter scene may be compared with those of the Great Palace mosaic; it is probable that the artists who did scenes of this sort had recourse to pattern books from which they drew, though they always knew how to make their renderings alive, and it is rare to find exact duplicates. The variants are, however, similar enough over long periods of time and in far removed regions to suggest that the pattern books were available.

Next in date was Magnus (518), in whose name there are five surviving ivories; then comes Justinian (521) with three. Those of Magnus are even more Constantino-
27 politan than those of Areobindus, for example one in the Bibliothèque Nationale at Paris. The frontally disposed attitude, the deeply cut eyes, the rounded cheeks and the precise elegance of the carving may be taken as typical of the figural work of the capital at this date, while the stylized palmettes surrounding an inscription at the centre, and the
31 acanthus leaves at the corner of a diptych in the name of Justinian, also in the Bibliothèque Nationale, are equally typical of Constantinopolitan ornament. A more restrained,
30 rather dry style, characterizes a leaf in the name of Philoxenus (525) in the same collection, but perhaps the most interesting thing here is the inscription, in beautifully formed letters, left in relief when the background was cut away; more often, and indeed even here at the centre, the letters of the inscriptions were incised. Almost the last of these ivories is a leaf at Oviedo in Spain in the name of Apion (539). It is similar to that of Justinian in the Bibliothèque Nationale, except that there is a bust of the consul at the centre instead of an inscription. The carving of the acanthus rosettes at the corners is perhaps a little harder, but the consul's bust is particularly well done, and the work is by a carver of com-petence; his hand was a good deal surer than that of the man who did the Philoxenus leaf at Paris.

In addition to the consular diptychs, which can be associated with Constantinople on the evidence of fact, there seems every reason to assign to the capital also a number of ivories of another class; these are usually called the imperial diptychs, though the name is a little misleading, since they can hardly all originally have been of diptych form. This is especially true of the most important of them, a supremely fine ivory made up of five
19 separate pieces, though one is now missing. It is in the Louvre and is known as the Barberini ivory. At the centre is an emperor on horseback; at one side, the figure of a

XII SILK. THE CHASUBLE OF ST ALBUIN. *c.* 1000. *Bressanone. The Cathedral Treasury.*

consul in military costume holding a statue of victory; at the top is a bust of Christ with winged victories on either side; below is a long panel which shows Gothic emissaries offering gifts on one side and on the other an embassy from India, presenting ivories and other oriental treasures. The emperor's head is in high relief and his features are individual and personal; they are indeed recognizable, on the basis of coins, as those of the Emperor Anastasius, and this identification is supported by history, for that emperor received an embassy from India in 496 and won a victory over the Goths two years later. The ivory is thus probably to be assigned to about 500. The round faces are similar to those on the diptych of Consul Anastasius (517), and the excellence of the technique and the quality of the carving, especially in the imperial portrait, all support an attribution to Constantinople; indeed, where else would one be more likely to find a work of this sort being produced? Two horizontal leaves at Milan, one with the bust of an empress supported by two winged victories, the other with tribute-bearing embassies like the section at the bottom of the Barberini ivory, must have belonged originally to another large composite panel.

The same brilliance of technique, the same round features, and the same high relief, are to be seen on two ivories representing an empress, one in Florence and the other in Vienna; on the former the empress is standing, orb in one hand, sceptre in the other; on the latter she is seated; the rich imperial costume is the same on each. Both are obviously to be assigned to Constantinople and both must date from around 500. An interesting portrait of Juliana Anicia which forms the frontispiece to a copy of the works of Dioscorides, now in Vienna, may be compared with these. It was done at Constantinople about 512.

Which of the other early ivories that have come down to us should be assigned to Constantinople is no easy question to solve. They comprise diptych leaves, pyxides, and panels from caskets or perhaps from great composite works like the famous throne of Maximian at Ravenna, and the authorities have but seldom been in accord one with the other in assigning them to the various possible centres; and curiously enough there has been a general tendency to neglect Constantinople in favour of other places, especially Alexandria. True, Alexandria was an important city and was closer to the sources from which the ivory came, but Constantinople was the capital; there were more powerful and more important patrons there than anywhere else, and sculptures and mosaics that have been found there, and which were certainly produced there, serve to give an indication of

30

III MOSAIC. THE ZOE PANEL. 1028–42. *Constantinople. Sancta Sophia.*

the amount and quality of the work on a large scale that was done there under imperial patronage. It surely stands to reason that many of the smaller things were made there also. One or two of the ivories, the origin of which is not firmly established, stand out particularly, notably the leaf of a diptych in the British Museum, bearing the Archangel Michael. The archangel has the full face and the elegant proportions, and the work shows the finished clear-cut style, that characterized the capital; but oriental elements have influenced the artist's approach here more than in any of the consular or imperial diptychs we have noted, for the understanding is spiritual and poetic rather than mundane and prosaic, as was that of so much Roman art. The angel stands above a flight of steps, but he is detached from them; he and the earth are dissociated: he belongs to the spiritual, the steps to the mundane world. We are in fact in the presence of an essentially Christian work, in which a new aesthetic, a new transcendental outlook, governs the nature of the sculpture just as it governs the understanding and spatial conceptions of a building like Sancta Sophia.

A more controversial problem is raised with regard to the place of origin of the famous throne of Maximian at Ravenna. It was carved for Bishop Maximian early in the sixth century. The bishop's monogram is in Greek, and there are assembly marks in Greek on some of the numerous plaques of which the throne is composed. At least four hands are to be distinguished. One was almost certainly an Alexandrian; he did the scenes from Joseph's life on the sides. Another may have been a Syrian; he did the ornamental scrolls. But the Bible scenes on the back and the evangelists and baptist on the front could well have been carved in Constantinople, and it is possible that some of the work was done there rather than elsewhere, though the case for Constantinople is on the whole less well substantiated than that for Alexandria.

That this new style should at some time or other have burst into flower was perhaps inevitable, but that it did so with such glory at the middle of the sixth century was to a great extent due to the patronage of one man, the Emperor Justinian (527–563).

XIV BOOK COVER. Gold and enamel. Twelfth century. *Venice. The Marcian Library*; Ms. Lat. Cl. 3, No. 111.

His name is familiar as the first to put the laws in order, and the code of Justinian is famous even today. He, with the aid of the great general Belisarius, extended the frontiers of the empire in the west far beyond Italy, and in the south into Africa; the advancing Goths and barbarians were beaten back in the north, Persia was menaced in the East; not since the hey-day of Rome had the empire been so extensive or so well organized. And along with this material prosperity the arts flourished anew, under a patronage more lavish even than that of such an emperor as Theodosios I. New cities were founded, a vast new building programme was put in hand which extended to every corner of the empire, and the decoration of the new buildings was conceived on a particularly lavish scale. San Vitale at Ravenna was set up under his patronage and Sant' Apollinare in Classe and Sant' Apollinare Nuovo were decorated with mosaics: the churches of the Nativity at Bethlehem and the Holy Sepulchre at Jerusalem were rebuilt; cities like Tsaritsingrad in Yugoslavia were founded. But it was the capital that benefited most from the emperor's munificence. Architects, mosaicists, craftsmen of every sort were assembled there, and a vast programme of work was set in hand both in the secular and in the religious field. Alas, we know but little of the additions that he made to the palace or of the other secular works for which he was responsible; the only structures that have retained anything like their original appearance are the great underground cisterns; the finest is that known today by its Turkish name of Bin-bir-derek, the 'Thousand and One Columns', the architect of which is generally supposed to have been Anthemios of Tralles, one of the two men 67 responsible for Sancta Sophia. Its immensely tall columns, jointed at the middle with sockets, are most original and are unparalleled in any of the numerous other cisterns of Constantinople, in all of which normal columns and capitals appear; often indeed they are old material re-used, as in a cistern near Sancta Sophia known by the Turkish name of Yeri-batan-Saray.

Of Justinian's major religious foundations three now survive—St Eirene, SS. Sergius and Bacchus, and Sancta Sophia. The first of these, completed soon after 532, is

XV BOOK COVER. THE ARCHANGEL MICHAEL. Enamel on gold. Eleventh century. *Venice. The Treasury of St Mark's.*

the most conservative of the three, for its ground plan is still that of a three-aisled basilica,

52, 53 though above it is roofed by two domes, set longitudinally one in front of the other. The extensive use of domes, set on pendentives over a basis square in plan, was perhaps the most outstanding of the Byzantine contributions to architecture; indeed Byzantine architecture from the time of Justinian onwards virtually consisted of an infinite series of variations on the themes of dome, cross, square and rectangle. The church of St Eirene has been considerably altered since the sixth century; the original columns that separate the aisles have been replaced by others, not uniform in size; the western dome and its substructures have been rebuilt, and there are other superficial changes, but apart from these details the general plan of the church is fairly typical of the sort of building that was the normal place of worship in the sixth century. The cross in mosaic at the east end is, however, an addition of the Iconoclast period (see p. 46). Originally there would probably have been a figure of the Virgin like that at Parenzo, or a scene like those in San Vitale or Sant' Apollinare in Classe at Ravenna.

The church of SS. Sergius and Bacchus has undergone less change, for its structure remains unaltered, though its interior decoration has been destroyed and none of the mosaics which must once have adorned its walls survive. But the rich ornamental

50, 51 cornices are there; they are more elaborate and show finer work than those in the closely similar church of San Vitale at Ravenna. The two churches have much the same plan, an open octagon surrounded by an aisle of the same form, but the projecting presbytery, which is such an important feature of San Vitale, is absent in the Constantinopolitan church. The latter was begun in 527 and finished in 536; San Vitale was completed rather later. It is perhaps to be regarded as a copy of the Constantinopolitan original, and certain features in it, notably the presence of an impost block above the capitals, suggest that the inventions of the Byzantine architects were followed in Ravenna without always being fully understood. In Constantinople the impost block was omitted, for the new type of capital that had been evolved there made it unnecessary.

XVI PAINTING ON SILK. ST JUST. Detail. Eleventh century. *Trieste. Cathedral of St Just.*

It was, however, in the great church of the Holy Wisdom, better known as Sancta Sophia, that the genius of Justinian's architects reached its culmination; there is probably no other building in the world which was in its day at the same time so original and so fully developed, for it was not only something that in its architecture and its decoration was entirely new, but also, in its style, completely perfect. It consists of a vast dome set over a square, on supports which are almost invisible from the inside, so that it seems, as a contemporary wrote, as if the arc of heaven were suspended on chains. Below, hints of the old basilican plan survive, for there are three aisles, separated by columns. But the spatial conception is quite distinct, for the basilica, however fine an individual building might be, was nevertheless based on an essentially limited plan, and the form inevitably lacked the aspiring qualities of Sancta Sophia. There is something profoundly spiritual in the conception of Justinian's great cathedral, symptomatic of the whole of Byzantine thought at this time. It serves to illustrate the fundamentally religious basis which had by the sixth century become characteristic of the new Christian world.

The outside of Sancta Sophia was severe and plain, and although it has been considerably altered, especially by the addition of the four minarets, it must have been much the same when it was built. Indeed, this is a feature of the Byzantine style, which again reflects the character of Byzantine thought; the interior, like the man's soul, is more important than the exterior, his body. The Parthenon, superb outside but restricted and limited within, forms an apt contrast. The decoration of the interior of Sancta Sophia, however, was as sumptuous as the exterior was plain. There were rich marble slabs on the walls below; they survive to this day, but are sorely in need of cleaning and polishing. Above there were mosaics, but the greater part of the original work has gone and such figural mosaics as are now to be seen—and there are some very fine ones—are of later date, for all those of Justinian's time were torn down in the eighth century (see p. 46). But perhaps even more important than all this were the rich furnishings of carved marble, of gold and silver, of ivory and of precious stones, the like of which are now to be found

---

XVII THE CROWNING OF DAVID. Miniature from a Psalter. 1066. *London. The British Museum;* Add. 19352. f106. r.

on a small scale only in museums and treasuries. It is possible to gather some idea of what
58, 59 the mosaics were once like in the churches of San Vitale or Sant' Apollinare Nuovo at
Ravenna. But superb though these are, it must be remembered that they were provincial
works, while those of Sancta Sophia were done by the finest craftsmen and the greatest
artists of the age, for its most important building. In the absence of figural work in Sancta
Sophia, a mosaic showing four archangels which was preserved in the church of the
76, 77 Assumption of the Virgin at Nicaea until 1922 may be cited. The complete destruction
of the church in that year during the Graeco-Turkish war is one of the greatest tragedies
of art history of recent times. The archangels were outstandingly lovely, and there is
reason to suppose that they represented the work of the best Constantinopolitan craftsmen
of the time of Justinian or slightly later.

Most of the other great imperial foundations of the capital were also decorated
with mosaics, while the poorer churches had wall paintings; their number was legion,
but practically nothing survives. There are, however, a few illustrated manuscripts that
belong to this age, notably a copy of Genesis at Vienna, a fragment of the Gospel of St
Matthew, known as the Sinope manuscript, in the Bibliothèque Nationale at Paris, and
a copy of the Gospels at Rossano in southern Italy. There has been a good deal of dispute
among the authorities as to where these manuscripts were illustrated. The Sinope fragment was almost certainly done in southern Asia Minor, for it is very oriental in style.
The Vienna Genesis is similar, but rather more refined; it is possible that it was done in
Constantinople itself, though western Asia Minor would seem more likely. The Rossano
Gospels is of a much more monumental character; the Bible scenes are painted with
great feeling, and there seems good reason to assign it to Constantinople and to the sixth
century, whatever may be concluded with regard to the others. The Bible scenes are
especially interesting, in that we see in them for practically the first time a developed
Christian iconography and a fully fledged Byzantine style. The scene of the Entry into
Jerusalem for example has in it all the features that were to characterize the illustration of

XVIII–XIX MINIATURES FROM MANUSCRIPT OF THE OCTATEUCH. Twelfth century.
Istanbul. Library of Topkapu Saray; Codex 8. f471. v. (above), f43. v. (below).

that scene for the next thousand years, while Christ is already the rather sombre bearded

II, III figure of developed Byzantine art. This rendering may be contrasted with that in the mosaics of San Vitale, where He is shown as youthful and beardless, like a classical Apollo. The mosaics that once decorated Sancta Sophia were probably more akin in style to the Rossano manuscript than to the apse of San Vitale, and this heavier, more colourful orientalizing style is to be seen in the two famous panels in San Vitale showing

58 on one side Justinian and his courtiers and on the other his Empress Theodora.

At one time there were few works of art that the authorities attributed to the centuries succeeding the death of Justinian in 565. It is true that he left the treasury empty, that the frontiers of the empire could not be maintained at their previous extent, and that none of the rulers between 565 and 726 was a personality of the same genius. But even so, the age was by no means a negligible one, and recent research tends to assign to it a number of works which were once associated with Justinian. Justin II (565–578) thus built in the area of the Great Palace and was responsible for the execution of wall mosaics in Sancta Sophia; vestiges of them survive in a chamber above the south porch. He sent a

71 fine silver cross to the Pope, which is still preserved at the Vatican, and there is at Poitiers

70 an enamel reliquary which he presented to St Radegonde about 570. It has subsequently

33 undergone repairs and alterations. A capital at Constantinople and some silver vessels

72–75 now in Russia and Cyprus are associated with the name of Heraclius (610–641), and the same emperor doubtless also sponsored church building and decoration, for his name is noteworthy as the rescuer of the True Cross from the Persians, who had captured it

70 shortly before. An interesting ivory at Trier may perhaps also be assigned to his reign; it shows relics being conducted to a church in a procession. It is likely again that many

IV, V, of the fine textiles which were at one time associated with the period of Justinian are

78, 79 actually to be dated to the end of the seventh or even to the first half of the eighth century rather than to the sixth.

XX–XXI MINIATURES FROM MANUSCRIPT OF THE OCTATEUCH. Twelfth century. *Istanbul. Library of Topkapu Saray*; Codex 8. f257 (above), f197. v. (below).

The importance of Constantinople as a centre of textile weaving is referred to in the texts, for Procopius notes that looms were established in the Royal Palace in the time of Justinian, and very soon after that Constantinople had begun to exercise a monopoly if not in the weaving, in any case with regard to the export of silks. Authorities have, however, tended to assign the majority of the textiles of this age that survive to Egypt, because so many of them have actually been found there. But it must not be forgotten that it is only in Egypt that such perishable things have been preserved, thanks to the dry climate, and that the absence of textile finds in excavations elsewhere is purely fortuitous. The silks that we do know elsewhere all come from treasuries in the west, where they were acquired at the time of their manufacture. On stylistic grounds certain of these savour strongly of the capital. The decoration of one from the tomb of Charlemagne at Aachen,

78 now divided between Aachen Cathedral and the Cluny Museum, showing a quadriga full face, has thus been compared to those of some of the consular diptychs. Its Constantinopolitan origin is not to be disputed, but it can hardly be dated as early as the sixth century, as was once proposed, for it seems inconceivable that Charlemagne would have been buried in a shroud already 200 years old at the time of his death. A date in the eighth century thus seems much more likely on general grounds, and it is borne out by a study of the style and technique. A number of other silks may also be assigned to the same period on the basis of technical and stylistic evidence. Outstanding among them is

V the magnificent silk in the Vatican, bearing the Annunciation and the Nativity in

II, III roundels. The figural work may be compared with that in the Rossano codex, but the ornamental part shows close similarity to the mosaics of the Dome of the Rock at Jerusalem (691–692) or the Great Mosque at Damascus (715); again a date in the early part of the eighth or the late seventh century seems probable. Technically it is related to a number of other textiles with different designs, like that divided between several different collections which

IV shows a man, probably Samson, struggling with a lion. Sometimes the 'Samson' stuffs have been assigned to Egypt, but once again Constantinople seems a more likely home.

XXII DETAIL OF ANGEL. From the Homilies of St John Chrysostom. *c.* 1078. *Paris. Bibliothèque Nationale*; Ms. Coislin. 79. f2. v.

44

Soon after these textiles were made, the production of figural work in the religious sphere was brought to a stop in Constantinople as the result of the accession to power of a new dynasty, the Isaurian. The emperors of this line, like Cromwell's puritans, disapproved of religious art. There had, ever since Old Testament times, been a dislike of three-dimensional religious sculpture in the East Christian area, and the 'graven image' had always been regarded with suspicion—that is why free-standing sculpture is almost non-existent in the Byzantine world. Feelings as to whether it was desirable to portray the divine or saintly form even in two dimensions in mosaic or paint were also divided. On the one hand there was a belief that the representation served as an intermediary between man and the divine, in itself unapproachable. On the other it was felt either that to depict it savoured of impiety or irreverence, the divine form being inconceivable; or that too great a veneration of the sacred images was dangerous, in that it might easily lead to superstition or even to idolatry. The Israelites seem to have been particularly susceptible to the dangers of such exaggeration, for the Old Testament is full of references to the tendency to lapse toward idolatry, and a belief in the dangers occurring from exaggerated veneration of the sacred images seems to have passed from Palestine along with the Christian faith itself. Even as early as the time of Justinian we read of regulations forbidding figural decorations in churches, and symbols like the fish or the peacock were used rather than direct portrayal at an even earlier date. A cross, rather than the head of Christ, which became so popular later, was normally figured on the reverse of the coins throughout the first period of Byzantine art, and non-figural work played a large part in the mosaic decorations, like those of the church of St George at Salonica or even Sancta Sophia itself. But a faction which favoured figural work was in the ascendency throughout these early years, and it was only in 726 that control swung to the other side. This does not mean that there was not a great deal of opposition from those who believed in the value of figural religious art; indeed, for the next century and a half a bitter war of words was waged on the subject. But, except for a brief interlude around 800, figural work in the churches was proscribed until 843, in any case in Constantinople and the larger cities. In more out-of-the-way parts of the empire wall paintings depicting Christ, the Virgin, or Saints may have been executed, but recent researches show that even in places as far distant as Cappadocia decorative pattern work rather than figural was done at this time.

In the central area the decorations that were set up—and a good deal of work was

III MOSAIC. THE JOHN PANEL. *c.* 1118. *Constantinople. Sancta Sophia.*

probably done—were completely non-figural; a great cross in mosaic, which adorns the
53 eastern apse of the church of St Eirene may be taken as typical. Similar crosses adorned
the apses both of St Sophia at Salonica and of the Church of the Assumption at Nicaea;
both were replaced by figures of the Virgin in the ninth century when the Iconoclast ban
was lifted, but the backgrounds were not re-done, and the outline of the cross can still be
faintly discerned at Salonica and is recorded as having been visible at Nicaea before the
mosaics were destroyed in 1922. Similar crosses were no doubt set up elsewhere, and wall
areas other than the apse were perhaps adorned with compositions like those in the court
of the Great Mosque at Damascus, where trees, rivers, and fantastic architectural compositions provide a decoration of very rare beauty. In fact, the art of this age was by no
means negligible, even if figural representation was excluded.

81   The doors of Sancta Sophia, which bear an inscription dated to 840, can be also
assigned at least in part to these years. Aesthetically speaking, they are perhaps more
successful and pleasing than the doors of a rather later date with figural decorations
like those at Salerno, which were made at Constantinople and exported to Italy. A good
deal of similar work that has now disappeared was no doubt done at Constantinople,
both for use in the churches there and for export. Smaller objects in metal, especially
crosses, were no doubt also important during Iconoclast times, and a special form of
cross, flanked below the traverse by a floral pattern, its leaves balancing each other on
either side, would seem to have been a favourite Iconoclast motif. At the sides are
usually the letters IC XC NI KA, signifying 'Jesus Christ conquers'. Two examples of
such a cross are to be seen in the fine manuscript in the Bibliothèque Nationale which
was done for Basil I between 867 and 888, that is, just after the Iconoclast period; they
represent a survival from Iconoclast art.

    It was at one time held that the artists driven, so to speak, underground by the ban
on religious art, turned their activities to the secular sphere, and that the mass of the ivory
caskets, on nearly all of which classical subjects appear, was produced in these years.

XXIV ENAMEL CROSS. Obverse. Twelfth century. *Cosenza. The Cathedral Treasury.*

48

THE VIRGIN

XXV–XXVII MOSAIC. THE DEESIS PANEL. Thirteenth century. *Constantinople. Sancta Sophia*

These caskets are made up of small plaques framed in narrow, strip-like borders, themselves decorated with rosettes, and are usually referred to as the 'Rosette caskets'. More recent investigations have, however, shown that these caskets were more probably made in the tenth and eleventh centuries, no doubt by the very same craftsmen who did the fine religious ivory plaques which were so important at that time. But in default of the caskets, and with the exception of coins, it is not easy to fill the gap of the Iconoclast age so far as small-scale objects are concerned. There are, though, a number of wall paintings in the West which there is good reason to attribute to men who had been trained in the Byzantine world, and these must serve to give an idea of the direction that developments would have taken. Most important is the lovely work at Castelseprio near Milan in Italy, which may well have been done by a man who favoured figures and who fled Constantinople when the Iconoclast ban came into force. But the sudden burst in the production of work of high quality that succeeded Iconoclasm in the Byzantine world does suggest that ivory sculptures, mosaics, and painting were not wholly suppressed; otherwise it is hard to explain how it was that skill and technical ability had not declined. Yet the character of much of the work produced when the ban was lifted was extremely classical, so it would seem that so far as subject matter was concerned the artists had recourse to old models which pre-dated the imposition of the Iconoclast ban.

Iconoclast rule ended in 843, and it would seem that the redecoration of the churches began at once, though there was still a faction which disapproved, and the sponsoring of figural work was at first certainly not universal. In any case the Patriarch Photios preached a sermon in Sancta Sophia in March 867 in which he referred to a newly erected mosaic of the Virgin in a way which suggests that it had aroused a good deal of opposition. There are, however, some fragmentary mosaics in an upper chamber on the south side of the church which were probably executed before that, perhaps as a sort of memorial to the lifting of the ban. But from the end of the century onwards figural work once more became normal and the redecoration of the great cathedral proceeded thenceforth, though in a somewhat piecemeal manner, for the mosaics that survive are all of different dates, covering the whole period from soon after Iconoclasm till the Latin conquest of 1204 or even later. The Virgin in the apse and two archangels on the vault in front of 88, 89 it—only one of them survives—are probably the earliest of the post-Iconoclast mosaics in the church. The Virgin can hardly be that described by Photios, for the pose is different,

54

XVIII MOSAIC. THE NATIVITY. *c. 1310. Constantinople. Kariye Cami.*

but it may well date from about the time of his sermon, except for the head which would appear to be later. The surviving archangel is very fine indeed; on technical grounds it is probably to be regarded as of the same date as the apse mosaic, though at first glance it might well be tempting to assign it to the centuries before Iconoclasm.

The next in date of the Sancta Sophia mosaics is a panel in the lunette over the main entrance from the narthex, which shows Christ enthroned, with the Emperor Leo VI 93 prostrate at His feet. This happily can be firmly dated to between 886 and 912. Next comes a panel of similar shape over the south door, showing Constantine and Justinian 129 presenting models of the city and the church to the Virgin. The records tell us that Sancta Sophia was shut for repair between 986 and 994, during the reign of Basil II, and there seems no adequate reason to dispute the suggestion put forward by Whittemore when he uncovered the mosaic that it should be assigned to that time, though some have sought to date it later.

Other large-scale mosaics were no doubt set up elsewhere in Constantinople at this period, but none has survived. We do know, however, that the age was economically prosperous and that patronage of the arts was lavish, and its role in the later ninth and tenth centuries is attested by works on a small scale that survive, if not by those on a large. Not only are these smaller things numerous, but they are also of the very first artistic importance, and this importance is no less because the things themselves are small. In the Byzantine world, as in Persia and China, the western distinctions between large and small, art and craft, were never applicable; and small things were to the Byzantine outlook just as significant as interpretations of divine power as were the large, and the men who produced them were just as highly revered. Indeed, at least one of the emperors, Constantine VII Porphyrogenitus (913–959), was noted as a worker in metal, and he was himself to some extent responsible for the execution of one of the finest of all the x, treasures of the great middle period of Byzantine art; it is the superb 'staurothèque', or 124–126 reliquary to hold a portion of the True Cross, which is now at Limburg in Germany. There are records to show that it was preserved in the Great Palace from the day it was made till the Crusading conquest of 1204, when it was taken back to Germany as loot. It was presented to the Nunnery of Stuben near Trier, and was transferred to Limburg in 1827. The inscriptions upon it show that it must have been made between 948 and 959.

The same emperor is also known to us through one of the most important of the 96 ivories that have come down to us. It is in the Museum of Fine Art in Moscow, and shows

IX MOSAIC. THE FLIGHT INTO EGYPT. *c. 1310. Constantinople. Kariye Cami.*

the emperor being crowned by Christ. The same theme appears again at a rather later date in an ivory in the Bibliothèque Nationale in Paris showing the Coronation of an emperor and empress who are probably to be identified as Romanos II (959–963) and his consort Eudoxia. The two serve to illustrate with particular clarity the essentially spiritual basis of Byzantine imperialism. The emperor reigned on earth as Christ's regent; his essence was spiritual as well as temporal, and his position sacred. Other emperors might set themselves up or be set up elsewhere in the Christian world, but their position in the Byzantine view was not to be taken seriously; they might make themselves powerful, but they could never rule by the same historical and divine right as the Byzantine emperor. Yet, with that curious realism and sense of expediency, that strange blend of spiritual and worldly, that characterized Byzantine thought—and still characterizes the outlook of the Orthodox monk today—it was nevertheless possible for Christ's regent to be deposed, even disposed of in the most ruthless manner, if his conduct did not seem to be all that could be desired.

In addition to the mosaics and the ivories, the art of the later ninth century is known to us also through the manuscripts. A few outstanding examples survive. First among them may be mentioned a copy of the Homilies of Gregory Nazianzus in the Bibliothèque Nationale (MS. gr. 510). Some of its pages bear crosses of a purely Iconoclast type; others bear scenes in two or even three registers which are primarily concerned with telling a story as a continuous narrative in a manner akin to that of the wall paintings of Cappadocia; others again bear individual scenes or single figures which are often very classical in character and suggest that the miniaturists must have had recourse to earlier models. The artistic quality of all is outstanding.

This manuscript is firmly dated to between 867 and 886, and is in this especially important, for the illustrations of a number of others, the age of which is not firmly fixed, can be grouped around it. Most important of them is a particularly significant manuscript known as the Paris Psalter (MS. gr. 139). Its date has been much debated, for some of its illuminations are so classical in style that they were at one time assigned to pre-Iconoclast times. But a comparison with the Homilies shows that it must surely belong to the same date. It contains a number of large-scale illustrations, all of quality, though five different hands can be distinguished and they were not all equally competent; the best of them was, however, a very able artist indeed.

The grand manner that we see here was followed in a number of other manuscripts

58

XXX MOSAIC. THE DONOR OF THE MOSAICS, THEODORE METOCHITES. *c.* 1310.
Constantinople. Kariye Cami.

of the ninth, tenth and early eleventh centuries, such as the Bible of Leo the Patrician

94, 95 (Reg. gr. 1), or an Old Testament (Palat. gr. 38), both in the Vatican. We see the

XXII, same grand manner again nearly two centuries later in a copy of the Homilies of

163 John Chrysostom in Paris (Coislin 79), which dates from between 1078 and 1081. Other important Constantinopolitan manuscripts comprise the Psalter of Basil II Bulgaroctonos (976–1025) in the Marcian Library at Venice, and a Menologion, or Book of the Saints, done for the same emperor, in the Vatican (gr. 1613). The former has only

XI, two pages of illustrations, one with six scenes from the life of David and the other with a

127 monumental portrait of the emperor with repentant Bulgars at his feet. The latter contains no less than 213 illustrations of saints, shown sometimes against architectural and some-

128 times against landscape backgrounds. There are also numerous Gospel books, usually with portraits of the evangelists at the commencement of each Gospel, which are to be assigned to the same 'Court' school and which cover the whole period from the mid-ninth to the end of the twelfth century. Examples are to be found in libraries all over Europe; some of the best are in the Bibliothèque Nationale in Paris.

This 'aristocratic' style contrasts markedly with that of the marginal psalters, which are illustrated with vivid scenes on a small scale in the margins only. Many of these were done in out-of-the-way monasteries, but one of the most important of them, now in the British Museum (Add. 19352), was written in the famous monastery of the Studion at Constantinople. It was there that the main opposition to Iconoclasm centred during the eighth and ninth centuries, and it is probable that work of this type had continued there in secret even during Iconoclasm; the British Museum manuscript is, however, a good deal later, being dated to 1066. Nevertheless, reminiscences of the 'picturesque' style of early

XVII days are present in many of its illustrations, notably that reproduced here showing the Anointing of David. A similar 'picturesque' outlook is to the fore in the illustrations of

113 one of the few secular manuscripts that survive, a copy of the Theriaca of Nicandor in the Bibliothèque Nationale in Paris (Suppl. gr. 247); it must belong to the tenth or the early

XXXI MOSAIC. THE DEESIS PANEL. *c.* 1310. *Constantinople. Kariye Cami.*

eleventh century. But most of the manuscript illustrations, especially those of the 'aristocratic' group, are of a different nature, for they seem to express the spiritual character of the subject rather than to present an attractive façade. The themes are essentially Christian, the conception is abstract, and the colours symbolic rather than naturalistic. Gold is used profusely, partly because the metal itself was of value and hence the colour helped to stress the importance of the picture, and partly because the use of unreal colours helped to transport the theme from the world of everyday to that of religious ecstasy.

Though many of the emperors whose names we know as patrons were also conquerors whose successes on the field of battle were notable, the frontiers in general tended throughout this age to become more restricted, and it can hardly be claimed as one of temporal expansion. Yet economically it was astonishingly prosperous, the treasury was in general well filled, and the riches that were collected in the churches and the Great Palace aroused the wonder and astonishment of travellers from the West who came to Constantinople at the time. It was an age of lavish expenditure in life, of sumptuous production in art. Works in gold, enamel, ivory and precious silks were the order of the day; all were turned out by the Imperial workshops, not only in profusion, but also with outstanding accomplishment and with impeccable taste. It is really the products of this age that have earned for Byzantine art the normal association of the adjective 'sumptuous'.

The most important of these small-scale things at this age were perhaps the ivories. Quite considerable numbers survive, and several different schools can be distinguished. One of the earliest is a plaque bearing the Archangel Gabriel, in the possession of Mr W. R. Tyler, which is perhaps to be dated to the ninth century. Another, with the Coronation of Constantine VII Porphyrogenitus in Moscow, comes next in the series, and is to be dated about 944. The Romanos ivory belongs to about 959, and a whole series of others may be assigned to the next four or five decades; all are in a delicate, elegant, highly finished style, and have been assigned by Goldschmidt and Weitzmann to what they term the 'Romanos' group; the 'Court' school would perhaps be a more accurate designation, for work was done both before and after the time of Romanos. The best examples are the fine panels with saints at Venice and Vienna, or the superb Harbaville Triptych in the Louvre, which is perhaps the most beautiful of all the Byzantine ivories. Triptychs in the Vatican and the Palazzo Venezia in Rome are closely akin to the Harbaville, though the workmanship is not quite so good; the former is perhaps

XXXII WALL PAINTING. THE ANASTASIS. *c.* 1310. *Constantinople. Kariye Cami.*

rather later, the latter rather earlier in date. The only example of free-standing sculpture in
106 ivory that is known, a Virgin and Child in the Victoria and Albert Museum, is also
to be assigned to this group.

In addition to this 'Court' school, which corresponds to that of the 'aristocratic'
manuscripts, several other groups may be distinguished. The most clearly defined is the
120, 121 'Nicephoras' group, of which an ivory at Cortona in the name of the Emperor Nicephoras Phocas (963–969) may be taken as the type example. The faces are here rather
fuller, the heads rounder, the lips thicker, the noses plumper, the figures less elongated,
and the general approach rather less idealized. A triptych at Luton Hoo, with the Virgin
123 in the centre and medallions of saints on the wings and a Crucifixion in Hanover show
122 the development of this style, and a marble sculpture of the Archangel Michael in Istanbul
is closely akin. A roundel of green porphyry in the Victoria and Albert Museum shows
150 the same style at a rather later date; it bears the name of the Emperor Nicephoras Bota-
151 niates (1078–1081). A marble relief in the Istanbul Museum is closely akin to it and is to
be assigned to the same date.

A third group of ivories is termed by Goldschmidt and Weitzmann the 'pictorial'.
Here scenes rather than figures constitute the subject matter, and they are more often than
not framed in openwork arcades, which must obviously have been inspired by manuscript models. The scenes are usually vivid and expressive and tell their story with great
force; they are less austere than the works of the 'Court' school, and attract more readily at
114 a first glance. Unfortunately none of the ivories of this group is actually dated; one with
116, 117 the Ascension in Florence, one with the Forty Martyrs, and another with the Entry into
115, 119 Jerusalem in Berlin or one with the Dormition of the Virgin in Munich, may be cited.
These are all works of extreme technical excellence and great beauty.

The ivories with classical scenes constitute another separate class, not only because of
the subjects they depict, but also because they nearly all take the form of small panels
which were made up into caskets. Goldschmidt and Weitzmann have listed 125 of these;

XXXIII MOSAIC. THE PANTOCRATOR. Early fourteenth century. *Constantinople. Church of St Mary Pammakaristos (Fetiye Cami).*

64

others exist which are not noted by them. They are almost all characterized by the presence of narrow ivory strips, ornamented with rosettes, between which are mounted the larger panels bearing the scenes or figures. They are usually known as the 'Rosette' caskets. It is a useful 'portmanteau' name, for though the majority of the caskets are ornamented with secular scenes, a few have purely religious decorations. Several of these caskets call for notice because of their outstandingly high quality. The Veroli casket in the Victoria and Albert Museum is perhaps the best, but there are fine ones elsewhere, like one in the Metropolitan Museum at New York, or one in the Cluny Museum at Paris; this is the latest of the three, and probably belongs to the end of the eleventh century. A few caskets of similar type are made up of plaques with religious subjects, usually Adam and Eve. There is a more unusual casket at Troyes, where there are no rosettes, but a series of hunting and similar scenes, and on the ends birds which must have been inspired by a Chinese textile. It is to be dated, on the grounds of costume, to the eleventh century. Indeed, most of the examples that survive are to be dated either to the tenth or the eleventh century, though a few are later, like the large casket in the Museo Nazionale at Florence, with busts of Christ, the Virgin and Saints, or an enchanting miniature casket with the Ascension on the top, at Stuttgart. The former has sometimes been regarded as an Italian work, but this is most unlikely for the style is metropolitan and the rather hard linear manner may be compared to that of a mosaic in Sancta Sophia known as the 'John Panel', which shows the Virgin and Child between John II Comnenos (1118–1143), and the Empress Irene. This hard linear manner that we see both in the mosaic and the ivory is to be regarded as typical of the Comnene period. A portrait of the Emperor Alexios Comnenos on a pier at right-angles to the 'John Panel', done in 1122, shows, however, a profusion of white highlights in the modelling, and heralds the style that was to become universal in the late thirteenth and fourteenth centuries.

Hints of this rather more linear style appear in one or two of the ivories which are clearly to be assigned to the 'Court' school, and which are probably to be dated to the late

---

XXXIV PORTRAIT OF THE HIGH ADMIRAL APOCAUCOS. From manuscript of Hippocrates. c. 1342. *Paris. Bibliothèque Nationale*; Ms. gr. 2144. f11.

143   eleventh century. The finest is one of the Virgin and Child at Utrecht. The rendering is rather more intimate and personal than is the case with the earlier ones, and it is tempting to suggest that we have here another instance of the tendency towards greater humanism which appeared in the art of the twelfth century and reached a peak at the

144   end of the thirteenth. The trend is carried rather further in the St John at Liverpool, and

145   we see it again in an open-work plaque in the Victoria and Albert Museum with medallions of the Baptist at the centre and four apostles at the corners. A very battered but

142   extremely fine marble slab of the Virgin at Constantinople may be compared, and a

XVI, 146   lovely painting of St Just on silk, which is almost Chinese in the reticence of its style, is again in the same manner. There are marble slabs that must have been modelled upon the former at Ravenna, Venice, and elsewhere, but all are clumsy in comparison and serve by contrast to attest the excellence of the Constantinopolitan workmanship. The same rather polished, elegant manner characterizes the carvings in steatite, like one with

162   the Archangel Michael in the Museo Bandini at Fiesole; it was originally coloured, for traces of gold remain. The material seems to a great extent to have replaced ivory in the twelfth century; the advance of the Seljuk Turks into Asia Minor may have made it harder to obtain ivory, and the general decline in economic prosperity after about 1100 no doubt influenced the substitution of the cheaper material.

    The ivories are perhaps the most important works of this great middle period from the artistic point of view, but the objects of metal, precious stones and enamel—the three were often associated together on the same object—possibly give a clearer impression of the richness of the 'Court' art of the period. These things were made in large numbers, and practically every church in Constantinople was lavishly supplied with such treasures as chalices, patens, bindings for Gospels or service books, cases in which sacred relics were kept, and so on, in addition to exquisitely carved ivories and precious silks. A few of those that can be firmly dated have already been mentioned. Of others attention may be called to one or two characteristic pieces in each of the most usual techniques. First may be

XXXV ICON. THE TWELVE APOSTLES. Fourteenth century. *Moscow. The Museum of Fine Art.*

158 mentioned cast metal; there is a fine bronze triptych, with the Virgin and Child on the central panel, in the Victoria and Albert Museum, which is late in date. Not very many examples of cast metal survive; perhaps such things were more often melted down than others, as each object would contain a considerable quantity of actual metal. Works in repoussé, where the designs were beaten out from the back, are more common, for not only was the technique very popular, but also, as the metal was thin, the temptation to melt it down proved less considerable. Perhaps the most important example of such work
136 is a paten at Halberstadt, which is probably to be dated to the tenth century. There is,
159 however, a very lovely plaque of gilt bronze showing the Virgin full length in the Victoria and Albert Museum, which may be as late as the early twelfth century. A reliquary in
166, 167 the Louvre is akin, but is probably later still, for the style is rather less refined. All were almost certainly made in the capital, but the technique was practised in many centres elsewhere and Constantinopolitan prototypes were widely copied, not only in the Byzantine world, but also in Italy and Germany; some book bindings in St Mark's at Venice were thus probably made locally. Enamel plaques were often attached to relics of this sort, to enliven the repoussé metal grounds; this was done on the lovely 'staurothèque', or reliquary
135 for housing a fragment of the True Cross, at Esztergom in Hungary. The enamels and the plain gold ground are of the eleventh century, while the repoussé border is a later addition and is to be assigned to the early fourteenth.

The greatest mass of examples where metal and enamel are associated together is, however, preserved in the treasury of St Mark's and in the Marcian Library at Venice.
XIV, XV, The treasures there comprise gospel covers, chalices, and reliquaries, all of which were
137–141 brought from Constantinople at the sack of the city during the Fourth Crusade in 1204. Usually the bodies of the chalices and patens are of precious stone, the stems and bases of metal, generally gold, and the borders of gold, in which are set smaller precious stones and enamels. The reliquaries and the book covers are of gold or silver gilt, studded with enamels and precious stones: to read a catalogue of them is reminiscent of the penultimate

---

XXXVI MINIATURE MOSAIC. SIX OF THE TWELVE FEASTS. Fourteenth century. *Florence. Opera del Duomo.*

chapter of the Book of Revelations, so varied and precious are the materials. Sometimes
139 the chalices are two-handled, like goblets, sometimes they are plain; sometimes the patens
137 are flat, sometimes they are of more elaborate shapes, like one in St Mark's of alabaster
with six lobes. The enamels on these vessels are usually very small, though often of superb
quality. But larger enamels were made, either as plaques for mounting on reliquaries,
138, 140, 141 book covers and so on, or even to stand alone. To this last category belong a book cover
XV with the Archangel Michael in relief in St Mark's and a magnificent cross in the
XXIV, 170 Treasury of the Cathedral at Cosenza; the latter dates from the twelfth century, and represents the culmination of a technique which was probably first used in the Byzantine
world in the sixth century, though on a much smaller scale. One of the earliest of these
enamels is a cross in the Victoria and Albert Museum, known as the Beresford Hope
90, 91 Cross. A book cover in the Marcian Library is perhaps of slightly later date. The most
impressive collection of enamels is that mounted up in a Gothic frame in St Mark's at
Venice, known as the Pala d'Oro, though the enamels themselves are of rather varying
quality and many of them date from the thirteenth century, when the peak of excellence
had been passed. Finer, and especially important, because they are exactly dated, are some
enamels in the Budapest Museum, which once formed a crown that belonged to the
134 Emperor Constantine Monomachos (1042-1054). Three of the plaques represent the
emperor, his consort and her sister; on others there are dancing girls of rather oriental
appearance.

This emperor was not very distinguished in the political sphere, for he seems to have
been both incompetent and dishonest, but he was important as a patron of art, and in
addition to the crown his name may be associated with mosaics at Chios, and also with
XIII, a fine group in the south gallery of Sancta Sophia, where he is shown with his consort
133 the Empress Zoe (1028-1057), with a figure of Christ between them. There is reason to
believe that the mosaic originally depicted Zoe and her first husband, Romanos III
(1028-1034), and that it was first set up in their reign. At a later date the inscription above

XXXVII MINIATURE MOSAIC. SIX OF THE TWELVE FEASTS. Fourteenth century. *Florence.
Opera del Duomo.*

72

the emperor was altered and the head remodelled to represent the last of her three husbands, Constantine Monomachos; her own head was also apparently somewhat refurbished at the same time. The raised eyebrows and sidelong glance of Christ in this composition are the first indications that a new, more personal style was beginning to develop.

The last of the materials for which this great 'Second Golden Age' of Byzantine art was famed were the silks, in the production of which a degree of excellence was reached in the imperial workshops which has probably never since been equalled. The imperial looms at Constantinople held a monopoly in the production of certain types of silks, and on one occasion an unfortunate ambassador from the West had the stuffs that he had acquired confiscated by the customs, for they were only allowed to be exported with imperial permission. But others reached the West as gifts, where they were used for the burial of emperors and saintly ecclesiastics. Except for a few small pieces that were re-employed for the insides of book bindings, it is from the tombs that have come the majority of the examples that survive. At Constantinople they were used for imperial and courtly costumes, as hangings in the Great Palace and the grander houses, and no doubt in the churches also. A few of the pieces that survive are dated, like the famous lion stuffs at Siegburg (920–931) and Düsseldorf (976–1025); the former is very fragmentary and the latter has now, alas, perished. Others bear inscriptions referring to the imperial work-
130 shops, like the great elephant stuff from Charlemagne's tomb at Aachen; it was probably inserted into the tomb about the year 1000. Others, such as the superb eagle stuffs at
132, XII Auxerre and Bressanone, or the stuff made up into stockings for Pope Clement (1047) at Bamberg, are to be attributed to Byzantium on technical grounds. Byzantine again is
131 the superb silk damask at Sens, known as the shroud of St Siviard. Stuffs like these, with essentially Byzantine designs, were much copied both in the West and in the Islamic world, but nowhere was the workmanship so proficient as at Constantinople, and the copies can usually be distinguished on technical grounds even though they are them-selves often of very high quality.

XXXVIII MINIATURE MOSAIC. THE ANNUNCIATION. Fourteenth century. *London. The Victoria and Albert Museum.*

ΟΕΥΑΓΓΕ ΛΙΣΜΟΣ

Apart from the stuffs with Greek inscriptions or with designs of Byzantine type, a number of other textiles exist which were perhaps also made at Constantinople, though the designs are of a rather more Persian character. The most Byzantine of them is that known as the Mozac rider stuff in the Musée des Tissus at Lyons; it is probably to be assigned to the tenth century, though an earlier dating is possible. Its design may be com-152, 153 pared with the imperial figures on the ivory casket at Troyes. Similar stuffs at Berlin and elsewhere are more probably Persian; Syria was also important as a centre of manufacture in early times, and it is possible that work of a Christian character continued to be done there well after the Islamic conquest.

Certain other 'sumptuous' arts must just be mentioned, for work was done in every possible technique and every possible material. Some interesting plaques of marble, in which the ground is cut out to permit the insertion of a design in coloured stones, were discovered in the church of St Mary Panachrantos at Constantinople in 1927; some of them represent ducks and other birds, but the majority probably bore saintly figures, and 149 one of St Eudoxia may be noted. A slab at Athens is similarly cut out, but the design is in coloured pastes, not stones. Glass was also made, but we know very little of it. Pottery was important, and a considerable number of different techniques were used. The most distinctive consisted in painting a design, sometimes of a decorative character, and some-times in the form of figures of Christ, the Virgin, or Saints, in vitrifiable colours; the whole was coated with a thin transparent glaze and then fired. Some fine examples, showing a great variety of designs, colours and manners, are preserved in the Istanbul Museum and in the Louvre. Most of the examples that are known are to be dated to the ninth and tenth centuries. 'Impressed' wares, where a moulded design underlies a monochrome glaze, were also important at this time. By the eleventh century these methods of decoration had given place to others, notably the well known 'sgraffito', which became the most usual technique after the twelfth. The earliest 'sgraffito' decorations were monochrome; at a later date coloured glazes were used to give a greater variety to the engraved designs.

XXXIX THE TRANSFIGURATION. From the Manuscript of John Cantacuzenos. 1370–75. *Paris Bibliothèque Nationale*; Ms. gr. 1242. f92.

In 1204 the Fourth Crusade set out from Europe with the object of freeing the Holy Cities from the Infidel. Instead, they attacked their fellow Christians in Constantinople; the Orthodox emperors were driven from the city and Latin ones ascended the throne in their stead; they continued in power until about 1261, when they were in turn expelled and the last Byzantine dynasty, the Palaeologan, was reinstalled in the capital.

The capture of Constantinople by the Crusaders meant that the galaxy of treasures assembled in the churches there was dispersed. The sack was wanton and uncalled for; a vast treasure of the first importance from the artistic point of view was destroyed. But much was also taken to the West and presented to churches and cathedrals in France, Italy and Germany, and there these things have subsequently been preserved; had all the treasures remained in Constantinople they would no doubt have been irrevocably lost at the Turkish conquest in 1453 when the town was again pillaged.

But this was not the only affect of the Latin conquest so far as art was concerned; it also had important economic results. The empire was divided, the civil service disrupted, the treasury exhausted, and the state impoverished; and though members of the royal family were able to re-establish themselves at Trebizond, at Nicaea, and in northern Greece, the scale of court and official life was seriously reduced, and trade with the east was broken off. The effect on art was obvious; rich materials like gold, silver and enamel became rare and unusual; ivory was either too expensive or was no longer available; the patronage of individual nobles was to a great extent substituted for that of the imperial family. This did not mean that there was any real cessation of artistic production or decline of quality; it meant instead that less sumptuous materials were employed and that new styles came into being. Steatite thus came to be used instead of ivory, and its soapy, svelte texture lent itself particularly well to the rather low relief carving that had become fashionable even before the conquest. Paintings and small-scale mosaics similarly replaced ivory, gold or enamels as the normal vehicles for sacred pictures and emblems. Indeed, it was really in this last stage of Byzantine culture that painting on a small scale first came fully into its own.

XL PORTRAIT OF CONSTANTINE COMNENOS AND EUPHROSYNE DUCAENA PALAEOLOGINA. From the Lincoln College Typicon. c. 1400. Oxford. The Bodleian Library; Ms. No. Gr. 35.

† ΚΩΝϹΤΑΝ
ΤΙΝΟ ϹΚΟΜΝΗ
ΝΟ Ϲ ΓΑΥΛΟ ΠΑ
ΛΑΙΟΛΟΓΟ Ϲ Ο
ΠΡΟΤΟ ϹΕΒΑϹΤ
Κ ΓΑΜΠΡΟϹ
Τ Κ Τ ΤΟ
ΡΙ ϹΗ Ϲ

† ΕΥΦΡΟϹΥΝΗ
Δ ΟΚΝΑ ΠΑΛΑΙ
Ο ΛΟ ΓΙΝΑ
Η ΠΡΟΤΟ ϹΕ
ΒΑϹΤΗ Κ ΕΓ
Κ ΟΝΗ Τ Ϲ
Κ Τ ΤΟ ΡΙ
ϹΗ Ϲ

Perhaps the finest work of this age is a large mosaic in Sancta Sophia; it represents the Deesis, that is, the Virgin and St John interceding with Christ for the sins of the world. It is to be dated to the thirteenth century, either to just before, or more probably to just after, the Latin inter-regnum. The work is distinguished by a delicacy of technique never before attained, by a minute manner, by a richer palette, and by a new, more humanistic outlook. At one time it was supposed that this new style came about thanks to the Latin influence introduced as a result of the Fourth Crusade, but recent research has shown that it was actually born in the Byzantine world long before any significant change in art had made itself felt in Italy, for it is already apparent in a great many works of the twelfth century; the icon known as our Lady of Vladimir, which was painted in Con-stantinople around 1130, may serve as an example. The tender, more personal approach was carried further in wall paintings of 1164 in the little church of Nerez in Macedonia, which were done under the patronage of a member of the imperial family by an artist who must have been brought from the capital. Other wall paintings of the later twelfth century show the influence of the same more intimate style, which must have already been conceived in Constantinople by about 1125, even if it did not become universal there till the thirteenth century.

The evolution of the new style is well exemplified in a number of portable mosaics. The earliest that we know are really wall mosaics on a reduced scale, made of com-paratively large cubes set in plaster; the most important is one representing the Virgin and Child now in the Patriarchate at Constantinople; it is to be dated to about 1065. But panels like this, made up of comparatively large cubes, soon gave place to smaller ones, where the cubes were no bigger than a pin's point; they are set in wax on a wooden ground. A fine panel of Christ at Florence, dating from around 1150, is still com-paratively large in size, though the cubes are small; a similar one at Berlin has rather larger cubes and is earlier. Work done after 1204 was usually on a smaller scale, the panels being little more than some twelve inches in height; outstanding examples are the two

---

XLI ICON. THE ANNUNCIATION. Fourteenth century. From St Clement's, Ochrid. *Skopolje. Macedonian State Collections.*

panels in the Cathedral Treasury at Florence, each with six Bible scenes, or one with the Annunciation in the Victoria and Albert Museum, which must date from the early fourteenth century. It was certainly made by a Constantinopolitan craftsman, and it would seem that illuminations and panels continued to be executed in Constantinople for Orthodox patrons even during the Latin inter-regnum; indeed, Weitzmann, in a recent publication, has listed a series of manuscripts which there is reason to assign to Constantinople and to date to these years.

But even if work on a small scale continued to be produced in the capital, no large-scale decorations survive that can be assigned to the inter-regnum, and the best work of this age on a large scale was probably produced in centres elsewhere where Orthodox patronage was available, notably at Nicaea and Trebizond, where members of the imperial house set up independent kingdoms. In the former place a dynasty was estab-lished, which was eventually strong enough to recapture Constantinople; at Trebizond the emperors of the old Comnene line ruled independently till the city fell to the Turks in 1461. Good work on a large scale was also done in Yugoslavia under the patronage of the Serbian kings, and it is largely thanks to the preservation of wall paintings at Mileševa and Sopočani that we can form a picture of what the best paintings of this age were like. In Constantinople the period of glory came with the early fourteenth century, when a whole series of churches were extensively decorated with mosaics and frescoes.

The most important surviving monument of the age is undoubtedly the little church 180, 181 near the walls now known as Kariye Cami. Small, but of good proportions, like all the churches of the time, it consists of a square 'naos' or main church, roofed with a dome and preceded by two transverse narthices, the most westerly of them extending not only across the axis of the church, but also across that of a longitudinal side aisle or chapel. This chapel was adorned not with mosaics, but with wall paintings, which are at present being brought to light by the Byzantine Institute of America from beneath subsequent layers of dirt and overpaint. The chapel was a mortuary one, and it is therefore not surprising

---

XLII ICON. THE ANNUNCIATION. Detail of the Angel's head. Fourteenth century. From St Clement's, Ochrid. *Skopolje. Macedonian State Collections.*

XXXII, 185 to find the Anastasis or Resurrection in the conch of its apse; the other scenes also illustrate texts of similar import; the iconography in many of them is rather obscure. The work is, however, of outstanding quality. The drawing is delicate, the colouring rich and strangely lovely, and the general effect of the whole most profound. White highlights are profusely employed; indeed, they are to be counted as a characteristic of the art of the period, though they had already been used in the twelfth century, as for instance in the 165 mosaic of Alexios Comnenos in Sancta Sophia of 1122. The paintings must date from the first decade of the fourteenth century. At much the same date Giotto was decorating the Arena Chapel at Padua. The Byzantine painter had other ideas and a different outlook, but in his own way he was just as great a genius.

XXVIII–XXXI, 182–184 The mosaics of Kariye Cami belong to the same period as the paintings. In the church itself the most impressive is a panel showing the Dormition of the Virgin, above the west door; the scene is beautifully balanced and very effective, but the quality of the work is perhaps most apparent in the details of the figures. In the narthices the lives of the Virgin and of Christ are told in a series of vivid scenes, and as well there are on the lower parts of the walls a number of panels representing individual saints. The scenes are full, elaborate, and particularly dramatic; they typify the new style in the great importance given to the picturesque backgrounds, as well as in the vivacity of the figures and the compositions. In details the minuteness of manner that has already been noted is perhaps carried rather further. A particularly interesting scene shows the donor of the church, Theodore Metochites, presenting a model of it to Christ, while an especially fine composition—from the point of view of artistic quality perhaps the finest in the building— XXXI shows Christ with the Virgin beside Him and with two figures below. This is in a rather more monumental style, and it was at one time believed to be of earlier date than the other mosaics; the cleaning has, however, established the fact that all the mosaics in the church are of the same period.

The inclusion of portraits of the donors is another of the characteristic features of this

---

XLIII ICON. THE ANNUNCIATION. Detail of the Virgin's head. Fourteenth century. From St Clement's, Ochrid. *Skopolje. Macedonian State Collections.*

age, and once more illustrates the new interest in personality, as well as the widening of patronage and the dilution of imperial power; in earlier times the portraits that were set up were nearly always imperial. That at Kariye is one of a series dating from the later thirteenth and fourteenth centuries depicting noble or court functionaries; others are to be found in churches all over the Balkans and on Mount Athos. A miniature in a manu‑ script of the works of Hippocrates in the Bibliothèque Nationale, showing the High Admiral Apocaucos and dating from about 1345, may serve as an example; a wonderful series of portraits in a book in the Bodleian Library at Oxford, the Lincoln College Typicon, must also have been done in the capital.

Mosaics of much the same date as those at Kariye survive in two other Constanti‑ nopolitan churches, namely that of the Virgin Pammakaristos, now known as Fetiye Cami, and that of St Theodore Tyro, now known as Kilisse Cami. Both are very de‑ lightful buildings. The former contains a fine dome mosaic, with Christ at the centre and the Twelve Apostles below; other scenes and figures on the pendentives and on the walls are now being cleaned. The mosaics in the latter church are very battered, for all the gold tesserae which covered the backgrounds have been stolen, and only a few figures survive. The tesserae are larger than those in Kariye and Fetiye, and the work is somewhat coarse, though not without vigour and forcefulness. Mosaics and wall paintings may survive beneath whitewash and plaster in other churches in the capital, and there is good reason to hope that more may be discovered in due course.

Panel paintings of this age are a good deal more numerous than those of the preceding centuries—the finest are in the Hermitage at Leningrad, the Museum of Fine Art and the Tretiakov Gallery at Moscow and in Yugoslavia. One showing the Twelve Apostles in Moscow and one with the Archangel Michael at Pisa may be noted, but the most lovely of all is perhaps an Annunciation from the church of St Clement at Ochrida in Yugo‑ slavia; it is on the back of a fine rendering of the Virgin. Illuminations of the age are often very close in style to the panel paintings, as for example one showing the Transfiguration

XLIV ICON. THE VIRGIN OF PIMEN. Fourteenth century. *Moscow. The Tretiakov Gallery.*

in a copy of the Homilies of John Chrysostom in the Bibliothèque Nationale in Paris (gr. 1242), which dates from between 1371 and 1375.

There is practically nothing of the fifteenth century surviving in Constantinople itself, but the number of churches and wall paintings of that and the following century to be found in Greece and the Balkans is legion. Many of the paintings on panel and wall that decorate them must have been done by men from the capital or under the close influence of Constantinopolitan artists, but by this time new local styles were developing, and a number of distinct schools are now to be observed; most important of them is the Mace⁄donian, characterized by a dramatic, rather exaggerated realism.

The lootings of the Latins, the advances of the Turks in Asia Minor, the setting⁄up of independent Slav states in the Balkans, and the constant wars had all helped to reduce the wealth both of the city and of the imperial palaces, and precious objects other than miniature mosaics are rare. But if the donor portraits can be taken as a guide, it would seem that the rich woven silks which constituted such superb and typical products of the 'Second Golden Age' were still being made. Unfortunately none has survived. But in addition a new type of textile began to become very important in the fourteenth century, namely that decorated with embroidery, and there exist in various collections a number of examples which are of real distinction. Attention may be called to one in the Vatican, 195 known as the 'Dalmatic of Charlemagne', though it is clearly of much later date, or to 194 one in the Victoria and Albert Museum which is firmly dated to 1407. Embroideries of this sort continued to be produced even after the Turkish conquests of the mid⁄fifteenth century, for they could be done in the home and depended on the skill of individuals— no great imperial workshop was required for their production. Wood carvings and jewellery were similarly executed, but though attractive they belong to the realm of folk rather than fine art. But icons of the fifteenth, sixteenth, and even the seventeenth century often retained something of the old grandeur and, even if there are few later than the fifteenth century that are to be regarded as real masterpieces, many were produced which are as significant from the artistic point of view as are, say, the general run of Dutch land⁄scape paintings.

Thus the story ends, with a decline, but not in insignificance. And if the art of the last phase was more limited in scope than that of Renaissance Italy, less personal than that of seventeenth⁄century France, less expressive than that of the Germany of Dürer, it was still an art of real consequence. It had inherited much of the mastery of technique, of the profound spiritual content, and of the austere beauty that characterized the earlier phases. It was, in the twelfth century, in many ways in advance of what was being done in Italy; in the early fourteenth century it was as good, though different. The major monuments are not easy of access; the smaller ones are unfamiliar, but it is hoped that the few examples that are illustrated here may serve at least to dispel the old conceptions that Byzantine art was at best monotonous, at worst of an inferior nature.

THE MONOCHROME PLATES

1   Coin. The Emperor Constantine. Gold solidus. 306–337. Mint of Nicomedia. Private Collection.

2 Head of Constantine. Bronze. 306–337. Belgrade. The National Museum.

3   Head of Constantine. Bronze. 306–337. Belgrade. The National Museum.

4   Head of Constantine. Marble. c. 325. Istanbul. The Archaeological Museum.

5 Base of the Theodosian obelisk. c. 395. Constantinople. The Hippodrome.

6 The Concesti Amphora. Details. Silver gilt. 5th c. Leningrad. The Hermitage Museum.

7 The Concesti Amphora. Silver gilt. 5th c. Leningrad. The Hermitage Museum.

8 Relief from Bakirkoy. Marble. Late 4th c. Istanbul. The Archaeological Museum.

9   The Sarigüzel sarcophagus. Marble. Late 4th or early 5th. c.
Istanbul. The Archaeological Museum.

10   The Golden Gate. c. 400. From the south. Constantinople.

11   The Golden Gate. c. 400. The main entrance. Constantinople.

12   The land walls of Theodosios II. Early 5th c. Near Top Kapu. Constantinople.

13 The land walls of Theodosios II. Early 5th c. The outer wall and moat. Constantinople.

14　The Church of St John of Studion. c. 463. The interior, looking west. Constantinople.

15 The Church of St John of Studion. c. 463. Above: Detail of west end. Below: Interior looking East. Constantinople.

16   The Entry into Jerusalem. From the Church of St John of Studion. Limestone relief. 5th c.
Istanbul. The Archaeological Museum.

17   Group of Apostles. From the Church of St John of Studion. Limestone relief. 5th c.
Istanbul. The Archaeological Museum.

18   Two horizontal plaques from a diptych. Ivory. c. 500. Milan. Castello Sforzesco.

19   The Barberini Ivory. c.500. Paris. Musée du Louvre.

20   The diptych of Areobindus. Ivory. 506. Paris. Musée du Louvre.

21   The Empress Ariadne. Ivory. c.500. Florence. Museo Nazionale.

22   The diptych of Areobindus. Ivory. 506. Zurich. Schweizerisches Landesmuseum.

FL TAVRVS CLEMENTINVS
ARMONIVS CLEMENTINVS

VII COM SACRIARÇ EXCONS
PATRIC ET CONS ORDIN

23   The diptych of Clementinus. Ivory. 513. Liverpool. The Archaeological Museum.

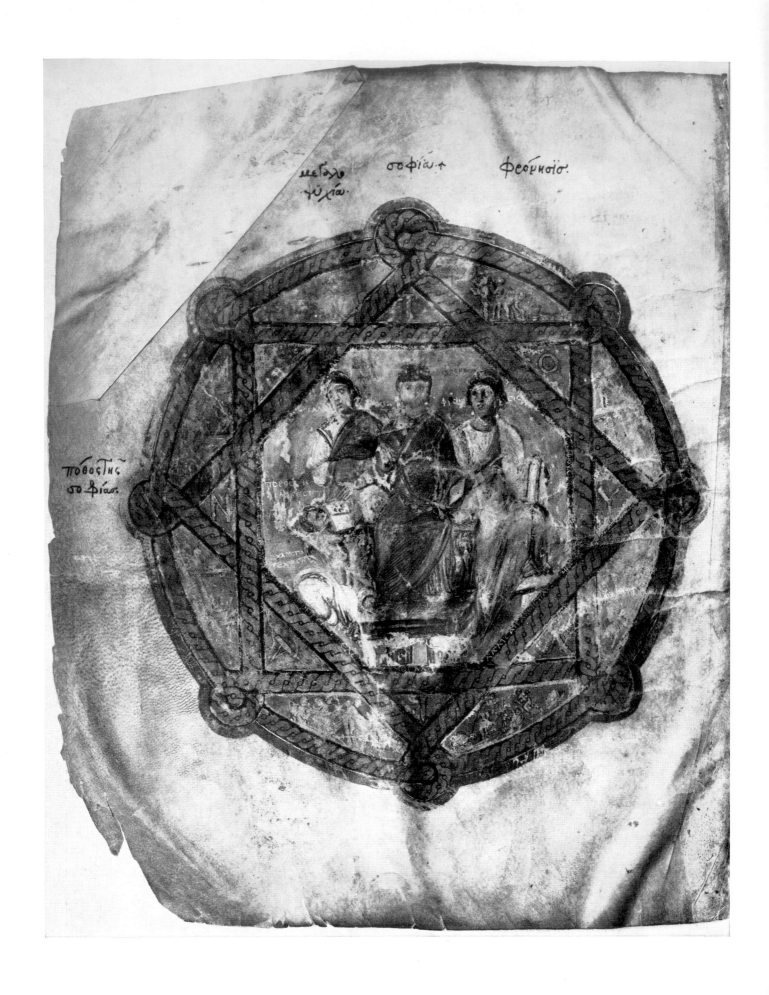

24   Portrait of Juliana Anicia. From the Manuscript of Dioscorides. c.512.
Vienna. The National Library. Cod. med. Gr. 1 f. 6.

25   Portrait of Dioscorides. From the Manuscript of Dioscorides. c. 512.
Vienna. The National Library. Cod. med. Gr. 1 f. 4.

26   The diptych of Anastasius. Ivory. 517. Paris. Cabinet des Médailles.

27 Leaf of the diptych of Magnus. Ivory. 518. Paris. Cabinet des Médailles.

28   The dish of Paternus. Details. Silver. 518. Leningrad. The Hermitage Museum.

29   The dish of Paternus. Silver. 518. Leningrad. The Hermitage Museum.

30   The diptych of Philoxenus. Ivory. 525. Paris. Cabinet des Médailles.

31   The diptych of Justinian. Ivory. 521. Milan. Castello Sforzesco.

32 Two capitals. Marble. Above: early 5th c. Below: early 6th c.
Istanbul. The Archaeological Museum.

33 Two capitals. Marble. Above: 6th c. Below: c. 540. Istanbul. The Archaeological Museum.

34 Two capitals. Marble. Above: 7th c. Below: 11th c.
Istanbul. The Archaeological Museum.

35   Statue base. Marble. c. 500. Istanbul. The Archaeological Museum.

36   Diptych with hunting scenes. Ivory. 5th c. Leningrad. The Hermitage Museum.

37   Plaque with hunting scenes. Bronze with silver inlay. 5th or 6th c. Paris. Musée du Louvre.

38   Mosaic floor. A seated "Philosopher". Early 6th c. Constantinople. The Great Palace.

39 Mosaic floor. Eagle and serpent. Early 6th c. Constantinople. The Great Palace.

40   Mosaic floor. A water mill. Early 6th c. Constantinople. The Great Palace.

41   Mosaic floor. Head, in the border. Early 6th c. Constantinople. The Great Palace.

42 A shepherd. Silver dish. 6th c. Leningrad. The Hermitage Museum.

43 The Personification of India. Silver dish. 6th c. Istanbul. The Archaeological Museum.

44   Vase from Homs. Silver. 6th c. Paris. Musée du Louvre.

45   Vase from Homs. Detail of ornament at shoulder. Silver. 6th c. Paris. Musée du Louvre.

46 Ambon from Salonica. Marble. Early 6th c. Istanbul. The Archaeological Museum.

47 Ambon from Salonica. Marble. Early 6th c. Istanbul. The Archaeological Museum.

48   The Archangel Michael. Ivory. Early 6th c. London. The British Museum.

49   The Archangel Michael. Detail. Ivory. Early 6th c. London. The British Museum.

50   The Church of Sts Sergius and Bacchus. Interior. 527–536. Constantinople.

51   The Church of Sts Sergius and Bacchus. Detail of cornice. 527–536. Constantinople.

52   The Church of St Eirene. Exterior. c. 532 and later. Constantinople.

53   The Church of St Eirene. Interior. c. 532 and later. Constantinople.

54   The Church of Sancta Sophia. Exterior. 532–537. Constantinople.

55   The Church of Sancta Sophia. Interior. 532–537. Constantinople.

56　The Church of Sancta Sophia. Interior. North side. 532–537. Constantinople.

57   Capitals in Sancta Sophia. Marble. 532–537. Constantinople.

58   Justinian and his court. Wall Mosaic. 526–547. Ravenna. San Vitale.

59   The Three Magi. Wall mosaic. c. 560. Ravenna. St Apollinare Nuovo.

60   Medallion of Justinian. 534–538. Electrotype of gold original,
formerly in the Cabinet des Médailles, Paris.

61   Head, probably the Empress Theodora. Marble. c. 530. Milan. Castello Sforzesco.

62   Portion of a ciborium arch. Marble. 6th c. Istanbul. The Archaeological Museum.

63   Portion of a ciborium arch. From the Church of St Mary Panachrantos. Marble. ? 6th c.
Istanbul. The Archaeological Museum.

64 Armlet and bracelet. Gold. 6th c. Istanbul. The Archaeological Museum.

65   Ear rings. Gold and precious stones. 6th–7th c. Istanbul. The Archaeological Museum.

66 Two medallions. Gold. 6th c. Istanbul. The Archaeological Museum.

67   Cistern known as "Bin-bir-derek" or "The Thousand and one Columns". c.528. Constantinople.

68 Liturgical fan. Silver gilt. 6th c. Istanbul. The Archaeological Museum.

69   Paten. The Communion of the Apostles. Silver, partly gilt. 565–578. Istanbul. The Archaeological Museum.

70　Above: Reliquary for fragment of the True Cross. Enamel. 6th c. Poitiers. Sainte-Radegonde.
Below: Procession, transporting relics. Ivory. 6th or 7th c. Trier. The Cathedral Treasury.

71   Cross of Justin II. Silver gilt. 565–578. Rome. Museo Sacro Vaticano.

72 Silver plates; with scenes from the life of David. Above: David receives Samuel's Message.
Below: David kills a bear. 610–629. Nicosia. The Archaeological Museum.

73 The Marriage of David. Silver plate. 610–629. Nicosia. The Archaeological Museum.

74   Athena deciding the quarrel between Ajax and Odysseus. Silver dish. 6th c. Leningrad. The Hermitage Museum.

75   Silenus. Silver dish. 610–629. Leningrad. The Hermitage Museum.

76 Mosaic on the vault before the apse. Two Archangels. 6th–7th. c.
Formerly in the Church of the Assumption, Nicaea.

77   Mosaic on the vault before the apse. Detail of Archangel. 6th–7th c.
Formerly in the Church of the Assumption, Nicaea.

78   A quadriga. Silk textile. 8th c. Paris. Musée de Cluny.

79 A lion hunt. Silk textile. 8th c. Rome. From Cappella Sancta Sanctorum. Museo Cristiano.

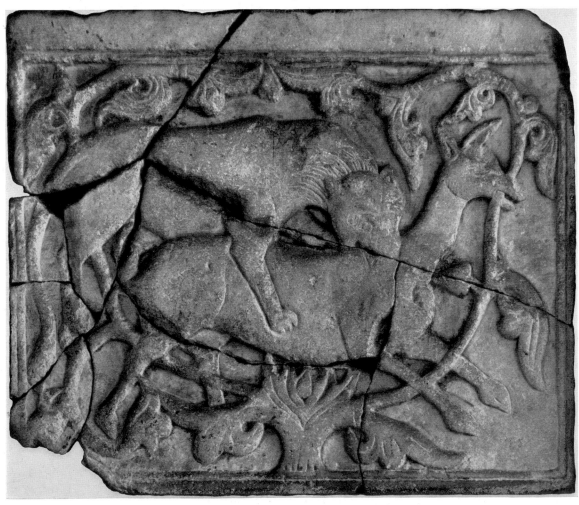

80   Above: A stag. Marble relief. 8th c. Istanbul. The Archaeological Museum.
Below: Lion attacking a deer. Marble relief. 11th c. Istanbul. The Archaeological Museum.

81   Bronze door. c.840. Constantinople. Sancta Sophia.

82   Gold goblet. 9th c. Istanbul. The Archaeological Museum.

83 Ivory. The Archangel Gabriel. 9th c. Washington D. C. W. R. Tyler, Esq.

84   Christ. From the Homelies of Gregory Nazianzus. 867–886.
Paris. Bibliothèque Nationale. Gr. 510 f. A, v.

85   The Transfiguration. From the Homelies of Gregory Nazianzus. 867–886.
Paris. Bibliothèque Nationale. Gr. 510 f. 75.

86   The Prayer of Jonah. From the Paris Psalter. 9th c. Paris. Bibliothèque Nationale. Gr. 139 f. 431 v.

87 Moses on Mount Sinai. From the Paris Psalter. 9th c. Paris. Bibliothèque Nationale. Gr. 139 f. 422 v.

88   Sancta Sophia. Mosaic on vault before the apse. An Archangel. 9th c. Constantinople.

89   Sancta Sophia. Mosaic in the semi-dome of the apse. The Virgin and Child. 9th c. Constantinople.

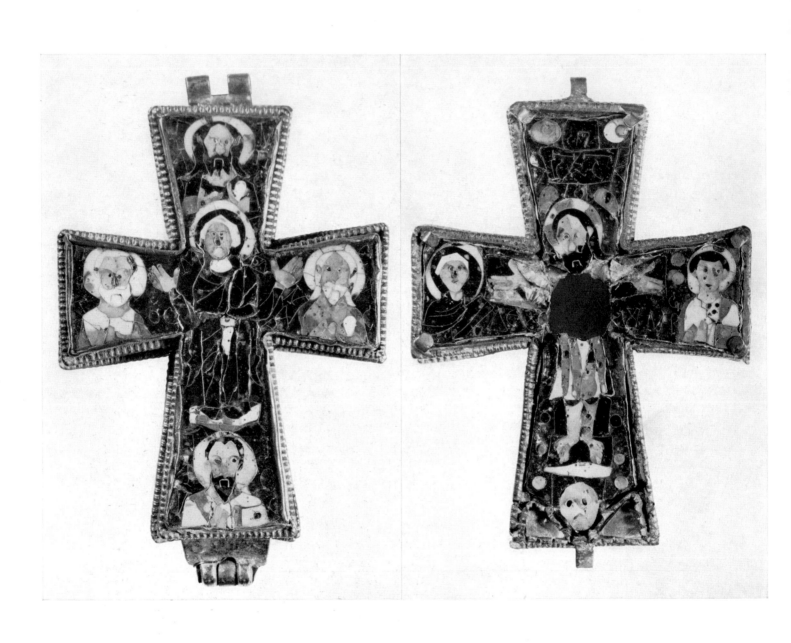

90   The Beresford Hope Cross. Enamel. 9th c. London. The Victoria and Albert Museum.

91   Enamel and jewelled Gospel cover. 9th c. Venice. The Marcian Library.

92   Christ. Ivory. 9th c. London. The Victoria and Albert Museum.

93 Sancta Sophia. Mosaic over the entrance from the Narthex. Christ and the Emperor Leo. 886–912. Constantinople.

94   Moses on Mount Sinai. From the Bible of Leo the Patrician. 10th c.
Rome. Biblioteca Vaticana. Reg. Gr. 1 f. 155 v.

95　David anointed King. From the Bible of Leo the Patrician. 10th c.
Rome. Biblioteca Vaticana. Reg. Gr. 1 f. 263.

96   The crowning of Constantine VII Porphyrogenitus. Ivory. c. 944.
Moscow. Museum of Fine Art.

97 The crowning of Romanos and Eudoxia. Ivory. c. 950.
Paris. Cabinet des Médailles.

98 Ivory triptych. Reverse. 10th c. Rome. Palazzo Venezia.

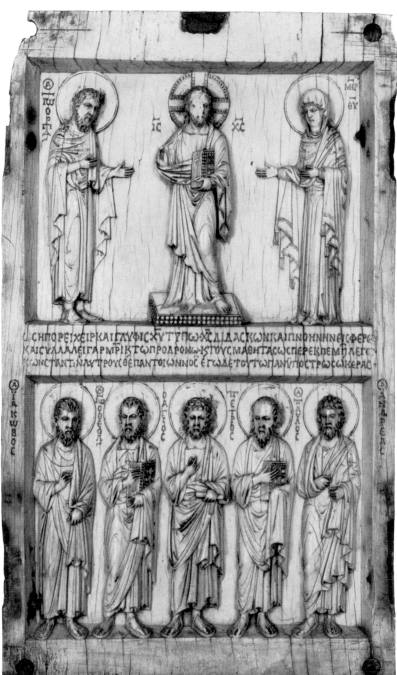

99 Ivory triptych. The inside, 10th c. Rome. Palazzo Venezia.

100   The Harbaville Triptych. The wings closed. Ivory. 10th c. Paris. Musée du Louvre.

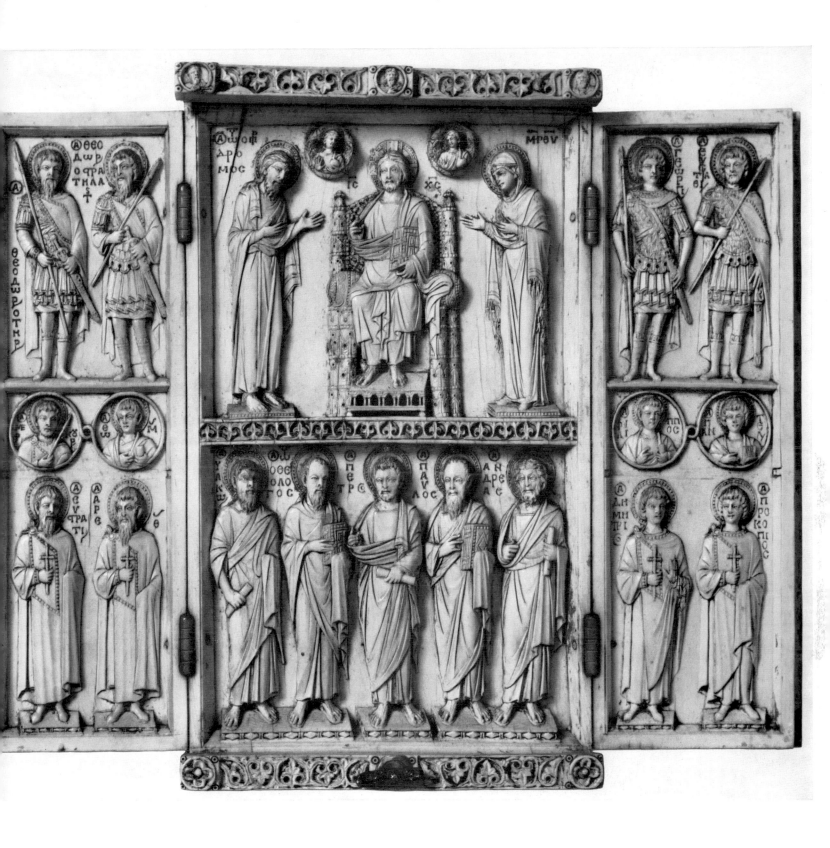

101   The Harbaville Triptych. The inside. Ivory. 10th c. Paris. Musée du Louvre.

102   The Harbaville Triptych. Reverse of the central panel. Ivory. 10th c. Paris. Musée du Louvre.

103   St John the Apostle and St Paul. Ivory. 10th c. Venice. Museo Archeologico.

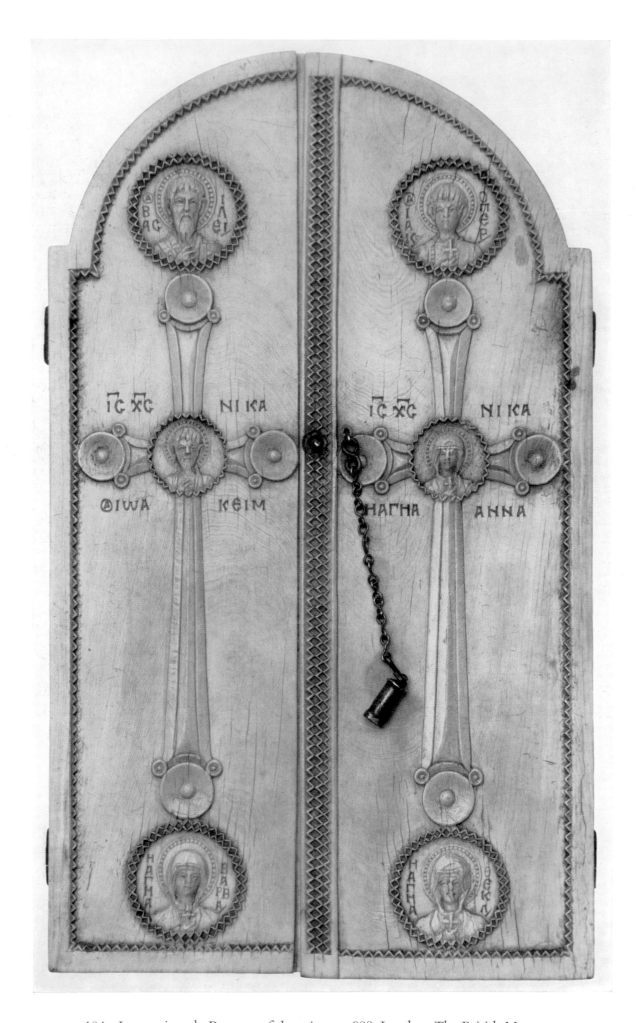

104   Ivory triptych. Reverse of the wings. c.988. London. The British Museum.

105   Ivory triptych. Interior. c. 988. London. The British Museum.

106   Statuette. The Virgin and Child. Ivory. 10th c. London. The Victoria and Albert Museum.

107   Christ. Ivory, affixed to metal book cover. 10th c. Oxford. The Bodleian Library.

108　The Veroli Casket. Ivory. 10th c. London. The Victoria and Albert Museum.

109   The Veroli Casket. Details. Ivory. 10th c. London. The Victoria and Albert Museum.

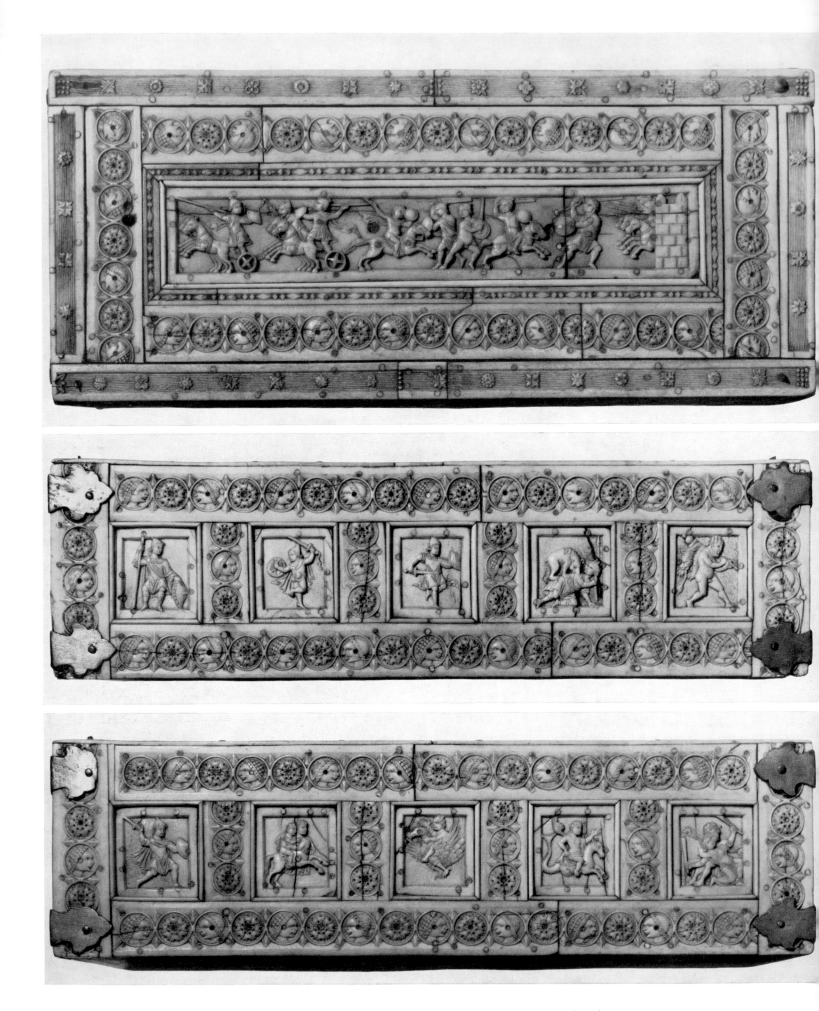

110 Ivory casket. Top and sides. 11th c. Paris. Musée de Cluny.

111   Ivory casket. Detail of panels. 11th c. Paris. Musée de Cluny.

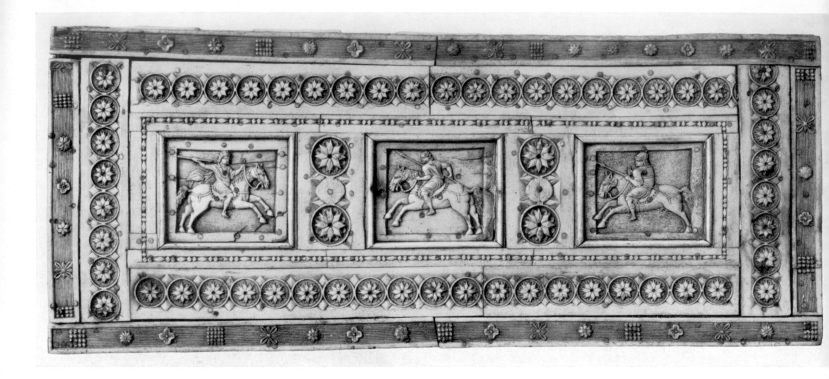

112   Above: Casket with warriors. Ivory. 10th–11th c. New York. The Metropolitan Museum.
Below: Panel from casket; scenes from the life of Joshua. Ivory. 10th c. London. The Victoria and Albert Museum.

113   Illumination from the Theriaca of Nicandor. 10th c. Paris. Bibliothèque Nationale. Suppl. Gr. 247 f. 47 v.

114   The Ascension. Ivory. 10th c. Florence. Museo Nazionale.

115   The Entry into Jerusalem. Ivory. 10th c. Berlin, Dahlem. Ehemals Staatliche Museen.

116   The Forty Martyrs. Ivory. 11th c. Berlin, Dahlem. Ehemals Staatliche Museen.

117 The Forty Martyrs. Detail. Ivory. 11th c. Berlin, Dahlem. Ehemals Staatliche Museen.

118   Ivory triptych. 10th–11th c. Paris. Musée du Louvre.

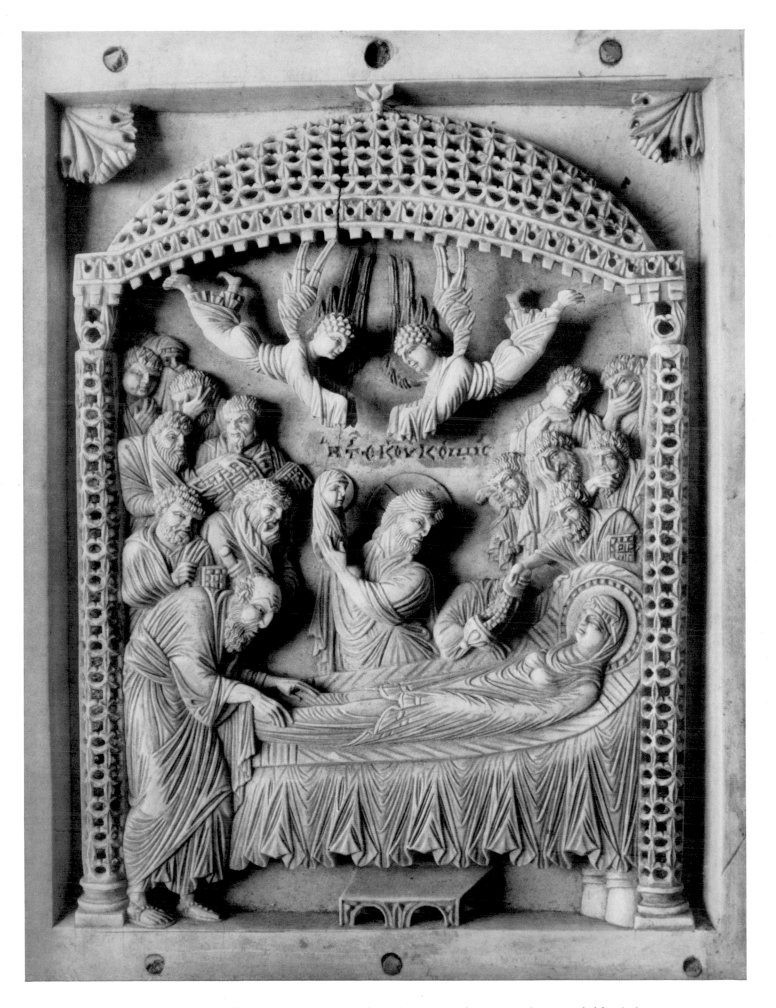

119 Dormition of the Virgin. Ivory. 10th–11th c. Munich. Bayerische Staatsbibliothek.

120   Ivory reliquary. Reverse. 963–969. Cortona. The Church of St Francesco.

121　Ivory reliquary. Obverse. 963–969. Cortona. The Church of St Francesco.

122 Head of the Archangel Michael. Marble. 10th c. Istanbul. The Archaeological Museum.

123   Ivory triptych. Late 10th c. Luton Hoo. The Wernher Collection.

124   Reliquary for the True Cross. Outer container. Gold and enamel. c. 960.
Limburg on the Lahn. Cathedral Treasury.

125   Reliquary for the True Cross. Inner compartment. Gold and enamel. c. 960.
Limburg on the Lahn. Cathedral Treasury.

126 Reliquary for the True Cross. Outer container. Gold. c. 960. Limburg on the Lahn. Cathedral Treasury.

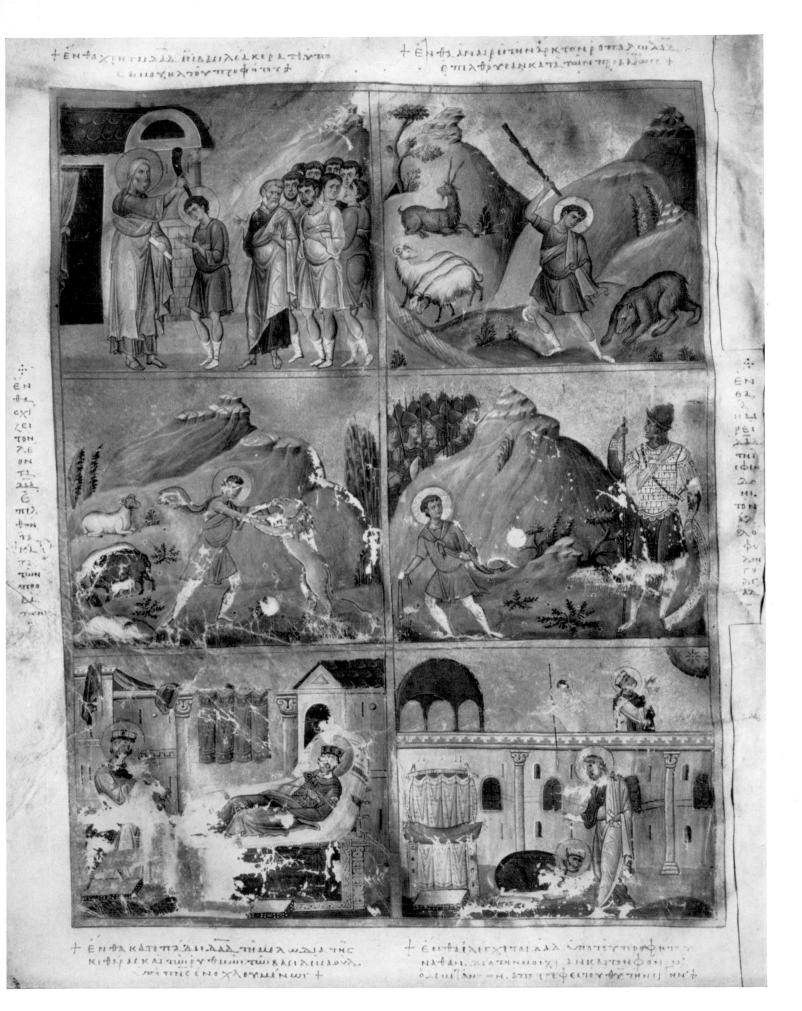

127 Six scenes from the life of David. From the Psalter of Basil II. 976–1025. Venice. The Marcian Library. Cod. Gr. 17 f. 2.

128　Above: Martyrdom of St Hermione. Below: The story of Moses. From the Menologion of Basil II. 979–984. Rome. Biblioteca Vaticana. Gr. 1613 f. 12.

129   Sancta Sophia. Mosaic over the south door. Constantine and Justinian. 986–994. Constantinople.

130 Silk with elephants in medallions. c. 1000. Aachen. The Cathedral Treasury.

131   The Shroud of St Siviard. Silk damask with winged gryphons. 11th c. Sens. The Cathedral Treasury.

132   The Shroud of St Germain l'Auxerrois. Silk. Late 10th c. Auxerre. The Church of St Eusebius.

133 Sancta Sophia. Mosaic. The Zoe panel. 1028–1042. Constantinople.

134   Enamels from the crown of Constantine Monomachos. 1042–1055. Budapest. The National Museum.

135 Reliquary for fragment of the True Cross. Wood, gold, and enamel. 11th c.
Esztergom. The Cathedral Treasury.

136   Paten. The Crucifixion. Silver. 11th c. Halberstadt. The Cathedral Treasury.

137 Paten of alabaster. 11th c. Venice. The Treasury of St Mark's.

138   Book cover of gold and enamel. 11th c. Venice. The Treasury of St Mark's.

139   Chalice. Onyx and enamel. 11th c. Venice. The Treasury of St Mark's.

140   Book cover. Silver gilt and enamel. 12th c. Venice. The Marcian Library.

141   Book cover. Silver gilt and enamel. 12th c. Venice. The Marcian Library.

142 Bas relief. The Virgin Orans. Marble. 11th c.
Istanbul. The Archaeological Museum.

143   The Virgin and Child. Ivory. 11th c.
Utrecht. The Archaeopiscopal Museum.

144   St John the Baptist. Ivory. 11th c.
Liverpool. The Archaeological Museum.

145   St John the Baptist and four Apostles. Ivory. 11th c.
London. The Victoria and Albert Museum.

146   St Just. Painting on silk. 11th c.
Trieste. Cathedral of St Just.

147   The Ascension. Top of ivory casket. 11th c.
Stuttgart. Württembergisches Landesmuseum.

148   Statue of an Emperor. Marble. 11th c.
Istanbul. The Archaeological Museum.

149 Plaque. St Eudoxia. Incrustation work. 11th c.
Istanbul. The Archaeological Museum.

150　Circular relief. The Virgin and Child. Green porphyry. 1078–1081. London. The Victoria and Albert Museum.

151 The Virgin and Child. Marble. 11th c. Istanbul. The Archaeological Museum.

152 Ivory casket. Sides. Hunting scenes. 11th c. Troyes. The Cathedral Treasury.

153 Ivory casket. Top and end. Mounted Emperors and phoenix. 11th c.
Troyes. The Cathedral Treasury.

154 The Virgin and Christ. Two ivory panels. 11th c. Bamberg. Staatliche Bibliothek.

155 Portative Mosaic. The Virgin and Child. c. 1065. Istanbul. Church of the Patriarchate.

156 Two marble slabs with geometric ornament. 12th c. Istanbul. The Archaeological Museum.

157   Pair of marble slabs sculptured in low relief. Peacocks. 12th c. Istanbul. The Archaeological Museum.

158   Triptych. Cast bronze. 12th c. London. The Victoria and Albert Museum.

159 Plaque. The Virgin and Child. Copper gilt. 12th c. London. The Victoria and Albert Museum.

160   Ivory casket. Busts of Christ, the Virgin and Saints. 12th c. Florence. Museo Nazionale.

161 Ivory casket. Details of panels. 12th c. Florence. Museo Nazionale.

162   The Archangel Gabriel. Steatite. 12th c. Fiesole. Museo Bandini.

163 The Emperor Nicephoras Botaniates, St John Chrysostom and an Angel. Miniature from the Homelies of
St John Chrysostom. c. 1078. Paris. Bibliothèque Nationale. Coislin 79 f. 2 v.

164   Sancta Sophia. Mosaic. The John panel. Detail of the Virgin. c. 1118. Constantinople.

165   Sancta Sophia. Mosaic. Portrait of the Emperor Alexios Comnenos. 1122. Constantinople.

166 Reliquary of silver gilt. Reverse. A leaved cross. 12th c.
Paris. Musée du Louvre.

167   Reliquary. The Maries at the Sepulchre. Silver gilt. 12th c. Paris. Musée du Louvre.

168   Portative mosaic. Christ. c. 1100. Berlin, Dahlem. Ehemals Staatliche Museen.

169   Portative mosaic. Christ. c. 1150. Florence. Museo Nazionale.

170   Enamel cross. Reverse. 12th c. Cozenza. The Cathedral Treasury.

171   Panel painting. Our Lady of Vladimir. c. 1130. Moscow. The Tretiakov Gallery.

172   Sancta Sophia. Mosaic. The Deesis panel. General view. 13th c. Constantinople.

173 Miniature Mosaic. The Crucifixion. Late 12th c. Berlin (East). Staatliche Museen.

174 Book cover. Silver-gilt repoussé work. 13th c.
Venice. The Marcian Library.

175   Scenes from the Life of Christ. Ivory. 13th c.
London. The Victoria and Albert Museum.

176   Moses on Mount Sinai. From Psalter. 13th c. Rome. Biblioteca Vaticana. Palat. Gr. 381 f. 169 v.

177 King David between Wisdom and Prophesy. From Psalter. 13th c. Rome. Biblioteca Vaticana. Palat. Gr. 381 f. 2.

178   The Palace of Constantine Porphyrogenitus. 12th or 13th c. Constantinople.

179 The Palace of Constantine Porphyrogenitus. 12th or 13th c. Constantinople.

180   The Church of St Theodore (Kilisse Cami). 10th to 13th cs. Constantinople.

181   The Church of St Saviour in Chora (Kariye Cami). 12th to 14th cs. Constantinople.

182   Mosaic. The Pantocrator. 1300–1320. Constantinople. Kariye Cami.

183   Mosaic. The Angel appears to Elizabeth at the well. 1300–1320. Constantinople. Kariye Cami.

184   Mosaic. The numbering of the people. 1300–1320. Constantinople. Kariye Cami.

185 Wall painting. The Anastasis. Detail, Christ. c. 1310. Kariye Cami. Constantinople.

186 Church of St Mary Pammakaristos (Fetiye Cami). South aisle. 13th c. Constantinople.

187   Church of St Mary Pammakaristos (Fetiye Cami). East end. 13th c. Constantinople.

188   Portrait of Hippocrates. From manuscript of Hippocrates. c. 1342. Paris. Bibliothèque Nationale. Gr. 2144 f. 10 v.

189 Icon. The Archangel Michael. 14th c. Pisa. Museo Civico.

190 The Emperor John Cantacuzenos enthroned. From manuscript of Cantacuzenos. 1370–1375.
Paris. Bibliothèque Nationale. Gr. 1242 f. 5 v.

191 Group of nuns. From the Lincoln College Typicon. c. 1400.
Oxford. The Bodleian Library. Gr. 35 f. 12 r.

192   The Virgin and Child. From the Lincoln College Typicon. c. 1400.
Oxford. The Bodleian Library. Gr. 35 f. 10 v.

193   Icon. The Virgin of Pimen. Detail. 14th c.
Moscow. The Tretiakov Gallery.

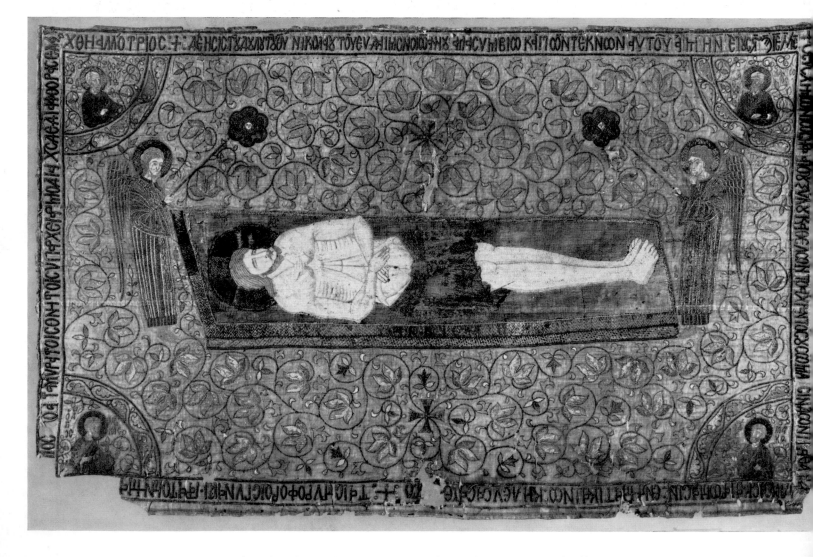

194   Embroidered Epitaphios. 1407. London. The Victoria and Albert Museum.

195   The "Dalmatic of Charlemagne". Embroidery. 15th c. Rome. Museo Sacro Vaticano.

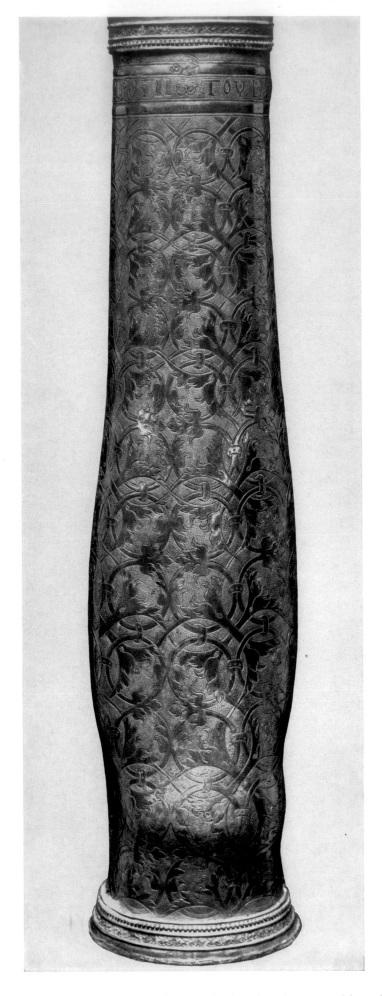

196   Reliquary for hand and arm. Gold. 15th c. Istanbul. Topkapu Saray.

NOTES ON THE PLATES

KEY TO SOURCES

BRÉHIER — L. Bréhier, *La Sculpture et les Arts mineurs* (Vol. III of Diehl, *Histoire de l'Art Byzantin*), Paris, 1934.

BYZANCE — *Byzance et la France Médiéval*, Paris: Bibliothèque Nationale, 1958.

B.Z. — *Byzantinische Zeitschrift.*

CATALOGO — G. Bovini and L. Ottolenghi, *Catalogo della Mostra degli Avori dell'alto medioevo*, Ravenna, 1956.

DIPTYCHEN — R. Delbrueck, *Die Consular-diptychen und verwandte Denkmäler*, Berlin–Leipzig, 1929.

EDINBURGH — *Catalogue of the Byzantine Exhibition*, Edinburgh–London, 1958.

EXPOSITION — *Catalogue de l'Exposition Internationale d'Art Byzantin*, Paris, 1931.

FIRATLI — N. Firatli, *A short guide to the Byzantine works of Art in the Archaeological Museum of Istanbul*, Istanbul, 1955.

G. AND W. — A. Goldschmidt and K. Weitzmann, *Die Byzantinischen Elfenbeinskulpturen der X. bis XIII. Jahrhunderts*, Berlin, 1931, I, Caskets; II, Other ivories.

J.H.S. — *Journal of Hellenic Studies.*

KOLLWITZ — J. Kollwitz, *Oströmische Plastik*, Berlin, 1941.

KUNST — W. F. Volbach and Max Hirmer, *Frühchristliche Kunst*, Munich, 1958.

KUNSTSCHATTEN — *Kunstschatten uit Vaticaanstad, Italiaanse Kerken en Musea*, The Hague: Gemeente Museum, 1955.

LAZAREV — V. N. Lazarev, *Istoria Byzantinskoe Jivopisi*, 2 vols., Moscow, 1947.

LONGHURST — M. H. Longhurst, *Catalogue of Carvings in Ivory*, London: Victoria and Albert Museum, Part I, 1927.

MATZULEWITSCH — L. Matzulewitsch, *Die Byzantinische Antike*, Berlin, 1929.

MENDEL — G. Mendel, *Catalogue des sculptures grecques, romaines et byzantines*, Constantinople: Musées impériaux ottomanes, I, 1912; II and III, 1914.

PASINI — A. Pasini, *Il Tesoro di San Marco*, Venice, 1886.

P. AND T. — H. Peirce and R. Tyler, *L'Art Byzantin*, Paris, I, 1932; II, 1934.

SEIDENWEBEREI — O. von Falke, *Kunstgeschichte der Seidenweberei*, Berlin, 1921.

SILKS — O. von Falke, *Decorative Silks*, London, 1936.

TRÉSORS — *Trésors d'art du Moyen Age en Italie*, Paris, 1952.

VOLBACH — W. F. Volbach, *Elfenbeinskulpturen der Spätantike und des frühen Mittelalters*, Mainz, 1952.

V.S.D. — W. F. Volbach, G. Salles and G. Duthuit, *L'Art Byzantin*, Paris, 1931.

WHITTEMORE — T. Whittemore, *The Mosaics of St Sophia at Istanbul: Preliminary Reports*, Oxford, I, 1933; II, 1936; III, 1942; IV, 1952.

WULFF AND VOLBACH — O. Wulff und W. F. Volbach, *Die altchristlichen und mittelalterlichen, Byzantinischen und Italienischen Bildwerke*, Berlin–Leipzig, Ergänzungsband, 1923.

NOTES ON THE PLATES

1 GOLD SOLIDUS: HEAD OF CONSTANTINE. *306–337. Private Collection. 4·52 gm.*

Constantine is shown facing right, wearing a diadem of laurels and rosettes, and looking upwards. On the reverse is a winged Victory facing right, seated on a trophy and writing on a shield held by a smaller Victory. On the shield are the letters VOT XXX. The inscription reads: SMNC VICTORIA CONSTANTINI AUG. The coin was struck at the mint of Nicomedia.

The bust of the emperor is full of life and marks a departure from the old Roman traditions. Indeed, it already seems to hint at changes in style and outlook which were to reach fruition in Constantinople in the course of the next few centuries.

Edinburgh, No. 248.

2, 3 BRONZE HEAD OF CONSTANTINE. *306–337. Belgrade. The National Museum. Ht. 36·7 cm.*

The head is crowned with a diadem. Traces of gilding remain, and the whole head was originally gilt. It was found at Nissa (Niš) in Yugoslavia.

Nissa was Constantine's birthplace and was used by him as a summer residence. The head is, however, of such remarkable quality that it is tempting to assign it to Constantinople, whither all the best artists had been summoned to work in the emperor's new city.

Kluge and Lehmann-Hartleben, *Grossbronzen*, III, Plate XVI and pp. 52 ff.; *Edinburgh*, No. 2.

4 MARBLE HEAD: PROBABLY THE EMPEROR CONSTANTINE. *c. 325. Istanbul. The Archaeological Museum. Ht. 39 cm.*

This head stood for many years in the garden of the museum, attached to a body to which it did not belong. In 1955 Professor Poulsen suggested the possibility that it represented Constantine; it was at once re-examined and was soon after published. It is perhaps not as fine as the famous head at Belgrade (Plate 3), but it is important in that it was almost certainly sculptured at Constantinople, for the resemblance to coins from the eastern mints is closer than to those from the western. It is probably to be dated to about 325.

Nazih Firatli, 'A portrait of Constantine the Great in the Museum', *Annual of the Archaeological Museum of Istanbul*, No. 7, 1956. See also *Firatli*, Plate 1.

5 THE BASE OF THE EGYPTIAN OBELISK. *c. 395. Constantinople. The Hippodrome.*

The upper part of the base is sculptured on all four sides, and shows the Emperor Theodosios I in the circus, with his court, guards, and other spectators. Below there is on one side an inscription in Greek, on the opposite side one in Latin, and on the other two sides low reliefs showing how the obelisk was transported and erected, as well as games in the Hippodrome.

The inscriptions tell us that the obelisk was set up by Theodosios I, the Great, in a space of thirty days, during the Consulship of Proclus; the exact year of this consulship is not known, but a date between 390 and 395 may be accepted as certain. No reliability can be placed on Wace's suggestion that the sculptures should be assigned to the time of Constantine (*J.H.S.*, XXIX, 1909, p. 60). In fact, they constitute a key monument for the age of Theodosios, and numbers of other sculptures that have been discovered at various times in Constantinople have been dated primarily thanks to evidence afforded by comparison with the Theodosios base.

The style of the work, with its vertical perspective, its rigid grouping, and its severe frontality, is, however, far more oriental than was that of much of the work done in Constantinople at the time or slightly later; a relief from Bakirkoy (Plate 8, *c.* 400), the Sarigüzel sarcophagus (Plate 9, *c.* 400), the 'antique' silver vessels published by Matzulewitsch (Plate 42), and the mosaic floor of the Great Palace (Plates 38–41, *c.* 500) may all be contrasted in this respect. These works and many others (e.g. Plate 43) are mostly in a 'neo-Attic' style, which may be regarded as typical of the capital; the carving of the Theodosios base approaches more closely to the orientalizing manner which may be taken as typical of work done in Syria, Palestine, and eastern Asia Minor. But there is every reason to believe that artists and craftsmen travelled freely in these early days of the East Christian Empire and the style of work at Constantinople was by no means unified at so early a date.

G. Bruns, *Der Obelisk und seine Basis auf dem Hippodrom zu Konstantinopel*, Istanbul, 1935; *Kunst*, Plates 54, 55.

6, 7 THE CONCESTI AMPHORA. *5th century. Leningrad. The Hermitage Museum. Ht. 42 cm.*

The amphora is of silver, its decoration is in repoussé in high relief; the details of the figures are gilt. The decoration is in three zones; on the shoulder is a hunting scene, in the centre

287

are warriors on foot fighting Amazons; below are three nereids riding sea monsters. Two handles, in the form of centaurs, were added later, for the relief decoration continues below the places of attachment. The vase was found in Moldavia in 1812.

Matzulewitsch assigned the find from Concesti to about the year 400, and suggested that the amphora was the work of a craftsman in the Black Sea area. Buscher, on the other hand, has argued for a seventh-century date and a Constantinopolitan workshop. It is, perhaps, noteworthy that the gold torque and the gold and enamelled fibula in the shape of a bird, also found at Concesti, are of a type usually dated to the seventh century, and there are aspects of style in the ornament of the dish from Concesti (Matzulewitsch, Plates 47, 48) which again look towards the later date. Further, the hunters are not concentrated on their task, but look outwards towards the spectators which is a feature characteristic of the later mosaics at Antioch, not the earlier. But the style is hardly that of the seventh-century 'Byzantinische Antike' as we see it in such a work as the Silenus plate in the Hermitage (Plates 74, 75), and on balance a date in the fifth century seems most likely.

Matzulewitsch, p. 132 and Plates 36, 43; E. Buscher, 'Bronzekanne aus Samos', *Abb. Ak. Berlin, Phil-Hist.*, No. 17, 1943, pp. 7, 9, 13, 24, 26; *Edinburgh*, No. 40.

8 MARBLE RELIEF: FOUR FIGURES. *Late 4th century. Istanbul. The Archaeological Museum; No. 2462. L. 150 cm. Ht. 74 cm.*

The lower portions of four figures, standing full length, survive; all wear the pallium and the leftermost of them holds a scroll.

The figures probably represent Apostles, and the foremost was no doubt depicted as receiving the scroll of the law from Christ; he must therefore be either Peter or Paul, and Kollwitz's study of the iconography serves to establish that the scene accords better with the composition usually associated with Paul than with that of Peter. He suggests a reconstruction which serves to stress the importance of East Christian as opposed to Italian developments in iconography in the fifth century (p. 156). The relief was found at Bakirkoy (Makrikeuy) near Constantinople. The work is of high quality and was no doubt executed in the capital.

Mendel, No. 1328; *Kollwitz*, p. 153 ff.

9 SARCOPHAGUS: WHITE MARBLE. *Late 4th or early 5th century. Istanbul. The Archaeological Museum; No. 4508. L. 150 cm. W. 63 cm. Ht. 155 cm.*

The sarcophagus is rectangular. On each side are two winged angels, upholding a circular medallion with a six-armed symbol in the form of a debased chi-rho inside it; at each end are two Apostles, full length, with a cross between them. It was found in a district of Constantinople known as Sarigüzel, not far from the mosque of Fatih—the site of Justinian's Church of the Holy Apostles. A Christian burial-ground existed in the area. The size of the sarcophagus shows that it was intended for a child.

The heads are well modelled and the sculpture is accomplished. It would seem that more than one man worked on the carving; even so, it was never completely finished. The marble is an import, probably from Greece, but it is likely that the carving was done in Constantinople. The quality of the work suggests that it was a commission for an imperial patron, but Airf Mufit, in his study of the work, was unable to suggest a personage, and for the time being any exact identification is impossible. The work is still close to the classical, but the style is Greek rather than Roman, and the sculpture is to be classed as 'neo-Attic', a designation which applies to a great deal of work done in Constantinople between the fourth and sixth centuries.

Arif Mufit, 'Ein Prinzensarkophag aus Istanbul', *Istanbul Asariatika Muzeleri Nessivati*, x, 1934; *Kollwitz*, p. 132; *Firatli*, Plate v; *Kunst*, Plate 75.

10, 11 THE GOLDEN GATE. c. *390. Constantinople.*

The Golden Gate is situated on the high ground, not far from where the land walls meet the Sea of Marmara, in a dominating position, clearly visible in every direction from a considerable distance. The gate itself and the smaller gate in front of it are Byzantine, the considerable fortress behind is a Turkish addition, set up by Mahommed II shortly after the conquest in 1453.

The Golden Gate itself takes the form of a triple entrance, with a great flanking tower on either side. The central arch is 8·5 m. and the two side arches 5·75 m. wide. All three gates are now in part walled up, but the walling dates from different periods, some of it being mid-Byzantine and some of Turkish date. In front of the gate is a paved court, and in front again a second gate or 'propylaea', on a modest scale, having one opening only, on the same axis as the central arch of the main gate. On either side of this arch are tall columns, topped by fine Corinthian capitals; on either side the outer wall was divided into a series of panel-like compartments, topped by carved canopies, in which sculptures in low relief were at one time situated. These reliefs survived in part till as late as 1791, and are mentioned by most of the travellers who visited Constantinople before then, often in very glowing terms. A few fragments of them were found during excavations conducted by the British Academy and the Istanbul Museum in 1927, which show that part at least was Graeco-Roman work of the second century A.D.

The foundations of the propylaean gate are to be assigned to the same date as the outer land wall, that is, to 447, but its upper structure is later, as is proved by the re-use of sculptured stones in its construction. It is impossible to give a definite date for this rebuilding, but the ninth or tenth century seems most likely. The date of the Golden Gate itself has also been disputed, though within narrower limits, some holding that it was built at the same time as the main portion of the land walls, that is, in 413, while others think that it was already there as a sort of free-standing triumphal arch when the land walls were erected. A third suggestion, that the gate is later than the walls, has also been put forward. Recent research conducted by Rüstem Duyuran has proved that the gate and the walls cannot be of the same date; either the gate is later than the walls, or, if it was earlier, a portion of the original structure must have been taken down before the walls were built. On the other hand, the inscriptions which adorned the two faces of the arch support an early dating. They were in metal letters, which have long since been robbed, but the holes for the attachment of the letters permit a reconstruction of the inscription. It read as follows:

> Haec loca Theodosius decorat post fata tyranni
> Aura saecla gerat qui portam construit auro.

It has been argued that this inscription could not refer to Theodosios II, the builder of the land walls, for the words 'post fata tyranni' refer to the suppression of a usurper, and no such event took place in his time. The text on the other hand might be very well applied to Theodosios I. If so, the most likely date would be between 388 and 391. It may be added that the whole style of the work tallies more exactly with what we know of Theodosios I and his foundations than with Theodosios II, and until further evidence of a strictly archaeological nature is available, the gate may be associated with the former emperor and be assigned to around 390 and to the same period at which he set up the Egyptian obelisk in the Hippodrome (Plate 5).

The upper portion of the main gate was once adorned with a cornice and with a number of statues, but none of these survives. Indeed much of the actual masonry has fallen as a result of earthquakes; the structure was very severely damaged by one in 1894. Its restoration is now in progress.

T. Macridy Bey and S. Casson, 'Excavations at the Golden Gate, Constantinople', in *Archaeologia*, LXXXI, 1931, pp. 63–82; A. Van Millingen, *Byzantine Constantinople: The Walls of the City and Adjoining Historical Sites*, London, 1899.

12, 13 THE LAND WALLS OF CONSTANTINOPLE. *5th century.*

Though they have in the course of centuries undergone numerous repairs and a great deal of destruction, the land walls of the city still retain very much the same appearance that they had when set up under the youthful Emperor Theodosios II between 413 and 447. From that day to this there has been no large-scale expansion of the city outside them. Most spectacular is the inner wall, a construction of the finest workmanship and of considerable height, reinforced by ninety-six towers; it was erected by the Prefect Anthemios in 413. Outside this is a second and rather lower wall, also with ninety-six towers, which stand in the spaces between the towers of the inner wall; this was erected by the Prefect Constantine in 447, who at the same time effected repairs to the inner wall, which had been damaged in an earthquake. Outside this is a moat divided into sections by walls at right angles; it has been suggested that these served to dam up water in the moat, but there has been some argument among scholars as to whether the moat was actually filled or was merely there as a protective ditch. Between the outer walls and the moat, as well as between the two walls themselves, are terraces each about 60 ft. in width.

A. Van Millingen, *Byzantine Constantinople: The Walls of the City and Adjoining Historical Sites*, London, 1899; F. Krischen and H. Leitzmann, *Die Landmauer von Konstantinopel*, Berlin, 1938.

14, 15 THE CHURCH OF ST JOHN OF STUDION
Fig. 1 (EMIR AHOR CAMISI). c. 463. Constantinople.

The church stands on the outskirts of the city, not far from the Golden Gate. Originally it formed part of the famous monastery of Studios, which for many centuries played a leading role in the religious life of the capital, especially as a centre of resistance against Iconoclasm in the ninth century. The church was erected by the Patrician Studios in 463 to replace an earlier building which had stood outside the city until the erection of the Theodosian land-walls. It underwent major repairs in the reign of Isaac Comnenos (1057–1059) and again in that of Andronicos II Palaeologos about 1290. It became a mosque about 1500, was severely damaged by fire in 1782, and finally fell into ruin at the end of the nineteenth century. The west end, however, remains more or less intact and shows the work of 463 to good advantage. The ornamental sculpture here is important, firstly because it is definitely dated, and secondly because it shows already a transition to the deeply undercut 'silhouette' manner which was to attain fruition under Justinian.

The ground-plan is interesting, for though the conservative basilical layout is followed, the proportions are very different from those prevalent in the west at this time, the building being much wider in comparison to its length; indeed, the proportions are far closer to those of a domed building like St Eirene than to those of the normal longitudinal basilica so prevalent in Rome. Another 'Byzantine' feature is the presence of a western transverse narthex. The central aisle terminates at the east in an apse, semicircular within, polygonal without. The side aisles are of rectangular plan and were two-storied, with a high gallery above the main arcades.

The church is now roofless and the carving of the capitals has perished as a result of fire. But some cornices remain, there is evidence that there was once a mosaic wall decoration, and there are vestiges of a fine floor in *opus Alexandrinum* which is perhaps to be assigned to the period of restoration under Isaac Comnenos.

A. Van Millingen, *Byzantine Churches in Constantinople*, London, 1912, Ch. 2.

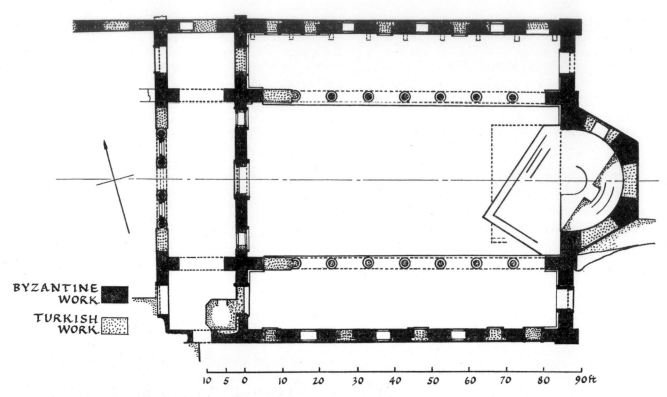

Fig. 1 Plan of the Church of St John of Studion (after Van Millingen)

16, 17 LIMESTONE RELIEFS. *From the Church of St John of Studion. 5th century. Istanbul. The Archaeological Museum; Nos. 2395 and 2394.*

There are three larger reliefs and several smaller fragments. Of the larger ones, the first (Plate 16, L. 1·5 m., Ht. 1·0 m.) depicts the Entry into Jerusalem. One figure follows our Lord, waving a branch; two welcome Him, one waving a branch, the other laying a cloak before His ass; behind is a tower-like structure representing Jerusalem. The border is composed of a vine scroll, with animals and birds interspersed.

The second slab found at the same time (Plate 17, Ht. 1·32 m., W. 60 cm.) bears a group of Apostles in front of a pedimented building. Above is the bust of another figure, with open book, presumably an Apostle, and between a bird pecking at a bunch of grapes. It is clearly by the same hand as the first relief.

A third relief, showing Christ and St Peter, though from the same place and of the same school, and probably of the same date, is by a different master, for the drapery is treated more formally and severely and the ornamental border is more stylized.

A number of other limestone reliefs in the museum, notably one bearing the sacrifice of Abraham (Mus. No. 4141), are related. They all show work of rather a primitive character, differing from that of the school responsible for such sculptures as the Sarigüzel sarcophagus (Plate 9) and the Bakirkoy

relief (Plate 8), both because of the coarser effect produced by the material—soft limestone as opposed to hard marble—and also in style. The work is rather oriental in character, but there is every reason to suppose that it was done locally, though it is possible that one of the masters came from Syria.

It has been suggested that the slabs originally formed part of a tomb or shrine in the monastery church. The church itself was built around 463, but there was an earlier building on the site, so this date is not conclusive. On stylistic grounds, however, the slabs might well have formed a part of the work done in 463.

Mendel, Nos. 668, 669, 670; *Firatli*, Plate VIII; *Kollwitz* mentions the slabs with Apostles (p. 163) and Christ and St Peter (p. 174), but not the one with the Entry. It was shown at Baltimore in 1947; see *Early Christian and Byzantine Art at the Walters Art Gallery*, 1947, No. 57; also K. Wessel, 'Ein Kleinasitisches Fragment einer Brustungsplatte', in *Forschungen und Berichte, Staatliche Museen zu Berlin*, 1, 1957, p. 71; *Kunst*, Plate 81.

18 TWO HORIZONTAL IVORIES. c. 500. *Milan. Castello Sforzesco; Nos. A 11 and A 12. L. 33·6 cm. Ht. 10·7 cm. and 10·4 cm. (lower plaque).*

The panels must have formed the top and bottom sections of a large composite diptych like the Barberini ivory (Plate 19). The upper one bears the bust of the personification of Constantinople in a medallion upheld by two winged

Victories. The inscription reads, AC TRIUMFATORI PER-PETUO SEMPER AUG(usto). On the lower is shown the swearing of allegiance of conquered barbarians in Phrygian costume; at either end are female figures suckling babies. In the corners are hanging crowns and the inscription VIR ILLUSTR(is) COM(es) PROTIC(torum) ET CONSUL ORDI-NAR(ius).

The work is of very high quality; comparisons suggested to Delbrueck a date around 500; Volbach thinks that the plaques are probably a little earlier than the Barberini ivory to which they are closely similar; the presence of the personi-fication, as well as the very accomplished style, show that the work was done in Constantinople.

Diptychen, No. 49; *Volbach*, No. 49; *Catalogo*, No. 52; *Edinburgh*, Nos. 41, 42.

19 THE BARBERINI IVORY. c. 500. Paris. Musée du Louvre. Total Ht. 34·1 cm. W. 26·6 cm. Central panel: Ht. 20·1 cm. W. 13·4 cm.

This superb ivory was originally made up of a large rect-angular panel in the centre, and four smaller panels, above, below, and at the sides; one is now missing. The central panel shows an emperor mounted; beside him is a winged Victory and behind his spear a figure in a Phrygian cap, the traditional way of indicating an Asiatic prisoner. To the left is a consul in military costume, presenting a statue of Victory. Above are two winged Victories, confronted, with a bust of Christ, youthful and beardless, between them. The panel below symbolizes the emperor's supremacy; on the one side barbarians bring tribute; on the other is an embassy from India bringing ivory and wild beasts; the figures and their head-dresses may be compared to those on a silver plate with the Personification of India in the Istanbul Archaeo-logical Museum (Plate 43).

There has been some discussion as to the identity of the emperor represented. Delbrueck has suggested Zeno (*Felix Ravenna*, fasc. 8, 1952, p. 5) and also Anastasius (*Diptychen*, No. 48); Constantine, Leo I, Basil, and Justinian have also all been proposed. Stylistic comparisons with the Ravenna throne, the diptychs of Anastasius and Areobindus, and other works suggest a date around 500. Anastasius defeated the barbarians in the Balkans on several occasions just before 500 and received an embassy from India in 496, and there seems every reason to suppose that this is the embassy that is depicted. The emperor may thus be identified with him.

Most authorities concur in assigning the ivory to Constan-tinople, and logic supports the evidence of style, for one would naturally assume that an ivory of this sort, depicting the emperor and signalizing his triumphs, would have been done in the capital and not in some provincial centre. But it is hard to see why Delbrueck (*Felix Ravenna*, 8, p. 6)

associates with it five other ivories, namely, a St Paul in the Cluny Museum, a multiple diptych in the Bibliothèque Nationale (Cod. Lat. Vet. 9384), a well-known book cover at Etchmiadzin, the centre of a multiple diptych at Lyons and another at Baltimore. All of these are in a very different style; they are in low relief and the faces are long and thin and the details are fussy. Indeed, these ivories bear little resemblance to the Barberini ivory, and are more likely to be of Syrian workmanship. More convincing is a parallel that has been suggested with certain of the ivories that compose the Ravenna throne, more especially the scenes on the back and the figures on the front. It is not, however, so close as to indicate absolute identity of workshop or date, and other of the ivories of the throne are in a style and of an iconography which there is reason to associate with Egypt.

Diptychen, No. 48; *Volbach*, No. 48; *P. and T.*, II, Plates 167–169; *Kunst*, Plate 219.

20 LEAF OF DIPTYCH OF AREOBINDUS. 506. Paris. Musée du Louvre. Ht. 36 cm. W. 11·6 cm.

The consul holds mappa and sceptre; he is shown as a bust in a medallion enclosed in a formal frame of acanthus leaves; above and below the medallion is his name in the form of a monogram in Greek letters. The reverse bears a very elaborate 'Paradise' scene in high relief, done in the west in the ninth century.

The style of the portrait recalls the Barberini ivory (Plate 19), and the rather severe nature of the acanthus frame accords well with the 'neo-Attic' tastes which we believe to have been characteristic of Constantinopolitan work. A diptych formerly in the Trivulzio collection, of which both leaves survive (*Diptychen*, No. 14), is closely similar, but it is rather less well preserved and can never have been of quite such high quality.

Diptychen, No. 13; *Volbach*, No. 12.

21 IVORY: THE EMPRESS ARIADNE. c. 500. Florence. Museo Nazionale. Ht. 36·5 cm. W. 13·6 cm.

The figure, in richly bejewelled imperial regalia, and carry-ing sceptre and orb, is shown standing within a niched recess with curtains drawn back on either side and topped by a dome. Above is an eagle at either side, with between them a chain held in their beaks. The empress's costume bears what is presumably an embroidered panel with upon it the representation of a prince or emperor as consul. The ivory must have formed the central panel of a composite diptych like the Barberini ivory (Plate 19). The central panel of a similar leaf which shows the same empress seated is preserved at Vienna.

Delbrueck suggests that the empress is to be identified as Ariadne, daughter of Leo I (457–474) and wife first of Zeno

(474–491) and then of Anastasius (491–518); she died in 515, and he suggested that the diptych should be dated to around 500. Peirce and Tyler on the other hand (II, Plate 27) compared the work to the diptych of Clementinus (513) and suggested that it was carved at the time of Ariadne's death. Grabar identified the empress as Constantina and dated the panel to the sixth century; de Loos-Dietz suggested Theodora and dated it about 530; others have identified the figure as the Empress Irene. The clear resemblance to the Barberini ivory tends to support the earlier dating. The eagles at the top follow a Roman model closely, but the style as a whole is Constantinopolitan, and there is every reason to believe that this and the Vienna ivory were both carved in Constantinople by a man who had been fully schooled in the style characteristic of the capital. Delbrueck identified a horizontal panel at Basle as the top of the diptych (No. 50).

Diptychen, No. 51; *Volbach*, No. 51; *Catalogo*, No. 53; *Edinburgh*, No. 39.

22 DIPTYCH OF AREOBINDUS. *506. Zürich. Schweizerisches Landesmuseum. Ht. 36 cm. W. 13·2 cm. and 11 cm.*

The two leaves are closely similar. On both the consul sits on an elaborate throne, the *sella curulis*, holding the mappa and sceptre. On either side, behind the throne, are two officials. Below again, but actually in front, as the 'vertical' system of perspective is employed, are circus games, with a row of spectators watching from behind a balustrade. On one leaf four *venatores* are spearing lions and a fifth stands behind; on the other men are lassooing bears. On both leaves there are inscriptions at the top which read on the one leaf, FL(avius) AREOB(indus) DAGAL(aifus) AREOBINDUS V(ir) I(nlustris), and on the second EX C(onsule) C(onsul) OR(dinarius). The left leaf is in better condition than the right.

Seven ivories with the name of Areobindus have come down to us; they belong to three distinct types, one where the consul is shown seated, watching circus games (Munich, Besançon, Paris, and Leningrad), one where he appears at the centre in a medallion enclosed by foliage (Paris—Plate 20—and Milan) and one where the decoration consists of crossed cornucopias (Lucca). The leaves at Zürich and Besançon are attributed to the same hand by Delbrueck (p. 110).

Areobindus was consul at Constantinople in 506, so there is reason to believe that the leaf was carved there. There is, however, little in the style of this leaf which points to Constantinople rather than to any other major centre.

Diptychen, No. 9; *Volbach*, No. 8; *Catalogo*, No. 56; *Edinburgh*, No. 48.

23 DIPTYCH OF CLEMENTINUS. *513. Liverpool. The Archaeological Museum; No. M. 100036. Ht. 39 cm. W. 13 cm.*

Both panels show the Consul Flavius Clementinus enthroned between personifications of Rome and Constantinople. At the top are medallions of the Emperor Anastasius and the Empress Ariadne, with a cross between. At the bottom youths pour money from sacks as a sign of liberality. The inscriptions read FL(avius) TAURUS CLEMENTINUS ARMONIUS CLEMENTINUS and V(ir) IL(lustris) COM(es) SACR(arium) LARG(itionum) EX CONS(ule) PATRIC(ius) ET CONS(ul) ORDIN(arius). On the back is a later inscription, a prayer in Greek, and the date 772.

Little is known about this consul, but he held office in Constantinople and the ivory was probably carved there. There is, however, nothing that is very markedly Constantinopolitan about the style of this ivory, though the faces, especially those of the imperial portraits at the top, are not dissimilar from those on the Barberini ivory (Plate 19).

Diptychen, No. 16; *Volbach*, No. 14; *Catalogo*, No. 58; *Edinburgh*, No. 26.

24, 25 MANUSCRIPT OF DIOSCORIDES. *c. 512. Vienna. National Library; Cod. Med. Gr. 1. Ht. 37 cm. W. 30 cm.*

The manuscript begins with a magnificent dedication page, showing the Princess Juliana Anicia enthroned between two personifications, 'Megalopsychia' and 'Phronesis' (Plate 24; diam. of circle 23 cm.). In the foreground is a prostrate figure representing the Gratitude of the Arts; between this and the Megalopsychia is a figure representing the Love of the Foundress. Around the scene is an acrostic, in which mention is made of a church founded by Juliana at Honoratae, a suburb of Constantinople, about 512. The putti in grisaille engaged in building operations on the outer margin also refer to the construction of this church.

The book also includes a fine portrait of Dioscorides himself writing (f. 4, Plate 25); it seems to herald the typical evangelist portraits of later times. There are also in the manuscript a few decorative pages, such as one with a peacock, and a large number of pictures of plants having medicinal value.

Juliana was the granddaughter of Valentinian III and the wife of Areobindus, who was consul in the east (see Plates 20, 22). She therefore presumably lived at Constantinople, and the fact that she founded a church there makes it well-nigh certain that the miniature was done there also. The style is in the main Hellenistic, but there are certain oriental elements, especially in the decorative detail.

P. Buberl, 'Die Antiken Grundlagen der Miniaturen des Wiener Dioscoridescodex', *Jahrbuch des deutschen archaeol. Inst.*, 61, 1936, p. 114; also *Die Byzantinischen Handschrifts I. Der Wiener Dioskorides und die Wiener Genesis*, Leipzig, 1937.

26 DIPTYCH OF ANASTASIUS. *517. Paris. Cabinet des Médailles. Ht. 36 cm. W. 13 cm.*

In the centre is a pediment-like tribune, before which the consul sits holding mappa and sceptre. At the bottom of one leaf is a circus scene, shown as a half-circle with spectators at the corners; at the bottom of the other are Amazons above and tragic actors below. At the top are inscriptions reading FL(avius) ANASTASIUS PAULUS PROBUS SABINIAN(us) POMPEIUS ANASTASIUS and VIR INL(ustris) COM(es) DOMESTIC(orum) EQUIT(um) ET CONS(ul) ORDIN(arius). Between these and the pediments are on each leaf three medallions, supported by *erotes*; they represent Anastasius, Ariadne, and the Consul Pompeius.

One complete diptych, three leaves, and two fragments of diptychs of this consul survive. That in Paris is the finest. The complete leaves all follow the same dispositions. The precise nature of the carving, the rather severe dispositions of the figures, and the round faces, shown frontally, are all characteristically Constantinopolitan, and this diptych might have been assigned to the capital even without the knowledge that Anastasius was consul there.

Diptychen, No. 21; *Volbach*, No. 21; *Kunst*, Plate 220.

27 LEAF OF DIPTYCH OF MAGNUS. *518. Paris. Cabinet des Médailles. Ht. 26·2 cm. (originally 38·5 cm.). W. 13 cm.*

The consul sits enthroned between the personifications of Rome and Constantinople, which are on a very large scale; above is a garland, looped up at the centre, with a crown of bay leaves suspended from it at that point. The leaf bears no inscription, but it is usually associated with Magnus.

Four other leaves of this consul survive, one at Milan, one at Leningrad, one at Liverpool, and another in the Cabinet des Médailles. The Paris and Milan leaves are closely similar, and Delbrueck suggests that they are to be regarded as a pair; Volbach, though he admits the possibility, does not agree, and he is perhaps right for the hinge-holes do not correspond. On the Milan example (No. A8) the central of the three cords which hold up the crown is missing, while the hair of the consul has been re-carved in the manner of a late Romanesque fresco, to give him a tonsure; this does not accord at all well with the frontal position and the large staring eyes. The staff held by the Personification of Rome has also been re-cut, and there are other minor changes apart from the re-cutting. The ivory at Leningrad and the second one in the Cabinet des Médailles are copies of the Carolingian period; that at Liverpool is a more recent copy. All three copies are rather coarse, though this effect is to some extent due to the material which is not real ivory. All retain, however, a scene at the lower extremity showing the bringing of tribute as well as the inscription at the top, whereas on the

two original leaves only the consular portraits survive. The disposition of the figures is the same on all.

Diptychen, No. 22; *Volbach*, No. 24; *Trésors*, No. 20.

28, 29 THE DISH OF PATERNUS. *c. 518. Leningrad. The Hermitage Museum. Diam. 61 cm.*

The dish is of silver, the relief decoration partly gilt. At the centre of the base is engraved a large chi-rho cross, with the letters A and Ω on either side. This is bordered by an inscription which reads EX ANTIQUIS RENOVATUM EST PER PATERNUM REVERENTISS(imum) EPISC(opum) NOSTRUM. AMEN. Around the rim is an elaborate 'inhabited' vine scroll in relief, interrupted by two gold crosses and four cabochon mounts for jewels, which represent a later addition of more barbarian character. On the inside of the base is a second inscription in Greek, referring to the quality and weight of the silver. On the base are also four control stamps, one of which is in the name of Anastasius I (491–518). The name of a Bishop Paternus is known from the Black Sea region and serves to suggest a date close to 518.

The vessel was found in 1912 at Malaya Perescepina in the Poltava district of Russia, together with a number of other pieces of silver, some in Constantinopolitan style, some Persian and some apparently of local manufacture. Most important of them is the great Perescepina amphora. They were taken there perhaps as loot, perhaps in exchange for local products or perhaps as gifts to placate some nomad chieftain. But the general effect of the work is already purely Byzantine. The control stamps prove that the dish was made at Constantinople; it is, both on account of its size and because of the dignity of its design, one of the finest pieces of silver made in the capital that has come down to us.

Matzulewitsch, Plate 6 and pp. 102ff.; *Edinburgh*, No. 28.

30 IVORY: DIPTYCH OF PHILOXENUS. *525. Paris. Cabinet des Médailles; No. 45. Ht. 38 cm. W. of each leaf 14·3 cm.*

Each leaf bears three medallions made up of interlinking bands. In the upper ones is the bust of the consul, mappa in one hand and sceptre in the other, in the lower the personification of Constantinople. In the central medallion are incised inscriptions reading FL(avius) THEODORUS FILOXENUS SOTERICUS FILOXENUS VIR ILLUST(ris) and COMES DOMEST(icorum) EX MAGISTRO M(ilitum) PER THRACIA(m) ET CONSUL ORDINAR(ius). Between the medallions are further inscriptions in relief in Greek, reading ΤΟΥΤΙ ΤΟ ΔΩΡΟΝ ΤΗ ΣΟΦΗ ΓΕΡΟΥΣΙΑ and ΥΠΑΤΟΣ ΥΠΑΡΧΩΝ ΠΡΟΣΦΕΡΩ ΦΙΛΟΞΕΝΟΣ The diptych is enclosed on a silver mount.

Diptychs of this type were made for members of the Senate. Philoxenus was a senator, and also 'Magister Militum'; that is, commander-in-chief, for Thrace. He was also made a 'Comes Domesticorum' in 518; this may be interpreted as a privy councillor. Philoxenus was consul at Constantinople, and there is every reason to suppose that the diptych was carved there, though the style is somewhat coarse in comparison with that of other ivories of the period. But the work is expressive and forceful none the less.

Diptychen, No. 29; *Volbach*, No. 28.

31 DIPTYCH OF JUSTINIAN. *521. Milan. Castello Sforzesco; Nos. A 13 and 13 bis. Ht. 36·8 cm. W. 12·7 cm.*

At the centre of each leaf is a medallion, enclosing an inscription in Latin, reading MUNERA PARVA QUIDEM PRETIO SED HONORIBUS ALMA and PATRIBUS ISTA MEIS OFFERO CONSUL EGO. There is another inscription at the top which reads FL(avius) PETR(us) SABBAT(ius) JUSTI-NIAN(us) V(ir) I(llustris) and COM(es) MAG(ister) EQQ(uitum) ET P(editum) PRAES(entalis) ET C(consul) O(r)D(inarius); there are rosettes enclosing lions' heads at the four corners. The Consul Justinian was later to become emperor (527–565).

A similar diptych is preserved in New York, and there is also a leaf in the Cabinet des Médailles. The Milan example is finer than the others, though Delbrueck thinks all are to be assigned to the same hand; the ivory of the New York example has, however, cracked rather badly, which some-what detracts from its appearance. The clear-cut style is typical of Constantinople, and the ornament may be com-pared with that on some of the silver plates done in the capital, more especially the dish of Paternus which is dated to 518 (Plates 28, 29).

Diptychen, No. 26; *Volbach*, No. 25; *Trésors*, No. 21; *Catalogo*, No. 61; *Edinburgh*, No. 50.

32–4 CAPITALS. *5th century and later. Istanbul. The Archaeological Museum.*

The changes that characterize the evolution of a purely Byzantine style in art between about 450 and 550 are perhaps more clearly to be seen in the form and decoration of capitals than in any other direction. The series illustrated (as Plates 32–4) have been selected from the large quantity of examples in the Constantinople museum to illustrate this evolution.

The first (Plate 32, above; Museum No. 2367, Ht. 4·9 cm.; side 63 cm.) is a Corinthian capital of the conventional type, except for the fact that the drill has been used very extensively in modelling the acanthus leaves, and though they still remain to a considerable extent naturalistic, signs of a new outlook, where the leaves are no more than the basis of an 'all-over' black-and-white design, are already apparent. The capital is to be dated to the early fifth century, and is of the class usually known as 'Theodosian'.

Mendel, No. 741.

The second capital (Plate 32, below; Museum No. 2253, Ht. 38 cm.; side 52 cm.) bears a decoration of a more original character, namely, four heads, probably representing Oceanus, framed in leaves. The faces are well modelled, the hair and beards have become inextricably confused with the foliage of the background, so that it is impossible to tell where hair ends and foliage begins. The motif was one fairly usual in Roman art, especially in mosaic floors; heads in the border of the floor of the Great Palace may be compared (*The Great Palace of the Byzantine Emperors: First Report*, Oxford, 1947, Plates 43 and 49). The capital is probably to be assigned to much the same date as the floor; the early sixth century seems likely.

Mendel, No. 749.

The next capital is decorated with four winged horses, and there are acanthus leaves below (Plate 33, above; Museum No. 2404; Ht. 52 cm.; side 76 cm.). The acanthus leaves are rather flat and the chisel has been used rather than the drill. The horses which form the four corners are very beauti-fully carved, in the cold, polished, classical style which is known as the 'neo-Attic'; the style is characteristically Constantinopolitan and the marble is from the Marmara Islands. The capital is to be dated to the sixth century, and shows the finest work of the age, comparable with that on ivories, like the Barberini ivory in the Louvre (Plate 19).

Mendel, No. 750.

The fourth capital (Plate 33, below; Museum No. 2655; Ht. 55 cm.; side 107 cm.) is of an entirely new type. The Corinthian form, which still persisted in the lovely horse's head capital, has here been replaced by a flatter variant, designed essentially to support a brick arch rather than a solid block of stone. The conventional volutes have, how-ever, been retained below. The upper surface is thus very extensive and the relief is low, so that there are no weak spots, as there tend to be with the normal Corinthian form. Indeed the foliage is so little undercut that it looks more like embroidery than carving. Its rather flatter monotonous effect is mitigated by the very lovely peacock that dominates the principal face. On the opposite face is a cross, and on the two other faces there are acanthus plants. The peacock is in quite high relief and the sculpture is accomplished. The capital is essentially Byzantine in design as well as in shape; except for the retention of the conventional volutes below there is little that is classical about it. It was found near the site of Justinian's Church of the Holy Apostles and very probably came from the building. It is certainly to be dated to Justinian's time; a date around 540 is likely.

Mendel, No. 1242.

The next capital (Plate 34, above; Museum No. 942; Ht. 52 cm.; side 75 cm.) is actually dated to the reign of

Heraclius (610–641) by an inscription in Greek, reading 'O God of the saints, succor Heraclius the Despot'. But there is little about it which suggests a date in the seventh rather than the sixth century. It has even been suggested that the inscription is a later addition, but this would seem unlikely unless an earlier inscription had been erased; moreover, the very conservative nature of so many of the silver vessels dating from the reign of Heraclius should not be lost sight of. The acanthus leaves below are well modelled, and there is still a feeling for sculpture in the round. The cornucopias form a very effective decoration.

Mendel, No. 755.

The last capital we illustrate (Plate 34, below; Museum No. 2810; Ht. 27 cm.) is a cubic capital of a distinct type, for the acanthus leaves are completely stylized and the design of two birds back to back is like an embroidered pattern; indeed the capital would seem to have been closely inspired by a textile. The feeling here is clearly 'medieval' rather than classical. The style is not far removed from that of Romanesque sculpture, the design is close to that of the great eleventh-century textiles, like the shroud at Auxerre (Plate 132), and the capital is to be dated to around 1000.

Mendel, No. 751.

35 MARBLE PEDESTAL. c. 500. *Istanbul. The Archaeological Museum; No. 4202. Ht. 1·52 cm.*

The pedestal is square; it is sculptured on three sides, the fourth being plain, so that it must originally have stood against a wall. It was presumably used as a base for a statue or large bust. The decoration follows the same scheme on all three sides, that is to say that below there are two rectangular panels, enclosing diamond-shaped plaques, within which are rosettes made of acanthus leaves, while above it terminates in what is really an acanthus capital; on the front the acanthus leaves are spiny and the drill has been used profusely; on the two sides the leaves are spineless and the carving has been mainly done with the chisel.

The occurrence of the two styles, the more progressive and the more conservative, together on the same stone is interesting; equally so is the presence on the same block of the rectangular patterns below, which herald a type of ornament which was to become extremely popular on closure slabs in the sixth and following centuries. The combination of motifs that we see here is typical of Constantinople, and the actual carving is definitely in that precise 'neo-Attic' manner which is also to be regarded as characteristic of the capital. The base is to be dated to around 500; it assumes a place midway between the carvings of the west end of the Studion (Plate 15) and the capitals and cornices of SS. Sergius and Bacchus (Plates 50, 51). It was found near the Hippodrome

and may have stood there or in the baths of Zeuxippos, where there was a noted collection of statues.

First published in *Second Report upon the Excavations carried out in and near the Hippodrome of Constantinople in 1928*, London, 1929, Fig. 51; *P. and T.*, 11, Plate 42.

36 IVORY DIPTYCH WITH HUNTING SCENES. c. 450. *Leningrad. The Hermitage Museum. Ht. 32·2 cm. W. of each leaf 10·6 cm.*

On each leaf are four *venatores*, fighting with lions. The *venatores* are intent on their tasks and do not look outwards towards the spectator as do the hunters in the later floors at Antioch or on the Concesti amphora. The open backgrounds, with no indications of shadows and little of the ground, are similar to those of the Great Palace mosaic (see Plates 38–41).

The rather hard, precise style may be compared with that of a diptych in the Museo Nazionale at Florence bearing on one leaf St Paul and on the other scenes of Paradise. The style, like that of the Florence ivory, is distinctly in the 'neo-Attic' character that is to be associated with Constantinople, and Delbrueck indeed assigned the diptych to the Eastern Empire, dating it to about 450. But he noted stylistic similarities with the Apotheosis leaf in the British Museum, which he believed to refer to the tercentenary of the *consecratio* of the Emperor Marcus Antoninus Pius in 463; both the subject and the monogram at the top of the leaf, which has been read as SYMMACHORUM, point to a Roman origin.

De Loos-Dietz grouped the Liverpool Venatio (*Edinburgh* No. 27) and the Leningrad Venatio together with a sequence of diptychs which included the Apotheosis leaf, the Dionysos-Selene diptych at Sens, the Andrews diptych in London, and others, and placed them in Italy in the first quarter of the fifth century. Incidentally, she was in favour, in company with Weigand, of the tercentenary of the birthday of Antoninus Pius being in 386. Wessel suggested a north Italian origin for the Leningrad Venatio and preferred a date in the first half of the fifth century, a date accepted by Volbach, who is not explicit about the origin, though he groups it in his western sequence. Beckwith assigns the group related to the Apotheosis leaf from the middle of the fifth century until the date 463; he accepts Delbrueck's suggestion that the leaf refers to the tercentenary of the consecratio and attributes the group to a Roman workshop. A Roman provenance is thus most likely; we illustrate the ivory here because it clearly heralds developments in style which were followed in the mosaic floor of the Great Palace.

Diptychen, No. 60; *Volbach*, No. 60; Wiegand, *Kritische Berichte*, 1930–1931, p. 48; E. P. de Loos-Dietz, *Vroeg-Christelijke Ivoren*, Assen, 1947, 123; K. Wessel, 'Eine Gruppe oberitalienischer Elefenbeinarbeiten', *Jahrbuch des deutschen archäol. Inst.*, 63–64, 1948–1949, pp. 3 ff.; Beckwith, *The Andrews Diptych*, London, 1958, pp. 34–37; *Edinburgh*, No. 23.

37 BRONZE PLAQUE WITH SILVER INLAY. *5th or 6th century. Paris. Musée du Louvre; No. 3448. L. 18·7 cm. W. 15 cm.*

Three huntsmen, one on foot and two mounted, are shown hunting wild animals with the aid of dogs.

Hunting scenes of this type were extremely popular; they constitute one of the principal motifs of decoration of mosaic pavements between the fourth and sixth centuries and they occur on silver vessels, on ivories (cf. Plate 36), on textiles and on stone sculptures. All resemble one another so closely that it is obvious that sketchbooks of some sort must have circulated among the craftsmen in widely separated areas. In the earlier hunting scenes the animals are spirited, the conception is naturalistic, and the hunters are preoccupied with their tasks; in the later ones the animals are more stylized and the hunters look outwards at the spectators rather than towards the animals they are pursuing, as for example in the later floors at Antioch of about 500. Here the hunters are preoccupied with their activities. The plaque shows certain resemblances to the mosaic floor of the Great Palace (Plates 38–41) and is probably to be assigned to much the same date or slightly earlier. It was probably made in Constantinople. There is a somewhat similar plaque in the Dumbarton Oaks collection (*Handbook*, No. 75).

P. and T., 1, Plate 67; *Edinburgh*, No. 22.

38–41 MOSAIC FLOOR. *Early 6th century. Constantinople. The Great Palace of the Byzantine Emperors.*

The floor originally occupied four sides of a great peristyle court, some 70 m. square; the peristyle was about 10 m. deep on each side, and comprised an inner and an outer border, each rather more than a metre wide, and four registers of figures or scenes in a rich variety of colours against a plain white background; they comprise every shade available in marble or similar hard stone; the blues, greens and yellows are of glass. Only on rare occasions is the actual ground shown, and cast shadows are never indicated, as they were in mosaics of the classical period. The subjects are very varied, comprising figures of classical character, hunting scenes, beasts, fantastic animals, horses, sheep, circus games, scenes of country life and so forth. The technique is of the highest possible excellence, and though several hands are to be distinguished, some more accomplished than others, the work is all extremely fine. Though the artists obviously studied natural models so far as the animals are concerned and though many of the figures are themselves very classical, the absence of ground below the compositions, as well as of shadows, and the way in which the figures are silhouetted against a plain background, already savour of the 'medieval'; we see here, in fact, the first hints of the new manner which was to mature fully in the time of Justinian and to constitute the new 'Byzantine' style.

Four separate compositions are here illustrated, selected from the very large variety that compose the floor. Plate 38 shows a man seated; he follows the 'philosopher' type of antique art. Plate 39 shows an eagle struggling with a serpent; it is one of the motifs of a basically symbolic character that are treated with such naturalness and freedom in the mosaic. Plate 40 shows a building with water gushing from two tunnels below it; it is treated in the picturesque style of the classical wall-paintings of Pompeii or Boscoreale. Plate 41 represents a part of the border, which consists of formal bands with an elaborate acanthus scroll between. The folds of the scroll frame birds, fruit and so forth and at intervals human heads appear. Most of these heads are stylized, bearded representations of Oceanus, but this head, beardless but moustached, is more personal and more characterful; in spite of the unnaturalistic colouring, blue being used for the moustache and in the hair, it might almost be taken for the portrait of some barbarian chieftain of the day.

There has been much dispute as to the date of this mosaic, but stylistic considerations, and those of topographical and archaeological nature also, support a dating early in the sixth century. The floor must have belonged to a very important section of the palace, but it is, unfortunately, impossible to identify the building.

Floors in North Africa, at Piazza Armerina in Sicily, and at Antioch and elsewhere in Syria and Palestine may be compared from the stylistic point of view, but the Constantinopolitan one is technically far more perfect than any floors of fifth-century date elsewhere, and it is also of a higher quality from the artistic point of view.

The Great Palace of the Byzantine Emperors: being a first report on the excavations carried out in Istanbul on behalf of the Walker Trust (The University of St Andrews), 1935–38, Oxford, 1947; D. Talbot Rice, The Great Palace of the Byzantine Emperors: Second Report, Edinburgh, 1958.

42 SILVER DISH: A SHEPHERD. *6th century. Leningrad. The Hermitage Museum. Diam. 24 cm.*

The shepherd is seated on a stone bench; beside him is his dog, and before him are two goats, the upper one standing on a 'coulisse' or conventionalized rock, nibbling the leaves of a tree. The dish was found at Klimova, in the district of Perm, in 1907.

The presence of the ground below one of the sheep, together with a marked feeling for naturalism, suggests a date in the fourth century, and one would have tended to date the dish slightly earlier than the mosaic floor of the Great Palace, were there not stamps on the back; one of them is in the form of a monogram which reads either as 'Anastasius' or as 'Justinian', thus indicating a date in the first half of the sixth century.

The series of silver plates bearing scenes from the life of David, which were found in Cyprus and which are now divided between the Nicosia Museum and the Pierpont

Morgan Collection, are in a very similar style, though they are dated by stamps to between 610 and 625 (see Plates 72, 73). A plate in the Metropolitan Museum showing David slaying the lion (*P. and T.*, II, Plate 183*b*) may also be compared.

Matzulewitsch, No. 4 and pp. 112f.

43 SILVER DISH: THE PERSONIFICATION OF INDIA. *6th century. Istanbul. The Archaeological Museum. Diam. 45 cm.*

The decoration, partly in relief, partly in niello, shows a figure seated on a cushioned stool, surrounded by monkeys and birds which were regarded as typical of India. Below are two figures wearing turbaned head-dresses, holding on a leash a tiger and a leopard. The border is of geometric form, edged with running scrolls. The dish was found at Lampsacus in north-western Asia Minor.

Peirce and Tyler suggested that the figure was to be identified as the Personification of India, and it may be that the dark tint of the niello used on the face, arms, and shoulder is intended to represent a dark eastern skin. The curious horned head-dress may be compared to those worn by members of the Indian embassy at the base of the Barberini ivory (Plate 19, *c.* 500), and the figures at the bottom of the plate are also similar. Peirce and Tyler have also noted similarities to the Concesti amphora (Plates 6, 7), and to some of the silver from Traprain in the National Museum of Antiquities, Edinburgh. The composition of the Istanbul dish is, however, much more reticent, notably in the way in which the animals are virtually silhouetted against an open background as they are in the mosaic floor of the Great Palace, and on these grounds it seems likely that the plate is to be dated to the early sixth century. It is to be regarded as a product of the very best Constantinopolitan workshops.

P. and T., I, Plates 175–177; *V.S.D.*, Plates 51, 52; *Firatli*, Plate XIV.

44, 45 SILVER VASE. *6th century. Paris. Musée du Louvre. Ht. 44 cm.*

The shape is that characteristic of a pottery vessel; at the shoulder is a band of ornament bearing medallions of Christ, the Virgin, saints, and archangels, with foliated scrolls between them; above and below this band is bordered by a rope-motif; there are similar rope-bands at the foot at the junction of neck and shoulder; otherwise the surface is plain.

This large silver vessel is without stamp or hall-mark, but the style of the ornament suggests a date fairly early in the sixth century. It was found at Homs in Syria, and this has led scholars to assign it to Syria. But the location of finds is no guide to their source, and the absence of hall-marks does not preclude a Constantinopolitan origin. Moreover, the floral portion of the ornament is in a style close to what one would expect to see at Constantinople at this time, while the figures in medallions are completely Byzantine, and

herald work of the tenth and following centuries. Wherever the vessel was made—and that it was made at Constantinople is a distinct probability—it does not show to any marked degree any of the characteristics of the Syrian or oriental styles; in fact, it is to be regarded as an important example of the new 'Byzantine' style which characterized the sixth century, as we see in Justinian's buildings and decorations.

P. and T., II, Plate 71; *Louvre: Catalogue des Bijoux Antiques*, 1924, Plate XXVI; *Bréhier*, Plate LIII; *Edinburgh*, No. 44; *Kunst*, Plate 246.

46, 47 STONE AMBON. *Early 6th century. Istanbul. The Archaeological Museum. Greatest actual height 1·79 m. W. 82 cm.*

The ambon must originally have been very elaborate. In plan it was semicircular in front and straight at the back, except for a projection at the centre, where the stair touched the ground. The curved front was elaborately decorated. Below were a series of conch-topped niches, with a figure in each; together these represent the Adoration of the Magi. Above was a carved entablature, and above again closure slabs to bound the platform. Four columns apparently rose from this level, presumably to support a canopy like that over a ciborium; this no longer survives.

The figures are unfortunately very battered, but enough is preserved to show the high quality of the sculpture. The ornamental work is better preserved than the figural. It is extremely full and ornate, and its style falls half-way between the more naturalistic approach of the Theodosian age and the fully stylized work of Justinian's time, as for example in the cornices of SS. Sergius and Bacchus (Plate 51). A date shortly before the end of the fifth century thus seems probable. The work was in all probability done in the quarries of the Marmara Islands; as there is reason to believe that much Constantinopolitan sculpture was done there also, the ambon may be regarded as a Constantinopolitan work, even though it came from Salonica.

Mendel, Plate 643; for a reconstruction see G. Sotiriou, 'The Ambon of Salonica', *Annual of the Association of Byzantine Studies*, I, Athens, 1933, p. 418 (in Greek); *Kunst*, Plates 78, 79.

48, 49 IVORY: THE ARCHANGEL MICHAEL. *Early 6th century. London. The British Museum. Ht. 43 cm. W. 14·3 cm.*

The archangel is shown inside a doorway or embrasure, with an arch above it. He holds an orb topped by a cross in one hand, and a staff in the other. Above his head is a medallion with a cross in it and at the top of the ivory an inscription in Greek, reading 'Receive these gifts and having learned the cause . . .'; the inscription was no doubt continued on the second leaf of the diptych. Below is a flight of six steps, but the angel is poised above them; he does not stand upon them.

The rather fussy detail of the ornament of the arcade is at first glance somewhat suggestive of Syria, but is paralleled closer at hand by the Salonica ambon (Plates 46, 47). The rounded face of the angel suggests a comparison with the Barberini ivory, and the proportions of the figure and the fine upstanding inscription in Greek are just what one would expect to find in Constantinople. The transcendent understanding is also essentially Byzantine. In spite of this apparent eclecticism, the quality of the work is outstanding and there is every reason to believe that the ivory was made in the capital.

There has been some argument as to its date. Delbrueck assigns it to about 400 or even before, and compares it to the disk of Theodosios. Dalton and Volbach favour the fifth century; Morey, Friend, and Peirce and Tyler assign it to the sixth or even the early seventh. It has been examined more recently by E. P. de Loos-Dietz, who dates it in the first half of the sixth, and this seems much the most likely date.

Diptychen, p. 2; *Volbach*, No. 109; *P. and T.*, II, Plate 35; de Loos-Dietz, 'La plaque en ivoire à l'archange du British Museum et le classicisme Justinien', *Bull. v.d. Vereen tot Bevord. v.d. Kennis v.d. Antiek*, 29, 1945, p. 75; E. Kitzinger, *Early Mediaeval Art in the British Museum*, 1940, Plate 8.

50, 51 THE CHURCH OF SS. SERGIUS AND BACCHUS (KUCUK AYA SOFIA). 527–536. *Constantinople.*

The foundations of the church were laid in 527, the year of Justinian's succession, and it was completed before 536, for it is mentioned in the proceedings of a synod held that year in the capital. It is thus the earliest of Justinian's numerous churches. This is an important fact, for the carvings of the cornices and capitals inside it are already in a fully fledged Byzantine style; indeed, they represent some of the finest work of the sixth century. The plan, an octagon enclosing an open octagon, on which the dome rests, represents a stage in the development of the centralized church, which begins with Sta Costanza in Rome in the early fourth century and ends with the Dome of the Rock at Jerusalem in the seventh. The Church of San Vitale at Ravenna is akin, but more elaborate, in that it has a projecting presbytery on the eastern side. San Vitale was founded at much the same time, but was only completed in 547 or 548. In some ways it represents an advance on SS. Sergius and Bacchus, for it is higher and its proportions are more elegant. But in other ways it is retrogressive; this is especially the case with regard to the capitals: in both churches they are of the new 'impost' type, where volutes are absent so that an extensive flat surface is available at the top to support the bricks of an arch or vault. In SS. Sergius and Bacchus the masonry is placed directly upon the capital, whereas in San Vitale an impost block ('pulvino'), which is virtually a second capital, is placed between the capital proper and the masonry above; as Diechmann has pointed out (*Baukunst Constantinopels*, 1956, p. 54), this represents a complete failure to realize the significance of the Byzantine invention, where the capital itself

was quite adequate to afford support without an intervening impost. The marble in both cases came from the Marmara Islands and was probably carved in the actual quarries, perhaps by the same workmen; the cornices of SS. Sergius and Bacchus are, however, rather more elaborate than those of San Vitale, and show some of the finest work of the period.

A. Van Millingen, *Churches*, Ch. 3; *Kunst*, Plates 186–190.

52, 53 THE CHURCH OF ST EIRENE. c. *532 and later.* *Constantinople.*

On the site stood one of the earliest Christian churches of Constantinople. Constantine enlarged the building, but his church was destroyed in the Nika riots of 532. A new church was at once erected by Justinian, but it was again partly destroyed by fire in 564, and in 740 severe damage was done by an earthquake. At the Turkish conquest the building became first the armoury and then a museum of arms; in 1950 it was vacated and left empty as an ancient monument.

The plan is basilical, with narrow side aisles and galleries above, and a very wide central aisle; the roof, however, is composed of two dome chambers on an east–west axis; the domes are supported by great brick piers. The eastern dome chamber has been but little altered, except that the original columns of the arcades must at some time or other have been removed and others of varying size and height have been put in to replace them; the original columns were no doubt used for one of the great mosques built by the Turks in the sixteenth century. The westerly dome chamber has been very considerably altered, and the whole structure shows the evidence of numerous repairs. Three major phases can, however, be distinguished, which correspond with the work of Justinian, the repairs after the fire of 564, and those after the earthquake of 740. The interior, however, as seen in a photograph taken from the west, presents much of the original appearance.

The mosaic in the eastern apse is interesting for its consists of a great cross. We know that such decorations were set up in several churches in Iconoclast times, in place of the figural compositions of earlier date, and there is every reason to believe that the mosaic in St Eirene dates from that time. The inner inscription is somewhat damaged and has been wrongly restored; it should probably read 'We shall be filled with the good things of Thy House. Holy is Thy Temple. Thou art wonderful in righteousness. Hear us, O God our Saviour, and hope of all the ends of the earth and of them on the great sea.' The inscription on the outer face of the sanctuary has been identified as a text from Amos ix, 6, 'He who builds his ascent up to the heaven and his command on the foundations of the earth.'

A. Van Millingen, *Churches*, Ch. 4; W. S. George, *The Church of St Eirene at Constantinople*, London, 1912.

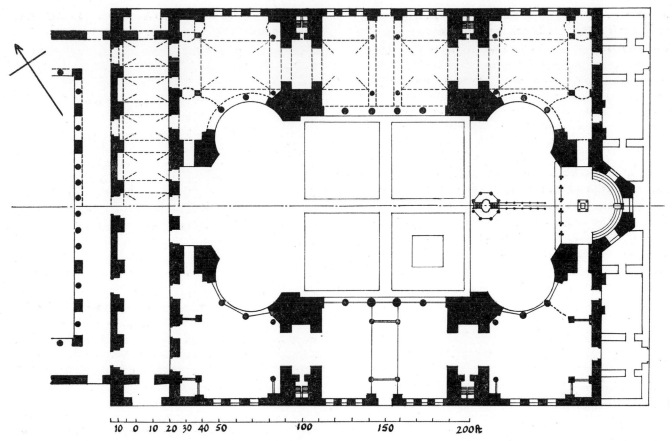

Fig. 2 Plan of the Church of Sancta Sophia (after Lethaby and Swainson)

54–6 THE CHURCH OF SANCTA SOPHIA. 532–537.
Fig. 2 Constantinople.

As is well known, the church was erected by Justinian to replace an earlier basilica, destroyed in the Nika riots of 532. It was dedicated in 537. In the astonishingly short period of five years and ten months this immense building—for long the largest church in the world—was completed. So miraculous did this seem to contemporaries that it was universally held that assistance was given to the work by angels. The Byzantine system of building, where courses of brick alternate with courses of mortar as thick or thicker than the bricks, was not well suited to such rapid work, for great weights were imposed before the mortar was properly dry, and as a result arches buckled and buttresses had almost at once to be erected. It was perhaps also to some extent as a result of this hasty construction that the eastern arch that upholds the dome and a part of the dome itself fell in the year 557, being unable to withstand the shaking of earthquakes which occurred in that year and in 553. The dome was then rebuilt 6·25 m. higher than before, though it still remains the flattest dome of large size in the world. That dome still stands, though it had to be repaired, first in the tenth century, and then again in the fourteenth. Its delicately proportioned vault is one of the greatest glories of architecture.

The plan is both surprisingly original and surprisingly conservative. Reduced to its simplest elements, it follows the old layout of a three-aisled building, the aisles separated by arcades in which piers and built columns both appear; the central aisle ends in an apse. What is new is that this conventional plan is fitted into an immense square instead of a rectangle, and that four great piers serve to delimit an upper square within the surrounding one; this is carried up to an unprecedented height. At the top of the central square is the dome, which rests on four great arches joining the piers, with pendentives at the corners; the vaults of the side aisles serve to buttress the central mass on north and south; at east and west are great semi-domes which must in turn have afforded some support, though their construction is so thin that it is clear that the architects looked upon them as parts of the roof of the basilica rather than as supports of the central dome.

The conception of the building is thus original; even more, it is profoundly spiritual, and it is to be doubted whether a more successful combination of a practical building, capable of holding a mass of worshippers, and a transcendental understanding, where thoughts and emotions are at once wafted to a spiritual rather than a mundane sphere, has ever been achieved in the history of the world's architecture. In this Sancta Sophia remains supreme. 'It seemed as if the vault of heaven were suspended above one,' stated the contemporary writer Procopius; a vault of subtle proportions and supreme loveliness, which at once evoked ideas of the infinite and corresponded to the spiritual conception of the faith to which the church was dedicated.

At their lower levels the walls were—and indeed they still are—adorned with slabs of marble, highly polished and carefully selected for their beauty; above, the walls, vaults, dome, and pendentives were entirely covered with mosaics. In many places these have fallen, and have been replaced by plaster. In other places the original mosaics of Justinian's day, comprising crosses or ornamental patterns, survive. In an upper chamber over the south porch there are some great scrolls that must date from the time of Justin II (Underwood, 'Notes on the work of the Byzantine Institute in Istanbul, 1954', *Dumbarton Oaks Papers*, Nos. 9 and 10, 1955–56, p. 291). Elsewhere, however, the mosaics are all of post-Iconoclast date; all belong to different periods between the mid-ninth and the thirteenth centuries. Most of the more accessible mosaics that survive have now been cleaned; there may, however, be others in the dome, below plaster of Turkish date.

The bibliography of Sancta Sophia is considerable for the church has interested writers at all periods. The best general account is still that of Lethaby and Swainson, *The Church of Sancta Sophia, Constantinople*, London, 1894, who list all the works published until their own day. W. R. Zaloziecky's *Die Sophienkirche in Konstaninopel*, 1936, is more in the nature of an inquiry into aesthetics than a pure architectural study. Of the more recent works, the most important are an article by K. J. Conant, 'The first dome of St Sophia and its rebuilding', *American Journal of Archaeology*, 43, 1939, p. 589, and 'A preliminary report of a recent examination of the structure', *loc. cit.*, 47, 1943, p. 403, which anticipates the publication of a full and prolonged study of the actual building. See also E. H. Swift, *Hagia Sophia*, New York, 1940, and *Kunst*, Plates 191–205. For the mosaics, see Whittemore, *The Mosaics of St Sophia at Istanbul: Preliminary Reports*, I, 1933; II, 1936; III, 1942; IV, 1952; and Plates.

57 CAPITALS: SANCTA SOPHIA. *532–537. Constantinople.*

The capitals of Sancta Sophia represent the finest early examples of an art that is wholly Byzantine. All hints of previous manners, western or eastern, have been blended together to form a new and distinct style, fully capable of holding its own against criticism. It is no longer to be described in any way as 'decadent', a term which could with justice be applied to some of the early Christian sculptures or capitals which are merely debased classical ones. The deeply undercut ornament is something new and original and succeeds in achieving a very effective result. We see work of the same type in Justinian's other buildings, but in none of them is it of such high quality as in Sancta Sophia.

58 WALL MOSAIC: JUSTINIAN AND HIS COURT. *526–547. Ravenna. San Vitale.*

The mosaics of San Vitale were set up during the reign of Justinian, and certain parts of the work were probably executed by craftsmen familiar with what was being done at Constantinople at that time, even if they were not actually trained there. In the absence of work of the period in Constantinople itself they may thus be cited as typifying Justinian's work at the capital. The panel of Justinian and his court is especially important, for it provides what is obviously a vivid portrait of the emperor, though not quite as vivid perhaps as that of Archbishop Maximian who stands on his left. It is, however, a far better portrait, and a better mosaic, than the rather similar panel in Sant' Apollinare in Classe; a portrait head in Sant' Apollinare Nuovo, which has sometimes been associated with Justinian, has been much restored and it is even doubtful if it actually represents the emperor. The corresponding panel in San Vitale, showing the Empress Theodora and her entourage, is closely akin; the two together give an admirable idea of the orientalizing style of much of the work done at this time, for the figures are posed rigidly and frontally rather than naturalistically. They are important too in that they reproduce an obviously true picture of the finest textiles of the age, a few actual examples of which have also come down to us.

G. Bovini, *The Mosaics of Ravenna*, Milan-London, 1956; *Kunst*, Plates 164–167.

59 WALL MOSAIC: THE THREE MAGI. C. *560. Ravenna. Sant' Apollinare Nuovo.*

The mosaics of Sant' Apollinare Nuovo belong to two periods: the figures and New Testament scenes high up on the walls were done in the time of Theodoric (493–526) and are in a vivid, expressive style; the processions of saints of either side, females on the north, males on the south, leading respectively to the Virgin and to Christ, are in a more elegant, flowing manner and are to be assigned to the time of Justinian (527–565). Between the foremost of the female saints and the Virgin are the three Magi, bearing gifts, the guiding star in the sky above them. The work is some of the best in Ravenna, being particularly brilliant and finished. An artist from the capital was almost certainly responsible for its creation.

Kunst, Plate 153.

60 GOLD MEDALLION OF JUSTINIAN. *534–538. Formerly in the Cabinet des Médailles, Paris. Diam. 8·6 cm.*

The medallion bears on the obverse a bust of Justinian in three-quarter face, in military costume and wearing an ornate helmet; around the margin is the inscription DN IUSTINIANUS PP AVG ('Dominus noster Justinianus Perpetuus Augustus'). On the reverse the emperor is shown mounted, with a figure of Victory holding a palm branch and a trophy of arms in front of the horse. Justinian is again in military costume and his horse has a rich saddle-cloth. The inscription above reads SALUS ET GLORIA ROMANORUM; below is the mint name CONOB (Constantinople).

The medallion was found at Caesarea in Cappadocia, but was minted in Constantinople some time between 534 and 538. It was preserved till 1831, when it was stolen and melted down; happily a number of satisfactory electrotypes are available.

Edinburgh, No. 254; W. Wroth, *Catalogue of the Byzantine Coins in the British Museum*, London, 1908, p. 11 and frontispiece; *Kunst*, Plate 244.

61 MARBLE HEAD: PROBABLY THEODORA. c. 530. Milan. Castello Sforzesco. Ht. 27 cm.

The neck is broken just below the chin; the hair is bound by a jewelled diadem, above which it is enclosed in a tight-fitting cap, while below the hairdressing is indicated by a series of vertical bands. The eyebrows form a flat plane with the bridge of the nose and the forehead, a convention found in other work of the sixth century (Plates 62, 63).

The head was found at Milan, but it is certainly the work of a Greek sculptor and was probably made in Constantinople. It has been variously dated. Peirce and Tyler compare it with the disk of Theodosios and with a head of Eugenius (392–394) in the Louvre, and associate it with Justina, wife of Valentinian and date it to 387. Delbrueck (p. 26) assigns it, primarily on the basis of the hairdressing, to the sixth century and identifies it as a portrait of Theodora. The later dating has found general acceptance, and the identification with Theodora is highly probable.

Trésors, No. 8; *P. and T.*, I, Plate 44; *Kunst*, Plate 68.

62 MARBLE: PORTION OF CIBORIUM ARCH. 6th century. Istanbul. The Archaeological Museum; No. 4268. H. 91 cm. Greatest width 1·4 m.

This was originally a rectangular plaque, pierced by an arch. Around the margin of the arch were the busts of the Apostles; in the two upper corners were busts of angels, their wings spread ingeniously to fill the triangular space. The outer border is formed of a double plaited band. The right-hand portion, with one angel and three busts, survives.

It is by no means easy to date this slab. The double plaited band at first suggests the eighth century, but such a date is precluded by Iconoclasm, when a figural relief of this sort could not have been made. Moreover the ornament is known in Asia Minor in the sixth and even in the fifth century. A date in the ninth or tenth century, though suggested by Mendel, seems hardly likely in view of the comparatively high relief of the busts of the Apostles; they accord more nearly with sixth- or seventh-century tastes. Moreover the style of the angel's hair is close to that of Theodora's head at Milan (Plate 61), while the technique of the figure sculpture, where the forehead appears as a wide flat plane, and the eyebrows constitute a single sharp line continuing around the nose, is one which is to be found on a number of sixth-century heads. The plaited band of the border could also belong to this date, so that on the whole a sixth-century date seems most likely. Peirce and Tyler publish a cross (II, Plate 175b) on which there is a rather similar interlace, which they date to the sixth century, though it must be admitted that so early a date for it is not very securely founded. The pattern is perhaps derived from the classical guilloche.

Mendel, No. 705.

63 MARBLE: PORTION OF CIBORIUM ARCH: FROM ST MARY PANACHRANTOS. 6th century. Istanbul. The Archaeological Museum.

A number of sculptured fragments were found in the filling below the floor of the Church of St Mary Panachrantos, now Fenari Issa Camisi, during the excavation conducted by Theodore Macridy Bey in 1928. Pieced together they form an archivolt of considerable size, on which were sculptured the heads of the Apostles.

The outstanding quality of the sculpture is not to be disputed; there has, however, been some argument as to the date. The church is a double one. The northern half was built by Constantine Lips in 908, the southern a few centuries later. Both were converted to the worship of Islam in 1496. The northern church was very richly decorated and fragments survive of fine architectural sculpture. Macridy's excavations showed, however, that Constantine Lips's church replaced a five-aisled building of the sixth century, and some of the capitals in the present building belong to that period. The arch could, on the basis of the archaeological evidence, have belonged either to the sixth-century edifice or to that of 908, for the fragments were found below a floor made at the time of the church's conversion into a mosque. At first glance its 'medieval' character appears predominant. But comparison with other stone sculptures in the Constantinople Museum as well as with the head of Theodora (Plate 61) and with ivories supports a date in the sixth century, and this tallies with the results of recent research which indicate very clearly that it was not only in architectural sculptures like the capitals and cornices of Sancta Sophia, but also in figural work, that the new style was developed at the time of Justinian.

P. and T., II, Plate 15a; *Firatli*, Plate VII; Macridy, *Archaeologischer Anzeiger*, 1929, pp. 343 ff.; Casson, 'Byzantine and Anglo-Saxon Sculpture', *Burlington Magazine*, LXI, 1932, p. 268.

64 GOLD ARMLET AND BRACELET. *6th century. Istanbul. The Archaeological Museum; Nos. 3534 and 3841. Greatest diam. of armlet 13·8 cm. Greatest diam. of bracelet 7·6 cm.*

The armlet (Museum No. 3534) is in the form of a plain gold ring with terminations adorned with granulated work; the granulations are small but the pattern somewhat irregular. The bracelet (Museum No. 3841) is also of gold, but the ends are widely separated and are flattened into heart-shaped terminations adorned with filigree ornament of a very delicate character. The bracelet was found at Reynaniye. Both are probably to be dated to the sixth century, and no doubt represent the work of the capital.

65 EAR-RINGS. *6th-7th century. Istanbul. The Archaeological Museum.*

The pair at the centre are of gold adorned with granulated work and stones set in cabochon mounts. There is a not dissimilar ear-ring in the Louvre (Bj 345), which is assigned to the third or fourth century by M. Coche de la Ferté. The Istanbul example is, however, probably rather later, and is perhaps Justinianic; the ear-rings worn by Theodora in the famous mosaic in San Vitale at Ravenna may be compared.

The pair at the sides in the middle, each with a single bird and a stylized scroll border, and the two ear-rings below, one with two birds confronted with the 'Hom' or tree of life between them, and the other, where they are confronted with a cross between, are of a type which was very popular in the Byzantine world from the sixth to the tenth centuries; examples exist in many collections; and ear-rings in the Stathatou Collection at Athens (No. 32 *bis*) and in the British Museum (No. 276) may be compared, though both show finer workmanship. The rather coarse cutting of the Istanbul examples suggests that they should be assigned to a fairly late date; the eighth century seems likely, though the one with the two birds, presumably peacocks, confronted with a cross between, might perhaps be as early as the sixth century for its workmanship is rather more delicate.

The pair at the top, of delicate filigree work, show finer craftsmanship than the others, and are certainly to be assigned to a fairly early date, probably to the sixth or even the fifth century.

E. Coche de la Ferté, *Les Bijoux Antiques*, Paris, 1956, Plate XLIII, No. 1, for the jewelled ear-rings. Coche de la Ferté, *Collection Helene Stathatos*, Athens, No. 32 *bis*; Dalton, *Catalogue of the Early Christian Antiquities in the British Museum*, 1901, Plate V, for the half-moon shaped examples.

66 TWO GOLD MEDALLIONS. *6th century. Istanbul. The Archaeological Museum; No. 82. Diam. 8 cm.*

The two medallions are identical and must have been cast from the same mould. They are decorated on both faces with scenes from the Life of Christ, in three registers, each designated by an inscription. The scenes are bounded by a border, on one side a Greek key-pattern, on the other busts in a stylized scroll. On the side with the former border the scenes are: in the top register the Annunciation and the Visitation; in the middle register, the Child in the Manger and the Flight into Egypt; in the third register the Adoration of the Magi. The additional figure at the back, thought by Leclerq to be the Baptist, is actually probably one of the shepherds who has strayed from the Nativity scene in the register above. On the other side there are seven scenes from Christ's life, namely, the Healing of a Blind Man, of the Leper, of the Woman with a Haemorrhage, of the Paralytic, and of the Man Possessed of the Devil, the Resurrection of Lazarus, and the Woman of Samaria. At the tops are two small projections for attaching a chain, so that the medallions could be worn, probably around the neck.

The medallions are recorded as found at Adana, but Leclerq assigns them to Iconium. Medallions of a similar type are known from elsewhere. One from Mersina, in the Hermitage, bearing three figures on its obverse, is published by Grabar ('Un medaillon en or provenant de Mersine en Cilice', *Dumbarton Oaks Papers*, No. 6, 1951, pp. 27 ff.); he assigns it to the fourth century. A fine one at Dumbarton Oaks, formerly in the possession of Professor Strzygowski, has recently been re-published by Marvin Ross ('A Byzantine Gold Medallion at Dumbarton Oaks', *Dumbarton Oaks Papers*, No. 11, 1957, p. 247). It bears the Adoration on one face and the Baptism on the other. He also notes a number of consular medallions which bear portraits on one face. The Dumbarton Oaks medallion was at one time assigned to Syria, but Ross puts forward convincing reasons for regarding it as a Constantinopolitan work. The style of the figures is not dissimilar from that of those on the plaque in the Istanbul Museum.

Though small and rather primitive, the figures are quite well proportioned; they are certainly more elegant than those in the Sinope Codex or on the paten from Antioch in the Istanbul Museum (Plate 69) or that from Riha on the Orontes in the Bliss Collection. Their character suggests a date quite early in the sixth century, and an association with Constantinople rather than the East seems likely.

P. and T., II, Plate 73*b*; Leclerq in F. Cabrol, *Dict. d'Archéol. Chrétienne*, I, Pt. 2, Paris, 1907, p. 1819; *Firatli*, Plates 33, 34.

67 CISTERN: THE 'BIN-BIR-DEREK'. *c. 528 (?).*
Fig. 3 Constantinople.

Though not the most picturesque, for it is half full of earth and rubbish, this is perhaps the most interesting of the numerous cisterns of Constantinople. In most of the others old columns and capitals have been re-used; at Bin-bir-derek, 'The Thousand and One Columns', the columns and capitals are all identical and were made for the building. The capitals are plain, but the columns are very unusual, being immensely tall, with a junction socket, rather like that used in modern water-pipes, at the centre. The cistern is

Fig. 3 The Bin-bir-derek cistern (after Wulzinger)

and Foolish Virgins, the Last Supper and the Washing of the Feet, the Giving of Bread (Plate III), the Giving of Wine, Jesus at Gethsemane, the Healing of the Man Born Blind, the Parable of the Good Samaritan, Christ before Pilate and the Repentance and Death of Judas, the Jews choosing between Jesus and Barabbas, and the Evangelist Mark.

There has been much dispute as to the date and proven-ance of this manuscript, for it has been attributed to Alexandria, Syria, Antioch, Asia Minor and Constan-tinople and dated to the sixth, fifth, and even fourth century. There can really be little doubt as to its sixth-century date, for the iconography of the scenes is of a character hardly developed before that time. The question of provenance is harder to settle. It has been suggested that the somewhat unusual sequence of the scenes supports an attribution to Antioch (Kantorowicz, 'The Baptism of the Apostles', *Dumbarton Oaks Papers*, Nos. 9 and 10, 1955-56, p. 220), and again that the style suggests Asia Minor (C. R. Morey, 'Sources of Medieval Style', *Art Bulletin*, VII, 1924, p. 37, n. 2). Stylistically, however, the work is much more sophisticated than that of other early manuscripts, namely, the Cotton Genesis in the British Museum and the Sinope fragment in the Bibliothèque Nationale, which are normally regarded as 'eastern'. If these manuscripts are to be assigned to Syria or eastern Asia Minor, as seems highly probable, the Rossano Gospels should, in contrast, be attributed to western Asia Minor or Constantinople. Indeed Morey goes so far as to say that the style of the Rossano Gospels is close to what may be regarded as a Constantinopolitan, in opposition to an Anato-lian style, the culmination of which was reached in the miniatures of the Leningrad Lectionary and the wall-paint-ings of the Cappadocian churches.

A comparison of the Rossano Gospels with the fourth great manuscript of this period, the Vienna Genesis, serves to narrow the possible location rather further, for though the single figures that top each column of text are very similar to single figures in the Genesis, the scenes at the top of the pages in the Rossano manuscript are a good deal more 'Byzantine'. The iconography is very advanced, as for example the Entry into Jerusalem; the type of Christ already foreshadows that which became supreme after the Iconoclast period, as for example in His Trial before Pilate; the scenes are vivid and expressive, but not exaggeratedly so; the figures are tall and elegant, as for example in the scene of Judas's repentance and death. In contrast the pictures of the Vienna Genesis are clumsier and less sophisticated, and are at the same time further removed from the style that may be regarded as characteristically Byzantine. It is thus tempting to assign the Vienna Genesis to the coastlands of Asia Minor, where one would expect to find a more polished style than in the uplands of Anatolia or in Syria, and to attribute the Rossano Gospels to Constantinople. The greater elegance and the more finished character of its illustrations would accord well with such an attribution. The quality of the

now almost half filled with rubbish, so that the original proportions are hard to realize. There are actually 224 columns, each 12·40 m. in height. The proportions are thus most unusual, but also most effective, and show clearly the genius of the architect responsible.

The cistern dates from the time of Justinian; it is probably to be identified as one constructed in the year 528. It has been assigned to Anthemios of Tralles, one of the architects responsible for Sancta Sophia, and though this attribution is not certain, the originality of the structure is such as might well be attributed to so great an architect.

Karl Wulzinger, *Byzantinische Baudenkmäler zu Konstantinopel*, Hanover, 1925, abb. 39. See also P. Forchheimer and J. Strzygowski, *Die Byzantinischen Wasserbeülter von Konstantinopel*, Wien, 1893, No. 6 and p. 215.

II, III ILLUMINATIONS FROM THE ROSSANO GOSPELS. c. *6th century. Rossano. The Cathedral. Ht. 30·7 cm. W. 26 cm.*

The text is in two columns; the miniatures, which are usually at the tops of the pages, extend from side to side. They portray the Raising of Lazarus, the Entry into Jerusalem (Plate II), the Cleansing of the Temple, the Wise

work is outstanding, especially as regards colour, and many of the scenes are of great beauty.

A. Munoz, *Il Codice purpureo di Rossano*, Rome, 1907; *Mostra Bibliografia per la storia della chiese in Campania e in Calabria*, Naples, 1950, Plate 8; *Kunst*, Plates 238–241.

68 LITURGICAL FAN: SILVER GILT. *6th century. Istanbul. The Archaeological Museum; No. 3758. Diam. 25 cm.*

The fan or flabellum is circular, with sixteen lobes and a projection at the base for attaching to a wooden or bone handle. It is decorated on each face in the same manner, at the centre a cherubim with two flaming wheels below, and around the margin a design like a peacock's feather corresponding with each lobe; similar designs are usual in the bowls of silver spoons of the sixth century (see Dalton, *B.A. and A.*, Fig. 448, p. 702). The decoration is lightly engraved.

The fan was found in 1908 at Stuma, near Aleppo, together with other silver objects, notably a paten with the Communion of the Apostles (Plate 69), another with an incised cross, and a third with an inscription; all are now in the Archaeological Museum at Istanbul. The paten bears stamps which date it firmly to the reign of Justin II (565–578). There are four control stamps on the stem of the fan. One was read by Ebersolt as 'Ioannou'; the second ends in the letters 'theou'; the third he read as 'Theodorou', and there is another name ending in 'ou'; the fourth is cruciform, with a monogram at the centre reading 'Theodorou'; in the arms of the cross is the word 'Diomidou'. The names of Joannes or Joannou and Theodorou are commonly found among the stamps on silver plates, especially those from Cyprus, which date from between 610 and 629 (see M. Rosenberg, *Die Goldschmiede Merkzeichen*, Nos. 5938, 5894 and 5927). The name of Diomedou does not appear on any of the stamps published by Rosenberg. There is a similar flabellum in the Dumbarton Oaks Collections (*Handbook*, Plate 128).

The character of the stamps suggests a date in the sixth century, and a similar date is indicated both by the nature of the decoration and the association of the flabellum with the Istanbul paten.

J. Ebersolt, 'Le Trésor de Stuma', *Révue Archéologique*, 4ième série, XVII, 1911, p. 407.

69 SILVER PATEN: PARTLY GILT. *565–578. Istanbul. The Archaeological Museum; No. 3759. Diam. 37 cm.*

The embossed design represents the Communion of the Apostles; in the centre is an altar covered with a cloth; above it is a ciborium from which hangs a lamp; on each side are six Apostles; Christ is shown as priest and He appears twice, on one side giving the bread, on the other wine. The figures are in repoussé and are gilt; certain details were done in little dots with a punch. The sloping side of the plate is decorated with a series of circular depressions, alternating with candelabra-like motifs and palmettes. Round the margin is a dedicatory inscription in niello which states that the dish was an ex-voto for the repose of the souls of Sergius the money-lender, his wife Mary, and their children. On the back are five control stamps, which must have been made before the decoration was embossed; they are well shown in Peirce and Tyler's illustration, and are to be identified as those of Justin II (565–578).

The vessel was found together with others at Stuma near Antioch in 1908, and has usually been regarded as of Syrian workmanship (L. Bréhier, 'Les Trésors d'Argenterie syrienne et l'école artistique d'Antioche', *Gazette des Beaux Arts*, I, 1920, p. 173; C. Diehl, 'L'Ecole artistique d'Antioche et les trésors d'Argenterie syrienne', *Syria*, II, 1921, p. 81); the rather clumsy but nevertheless expressive style of the figures bears out this suggestion. On the other hand, the presence of stamps on the back militates against it, if Matzulewitsch's assumption is correct, namely, that the presence of a stamp indicates that vessels were made at Constantinople. Peirce and Tyler also point out that the faces show a resemblance to those on the cross of Justin II in the Vatican (Plate 71), which there is every reason to associate with Constantinople. It is also significant in this connexion that in the rendering of the scene of the Communion of the Apostles in the Rabula Gospels, the only work we know which is undoubtedly Syrian, the figures are far more rigid than on the Stuma paten. There is a closely similar paten in the Dumbarton Oaks Collection at Washington, which is said to have been found at Riha on the Orontes; it also bears stamps of Justin II, though it is probably a little earlier than the Constantinople example. It bears an inscription reading 'For the repose of the souls of Sergia, the daughter of Ioannes, and Theodosios and the salvation of Megalas and Nonnas and their children.'

The question of the location of the workshop where these patens were made is not easy to determine. All that can be said is that the style is close enough to that of the great vase from Homs in the Louvre (Plates 44, 45) and to the Cyprus plates (Plates 72, 73) to suggest that all these vessels may well have been made in the same place. If that place was Constantinople, as seems most likely, one may assume that craftsmen trained in Syria were employed in the capital.

P. and T., II, Plate 140; *Firatli*, Plate XIII; J. Ebersolt, 'Le Trésor de Stuma', *Revue Archéologique*, 4ième série, XVII, 1911, p. 410; *Dumbarton Oaks Handbook*, No. 129; *Kunst*, Plate 247.

70 RELIQUARY FOR FRAGMENT OF THE TRUE *(above)* CROSS. *6th century. Poitiers. Convent of Sainte-Radegonde. Ht. 6 cm. W. 5·5 cm.*

The relic itself takes the form of a cross with two transverse arms; it is inserted into a square frame of cloisonné enamel work, adorned with a scroll pattern. This square originally constituted the central panel of a triptych, but the side panels were destroyed, together with a *chasse* in which it was kept, at the time of the French Revolution.

According to tradition the relic was presented to St Radegonde by Justin II (505–578). There is no reason to dispute the genuine character of the actual relic, but doubt has been expressed as to whether the enamel frame is indeed as early as the sixth century. The treasure has only been studied at a distance, and by few authorities. Of these Conway considers it to be sixth century, and his conclusions are supported by Dalton writing in the same article. Peirce and Tyler, on the other hand, compare the enamel to the Limburg reliquary (Plates x, 124–126) and date it to the tenth century (*P. and T.*, II, Plate 139). The similarity is, however, not very striking.

Conway notes that the enamels are lapis blue, turquoise blue, red, and translucent green. There are little green squares in cells round the outside of the plaque which are probably emeralds. His plate, however, does not give a very exact idea of the colours, for they are not really as brilliant; indeed, they are a good deal closer to those of the very few Christian enamels which have survived that are generally believed to be of pre-Iconoclast date, the most important of which is a reliquary cross in the Vatican from the Capella Sancta Sanctorum. The general tone is similar, even though the green that predominates is distinct from that of the Poitiers reliquary. But this may be due to the fact that the Vatican cross was probably made in Italy, whereas the reliquary of St Radegonde was Constantinopolitan. M. Rosenberg (*Zellenschmelz*, III, Frankfurt-am-Main, 1922, p. 41) gives an adequate coloured plate of the cross. He considers the Poitiers relic to be of the sixth century (p. 17), although he admits the difficulty of dating it on stylistic grounds.

So far as the actual ornament is concerned, the reliquary could well be early, for the scrolls, though minute, are close to those in the mosaics of Sta Pudenziana (*c.* 440) or those on some of the sculptured slabs at Ravenna of the sixth century. On the whole the date sanctioned by history seems probable and unless further evidence to the contrary is forthcoming, there seems no reason to accept Peirce and Tyler's suggestion that the reliquary is a tenth-century substitution for the sixth-century original.

M. Conway, 'St Radegonde's Reliquary at Poitiers', *Antiquaries Journal*, III, 1923, p. 1; *P. and T.*, II, Plate 139.

70 IVORY: PROCESSION OF RELICS. *6th or 7th*
(below) *century. Trier. The Cathedral Treasury. L. 26·1 cm. Ht. 13·1 cm.*

This ivory was probably originally part of a reliquary casket. To the right is shown a church, with before it an empress, holding a tall cross. An emperor leads a procession towards the empress: the rear is brought up by a wagon drawn by two horses on which are seated two ecclesiastical figures holding a reliquary. Behind is a three-storied building, in the windows and on the roof of which are grouped a mass of spectators. Behind the wagon is the entrance to the building, with a bust of Christ above it.

The figures and the event have been variously identified, some suggesting that the imperial figures are Constantine and Helena, others that it shows the procession of the Forty Martyrs to the Church of St Eirene in 544. More recently Pelekanides has suggested that the dedication of Sancta Sophia under Theodosios II in 415 is depicted. Grumel, however, has criticized this proposal. Grabar believes that the ivory is to be associated with the rededication of the church in 544. Volbach suggests a date in the sixth century; Delbrueck proposes one around the year 690, thinking that the ivory commemorates the building of a new church by an empress, to which relics are being brought. He suggests Constantinople as the place of manufacture, and in this other authorities concur.

The work is unusual, and the figures are curiously squat. Their character betokens a comparatively late date. The sixth and the seventh century are both equally possible on stylistic grounds; on the whole a date in the sixth century seems the more likely.

Diptychen, No. 67; *Volbach*, No. 143; Pelekanides, 'Date et interpretation de la plaque en ivoire de Trèves', *Mélanges Grégoire*, IV, 1952, p. 361; Grumel, 'A propos de la plaque d'ivoire de Trèves', *Revue des Etudes byzantines*, XII, 1954, p. 187; A. Grabar, *Martyrium*, II, Paris, 1946, p. 352, No. 4 and Plate LXX.

71 CROSS OF JUSTIN II: SILVER GILT. *Rome. Museo Sacro Vaticano. Ht. 40 cm. W. at arms 31 cm.*

The cross is decorated on one face with inlaid precious stones; they border a Latin inscription stating that this reliquary was presented to Rome by Justin. The opposite face is elaborately decorated in repoussé work; there are formal scrolls on the shaft and arms and medallions at the ends and centre. Above is Our Lord, holding a book; at the centre the Agnus Dei, at the foot Our Lord holding a cross.

The central medallion is a restoration and the others are rather coarse. Indeed, the work as a whole is somewhat ungainly in comparison for instance to the Homs vase (Plates 44, 45). A suggestion that it is to be associated with Justin I need hardly be considered, for the work clearly represents decadence after the brilliant age of Justinian. The emperor who presented it can in fact be no other than Justin II, and the cross is probably to be dated to about 575.

Kunstschatten, No. 13; *P. and T.*, II, Plate 136. For the association with Justin I, see A. A. Vasiliev, 'Justin the First', *Dumbarton Oaks Studies*, No. 1, 1950, pp. 85 f.

72, 73 SILVER PLATES. *610–629. Nicosia. The Archaeo-logical Museum; Nos. 452, 453, and 454.*

The two smaller plates show respectively David receiving Samuel's message (Plate 72A, diam. 14·1 cm.) and David slaying a bear (Plate 72B, diam. 14·1 cm.). The larger (Plate 73, diam. 27 cm.) shows the Marriage of David. In the first David is seated on a rock holding his harp; there are two sheep below and the landscape is treated very naturalistically. In the second there is a similar feeling for naturalism; David himself shows great spirit and vigour. The arrangement of the third plate is more formal. In front of an arcade supported on columns with Corinthian capitals stand five figures, in the centre the priest, on his right David, whose right hand is extended to clasp that of the bride, who stands on the priest's left. At either side are musicians playing pipes. In front are two wine flasks and a basket of bread.

These plates, together with a number of others, several bearing scenes from the life of David, and others with non-figural patterns of crosses or monograms, were found in a hoard near Kyrenia in Cyprus in 1902; another similar hoard was found at the end of the previous century. The latter is now in the British Museum, the former is divided between Cyprus and the Pierpont Morgan Collection and the Metropolitan Museum in America. The plates of the second hoard all bear control stamps which have been identified as those of the Emperor Heraclius; they indicate a date between 610 and 629.

Edinburgh, Nos. 34, 35, 36; *B.A. and A.*, Figs. 57, 62, and 358; *Archaeologia*, LX, 1906, p. 1.

74 SILVER DISH: ATHENA DECIDING THE QUARREL BETWEEN AJAX AND ODYSSEUS. *6th century. Leningrad. The Hermitage Museum. Diam. 26·5 cm.*

Athena sits on a cushioned stool; she wears a helmet and holds in her hand a spear and a shield. On her right is Ajax, on her left Odysseus; the armour of Achilles lies in the foreground. Above is a male figure appearing from a cloud. On the back are vine scrolls issuing from an amphora, on either side of which are birds; the vases alternate with a scroll, also with birds on either side. The dish was found near Sludka in the Perm district of Russia. There are no control stamps, but Matzulewitsch suggests a date in the first half of the sixth century on stylistic grounds, and a Constantinopolitan provenance is likely.

Matzulewitsch, pp. 54 ff.; *Edinburgh*, No. 51.

75 SILVER DISH: SILENUS. *610–629. Leningrad. The Hermitage Museum. Diam. 25·7 cm.*

A maenad, holding in her left hand something like a small bell on a thong and in her right hand a stick, leads the way; Silenus, with both hands clutching a wine-skin about his shoulders, capers after. Below are a bunch of grapes and

possibly a wine-container with a cup attached. The design is in part gilt. On the back are five control-stamps, including a monogram and the bust of a bearded emperor without nimbus. It was found near the river Kalganowka, in the Silkamsk district of Russia.

Matzulewitsch has identified the monogram and the bust of the emperor as Heraclius (610–641) and suggests that the dish should be dated between 610 and 629. It is to be assigned to Constantinople.

Matzulewitsch, No. 2, pp. 18 ff., 59 ff.; *Edinburgh*, No. 47.

76, 77 MOSAIC: ARCHANGELS. *Early 8th or 9th century. Formerly at Nicaea, in the Church of the Assumption. Ht. of angels 183 cm.*

There were four archangels disposed in pairs on either side of the vault in front of the apse; two of them, Arche and Dynamis, are shown here, and the head of Dynamis is reproduced in detail. Their names are written above their heads; below their feet is the second part of the following text which began on the opposite side, below the two other angels: 'May the heavens rejoice with Him and may all the angels adore Him.' It is the text indicated in the Painters' Guide for the scroll of Moses (A. Papadopoulos-Keramaeus, *Manuel d'Iconographia Chrétienne*, St Petersburg, 1909, p. 77).

When they first came to be noticed, the Nicaea mosaics were all assigned to the tenth or eleventh century; subsequent study has shown that they belonged to at least three periods. The archangels are the earliest, and Geza de Francovich has in a recent study put forward a case for assigning them to the sixth century. It is however hard to believe that such works would have escaped destruction by the Iconoclasts. A comparison with other works of the period, though it seems on one hand to support the early date brings out on the other certain obvious differences. They are in part those that distinguish the art of Constantinople from that of other areas of the Byzantine world, notably Italy on the one hand and Syria on the other. But they are also those of date, and a comparison with the archangel in a similar position in Sancta Sophia (Plate 88) supports a ninth century date. The date of these mosaics is thus uncertain; they are however very fine. Happily we have good photographs of them, for the building that they adorned was wantonly destroyed in the Graeco-Turkish war of 1921–1922.

G. de Francovich, 'I Mosaici del Bema della chiese della Dormizione de Nicea', *Scritti de storia dell' arte in onore di Lionello Venturi*, Rome, 1956, p. 1. The best plates are given in Th. Schmit, *Die Koimesis-Kirche von Nikaia*, Berlin and Leipzig, 1927. See also O. Wulff, *Die Koimesiskirche in Nicaea*, Strasburg, 1902.

78 SILK TEXTILE: A QUADRIGA. *8th century. Paris. Musée de Cluny. Ht. 75 cm.*

The silk is woven in compound twill. The design, on a blue ground, shows a pattern in yellow roundels joined together horizontally and vertically by medallions. The roundels contain a charioteer driving a quadriga; he wears armour but is bareheaded, without a nimbus, and appears to be grasping the sides of the chariot. On either side an attendant runs forward holding a crown and a whip. Below, two officials or attendants pour money from sacks into a receptacle or on to an altar. The borders of the roundels contain a series of floral forms consisting of heart-shaped petals and pairs of pear-shaped leaves. The medallions contain four similar floral forms symmetrically placed around a circle enclosing a quatrefoil of heart-shaped petals. In the space between the roundels a pair of rams or ibex are confronted holding in their mouths branches linked together by a collar, from out of which spring trefoil leaves; beneath their hooves is a palmette device. The silk came from the shrine of the Emperor Charlemagne in Aachen Cathedral.

Another piece of the same silk, also from the shrine of Charlemagne, is in the Münsterschatzkammer at Aachen. The Emperor Charlemagne died in 814. The tomb was opened about the year 1000 by the Emperor Otto III, at which time new silks were introduced. A second recognition was made in 1165, and in 1215 the bones and silks were placed with new silks in a shrine. Since that date there have been further recognitions.

Falke suggested that the scene in the roundel represented a victor in the circus games but not an emperor. He assigned the silk to a Byzantine workshop and as a result of comparisons with consular diptychs and gold coins, dated it without hesitation to the middle of the sixth century. He pointed out that the office of consul was abolished by Justinian in 541, and since the attendants pouring money out of sacks were close in style to similar figures on the consular diptychs (cf. diptych of Justinus, 540), the silk must be close to that date. He also noted that the style of the floral border was a coarsened, simplified version of the borders in examples of his 'Alexandrian' group of textiles, which he dated between the sixth and seventh centuries. The example of the 'Alexandrian' group singled out for comparison, an Amazon silk, is reputed to have been the shroud of St Fridolin, who was an apostle of the Upper Rhine in the sixth century and was buried at Säkkingen; Falke assigned the silk to about 550. Scholars have generally tended to follow Falke's attribution, though Volbach, accepting a sixth-century date, queried the Byzantine origin. Peirce and Tyler accepted the attribution to Byzantium, but suggested a date towards the end of the sixth or in the beginning of the seventh century. At another time they juxtaposed the charioteer with a silk at Sens woven with the bust of an emperor (?) and with gold *solidi* of Justinian II (685–711) and of Anastasius II (713–716), by which a significant comparison of hair-styles was inferred ('The Prague Rider Silk and the Persian-Byzantine Problem', *Burlington Magazine*, LXVIII, 1936, p. 219 and Plate III). They later compared the charioteer with imperial medallions ranging from Constantius II (337–361) to Maurice (582–602) ('Three Byzantine Works of Art', *Dumbarton Oaks Papers*, No. 2, 1941, p. 22).

The stylistic similarities between the Quadriga silk and the consular diptychs are not so close as Falke supposed, and the fact that the office of consul was terminated in 541 has little bearing on the date of the silk. Circus games continued for a considerable time afterwards, and the Emperor Theophilus (829–842) prided himself on his skill in chariot-racing. Falke's 'Alexandrian' group is no longer generally accepted as dating from the sixth century; three of the key pieces of this group have indeed been dated by Volbach to the seventh–eighth century (*I Tessuti del Museo Sacro Vaticano*, Plates T-103, T-104 and T-105), and there seems no reason to doubt that the group as a whole is contemporary with tapestry-weaves with closely similar ornament bearing Cufic inscriptions dated to the eighth century. In addition, if this silk actually came from the tomb, there seems no reason to suppose that Charlemagne would be buried with a silk nearly two hundred years old at the time of his death. The more plausible hypothesis would seem to be that the silk was woven at Constantinople in the late eighth century and that the emperor was buried with silks acquired a short time before he died.

Lessing, Plate 13; *Seidenweberei*, I, p. 68 and Fig. 87; *Silks*, Fig. 56; Volbach, *Cat. des Römisches-Germanisches Museums, Spätantike und frühmittelalterische Stoffe*, Mainz, 1932, Plate 49; *P. and T.*, I, Plate 187a; *V.S.D.*, Plate 82.

79 SILK TEXTILE: A LION HUNT. *8th century. Rome. Museo Cristiano; from the Cappella Sancta Sanctorum. L. 42·2 cm. W. 34·7 cm.*

The design is made up of medallions, in each of which are four hunters, two above, facing inwards and spearing lions with a formal date palm between them, and two below, facing outwards and spearing leopards. Their head-dresses terminate in crosses and are of a distinctly Byzantine type; the costumes are also Byzantine.

The figures may be compared with that on the Mozac rider stuff. Though there are Sasanian elements in the design, the textile is certainly not Persian; and it is probably to be attributed to Constantinople rather than to Syria or Egypt. The style and iconography suggest a date in the eighth rather than one in the sixth century as was at one time proposed.

Volbach, *Tessuti*, Plate T-118; *Kunstschatten*, Plate 18.

IV SILK TEXTILE: A LION STRANGLER. *8th century. London. The Victoria and Albert Museum. Ht. 39·5 cm. W. 31 cm.*

The silk is woven in compound twill. It bears on a red ground a pattern in red, dark blue, yellow, green, and white, of a man, clothed in a short tunic and a chlamys, wrenching open the jaws of a lion. The group is reproduced, facing alternately to right and left in horizontal rows. Above and below each row is a continuous horizontal scalloped band (one scallop for each repetition of the group) containing square panels with a floral device in between.

A considerable number of fragments woven with this pattern are known: from Chur, now in the Musée de Cluny (Paris), in the Musée Historique des Tissus (Lyon—from Chur), in the Dumbarton Oaks Collection (Washington, D.C.—also from Chur), at Berlin (Schlossmuseum), Dusseldorf, Nürnberg, and Ottobeuren; in the Museo Nazionale (Florence), in the Museo Sacro Vaticano, and in the Museo Nazionale, Trento. The fragments are basically all in the same type of weave—a compound twill weft-faced, with single-figure warps and a binding warp—but they vary considerably in quality.

The subject, the origin, and the date have all aroused controversy. Samson, David, Hercules, a gladiatorial combat, have at one time or another been mooted, and reference has been made to a silk in an inventory of the time of Pope Gregory IV (827–844), 'de tyrio, habentem historiam Danielis', although, as Kendrick pointed out, the struggling figure on the silk could hardly be taken for Daniel. For iconographical reasons, David seems unacceptable. The majority of scholars have opted for Samson.

Dates ranging from the sixth to the tenth century have been proposed. Two examples are connected by circumstantial evidence with the ninth century; one fragment lines the book-cover of a ninth-century Gregorian Sacramentary at Trent; another silk, at Ottobeuren, is connected with a tradition that it served to wrap the relics of St Alexander when they were brought in the time of Charlemagne from Rome to Vienne and from there by Toto, first abbot of Ottobeuren, to his abbey. If the tradition is correct, it seems reasonable to suppose that the relics were wrapped in a silk contemporary with the translation; therefore a date in the late eighth or early ninth century cannot be lightly dismissed. It seems equally reasonable to suppose that the lining of the ninth-century book-cover should not antedate the binding by much more than fifty years or so.

As to the origin, Alexandria, a factory in Syria, and Constantinople have all been suggested. So far, no example has been found in Egyptian burial grounds, which would appear to rule out an Alexandrian origin, but the Liber Pontificalis, listing the gifts of the Popes in the eighth and ninth centuries to the churches of Rome, includes a surprising sequence of silks called Alexandrian, of which a number bore patterns so far not discovered in Egypt. At the same time the papal gifts included several Syrian silks (S. Beissel, 'Gestickte und gewebte Vorhänge der römischen Kirchen in der zweiten Hälfte des VIII. und in der ersten Hälfte des IX. Jahrhunderts', *Zeitschrift für christliche Kunst*, VII, 1894, p. 358, and U. Monneret de Villard, 'Le Transenne di S. Aspreno e le stoffe alexsandrine', *Aegyptus*, IV, 1923, pp. 66–67).

As a number of silks related to the Lion-strangler are known to have Christian subjects, it seems unlikely that these were woven at Constantinople under the Iconoclast emperors, but they may well have been made there just before Iconoclasm.

Seidenweberei, pp. 54–55, Fig. 7; *Silks*, Fig. 46; Kendrick, *Cat. of Early Med. Woven Fabrics*, No. 1001, Plate 11; *P. and T.*, 11, Plate 180a; Volbach, *I Tessuti del Museo Sacro Vaticano*, Plate T-103; F. Morris, 'Notes on an early silk weave', *Bull. Needle and Bobbin Club*, XXVII, 1934, pp. 40ff.; E. Vogt, 'Frühmittelalterliche Seidenstoffe aus dem Hochaltar der Kathedrale Chur', *Zeitschrift für Schweizerische Archäologie und Kunstgeschichte*, XIII, 1952, p. 20, Plate 38; A. C. Weibel, *Two Thousand Years of Textiles*, New York, 1952, Plate 44; S. Müller-Christensen, *Sakrale Gewänder des Mittelalters*, Munich, 1955, No. 2 (for the Ottobeuren silk); *Kunst*, Plate 256.

V SILK TEXTILE: THE ANNUNCIATION. c. *800*. Rome. *Museo Sacro Vaticano; from the Cappella Sancta Sanctorum. Annunciation L. 68·7 cm. W. 33·6 cm. Nativity L. 31·5 cm. W. 27·5 cm.*

The stuff is now in two parts, one with medallions containing the Annunciation, the other with the Nativity: they must originally have belonged to the same textile. The design is based on a series of interlinking medallions adorned with a floral pattern. In the interstices between are stylized palmettes; in the medallions are the scenes of the Nativity and the Annunciation, in alternating bands. In the latter scene the Virgin is seated on a jewelled throne, and the angel approaches from her right.

An entry in the Liber Pontificalis refers to a stuff illustrating the Annunciation and the Nativity as being presented by Pope Leo III, which gives a date between 795 and 806. It is very probable that this entry refers to this actual silk.

The technique of the weave is the same as that of certain other fine silks, notably the 'Samson' stuffs. Von Falke assigned the group to Alexandria, and the suggestion is supported by certain iconographical parallels with paintings in Egypt. The fact that the angel approaches from the right is, for example, an eastern disposition, though owing to the habit of reversing designs in a textile it is hardly to be reckoned a sure guide in this case. The figures are, however, rather Syrian in style, akin to those on the early ivories like that with the Adoration and Nativity in the British Museum, and the palmettes are close to those on Persian works and also those in the mosaics of the Great Mosque at Damascus. Further, the reference in the Liber Pontificalis already noted speaks of 'notas siricas', which suggests that they came from Syria. Constantinople is also a possible home, for there are frequent references in the texts to the importance of the imperial looms there, and majestic designs like those on the Vatican textile are just what one would expect to associate with them. But if the dating of the stuffs to around 800 is to be accepted, Constantinople seems less likely, for by then the Iconoclast ban was in force in the capital. But we do not know how strongly it was enforced with regard to stuffs intended for export. Alexandria, Syria, and Constantinople are all possible centres, and it would be rash to suggest any provenance more definite than 'East Christian'. But the style is close enough to what we know about the capital to permit of the inclusion of this textile in a book devoted to the work of Constantinople.

Seidenweberei, Fig. 68; *Silks*, Plate III; W. F. Volbach, *I Tessuti del Museo Sacro Vaticano*, 1942, Plates T-104 and 105 for discussion and a full bibliography; see also *Kunstschatten*, Nos. 16 and 17; *Kunst*, Plate 257.

80 MARBLE RELIEF: A STAG. *8th century.*
(above) *Istanbul. The Archaeological Museum; No. 2156. Ht. 89 cm. W. above 98·5 cm.*

One stag only survives, with a plant below its legs and a hare in the space behind its horns and before its body. The border consists of a very stylized leaf design. The ground has been cut away and the subject and border left in relief. On the back is a cross in a circle, in low relief. The slab must originally have depicted two stags confronted.

The stag is no doubt symbolic, and illustrative of Psalm 42, 1, 'As the hart panteth after the water brooks, so panteth my soul after thee, O God.' Stags drinking at a pool in the mosaics of the Mausoleum of Galla Placidia at Ravenna illustrate the same theme. The slab was found on the Island of Thasos, and was perhaps carved there, though the style is akin to that of Constantinople. It is to be attributed to the seventh or early eighth century.

Mendel, II, No. 683.

80 MARBLE RELIEF: LION ATTACKING A
(below) DEER. *11th century. Istanbul. The Archaeological Museum; No. 1652. Ht. 86 cm. W. 106 cm.*

The slab depicts a deer being attacked by a lion, the whole surrounded by a free-flowing scroll. The work is in low relief and is surrounded by a border of the same height.

The motif was an old and very popular one, and the plaque is typical of an extensive group of 'animal' closure slabs, especially common from the ninth century onwards; often they appear to have been inspired by textile prototypes. The slab comes from a site on the Gulf of Ismid, but the style is Constantinopolitan; it is to be attributed to the tenth or eleventh century.

81 BRONZE DOOR: SANCTA SOPHIA. C. *840. Constantinople.*

The doors are of solid bronze, with elaborate borders of acanthus scrolls and formal patterns in fairly high relief. They bear incised inscriptions and monograms giving the names of the Emperors Theophilus and Michael and thus date from about 840. It has been held that the scrolls in relief which surround the doors represent work of the sixth century, reused, but this does not seem likely; the work is more probably all of one date. The doors are still in the place for which they were made, namely, the south entrance.

Apart from their high quality, the doors are an interesting example of art produced in a major building during the Iconoclast period, and their figureless, rather austere ornament contrasts with that of several sets of bronze doors in Italy, some of which were made locally, following Byzantine models, while others were actually ordered in Constantinople. Of the latter group the most important are those at Salerno, which date from about 1040. There are thirty-seven panels on each leaf; in most of them is a design in relief of a cross standing on a stepped base, with a floral sprig on either side of its stem; six panels on each door have engraved designs. There are similar doors at Amalfi, ordered at Constantinople in 1066, and at Monte Sant' Angelo, dating from 1076, where the decorations, depicting angels, are done in damascene work. Bronze doors that survive in the Greek world, like those at Vatopedi on Athos, are mostly of fourteenth- or fifteenth-century date.

Bréhier, Plates XLVII, XLVIII.

82 GOLD GOBLET. *9th century. Istanbul. The Archaeological Museum; No. 1531. Ht. 16 cm.*

The goblet stands on a tall plain stem; the bowl is ornamented in repoussé work forming a number of interlinked medallions, which contain birds in various positions.

The stem is similar in type to that usual on chalices of the sixth and seventh centuries; there are examples in the British Museum, in the collection of the Marquis de Ganay and at Dumbarton Oaks (*V.S.D.*, Plate 53A). The decoration is, however, of a purely secular character, and suggests that the vessel was a goblet rather than a chalice. Birds of the same type were usual on orientalizing pottery of the twelfth century onwards from all over the near-eastern world, but the closest parallels are probably to be found on some of the vessels of the proto-Bulgarian treasure of Nagyszentmiklos, which is to be dated to the ninth century (N. Mavrodinov, 'Le trésor protobulgare de Nagyszentmiklos', *Archaeologica Hungarica*, XXIX, 1943). The goblet is hardly likely to be much earlier in date. It was found at Skodra in Albania and may have been made in Bulgaria. It is included here to give an idea of what secular art at the close of the Iconoclast period was like.

83 IVORY: THE ARCHANGEL GABRIEL. *9th century. Washington, D.C. W. R. Tyler, Esq. Ht. 15 cm. W. 8 cm.*

The archangel stands full face and half length; his right wing and the lower part of the shoulder are missing. The ivory was noted in an inventory of 1786 in St Urbin at Troyes.

The work is of high quality and is in a severe monumental style. It is similar to the Christ in the Victoria and Albert Museum (Plate 92), but is perhaps slightly earlier in date. It is to be assigned to the second half of the ninth or the early tenth century rather than to around 1000, as Goldschmidt and Weitzmann suggest.

G. and W., II, No. 67; V.S.D., Plate 24b; Edinburgh, No. 62.

I, VI, MINIATURES FROM HOMILIES OF ST VII GREGORY NAZIANZUS. 867–886. Paris. Biblio- 84, 85 thèque Nationale; Ms. gr. 510. Ht. 41 cm. W. 30·5 cm.

The manuscript contains forty-six large miniatures depicting Bible scenes; they are of varying quality and character. There are also five additional leaves at the beginning. The first (Av.) shows Christ enthroned; much of the colour has gone, but the rendering still retains something of its original grandeur (Plate 84). On the next (B) there are three figures sadly damaged; on the next (Bv.) there is a leaved cross in gold on a blue ground; the leaves are purple. On the next (C) there is a similar leaved cross. On the last (Cv.) there are three more portrait figures.

Of the other illustrations perhaps the most important is that of the Vision of Ezekiel (f. 438v. Plates I, VII), where the prophet is conducted to the valley of dry bones by an angel. It is in a monumental, classical style, close to that of the illustrations of the Paris Psalter (Ms. gr. 139; Plates VIII, IX, 86, 87). The angel is of outstanding beauty. There are several other large compositions, like the Transfiguration (Plate 85; f. 75), which are in a completely Byzantine manner, and herald the style of the next century. Most of the other pages, however, are divided into two or three registers, in which various New Testament scenes are depicted. One, showing the Raising of Lazarus above and the Entry into Jerusalem below, is reproduced here (Plate VI, 88; f. 196v.). The colours are brighter and less subtle than those of the Vision of Ezekiel and the work is coarser; it is certainly by a different hand. But though the disposition in registers of this and other pages is suggestive of the wall-paintings in the rock-cut churches of Cappadocia, the style is nevertheless Metropolitan, and the manuscript is certainly to be assigned to Constantinople.

The leaved cross ornament is of an essentially Iconoclast character, and represents a survival from that phase of art (see D. Talbot Rice, 'The Leaved Cross', Byzantinoslavica, XI, 1950, p. 72). The manuscript was, however, done for Basil I and is therefore firmly dated to between 867 and 886. It represents the grandest 'Court' art in the period immediately succeeding Iconoclasm.

Omont, Miniatures des manuscrits grecs de la Bibliothèque Nationale, Paris, 1929; K. Weitzmann, Die byzantinische Buchmalerei des IX. und X. Jahrhunderts, Berlin, 1935; Byzance, No. 9.

VIII, IX PSALTER. 9th century. Paris. Bibliothèque Nationale; 86, 87 Ms. gr. 139. Ht. 36 cm. W. 26 cm.

The Psalter contains 449 leaves of text in miniscule of tenth-century character; the illustrations, fourteen in number, are on different parchment, bound up with the script. The subjects illustrated are: 1, David composing the Psalms; 2, David slaying the lion; 3, David anointed by Solomon; 4, David and Goliath; 5, the women of Israel glorifying David; 6, the crowning of David; 7, David between Wisdom and Prophecy; 8, the Penitence of David; 9, Crossing the Red Sea; 10, Moses on Mount Sinai (Plate 87); 11, the Prayer of Hannah (Plate VIII); 12, the Prayer of Jonah (Plate 86); 13, the Prayer of Isaiah (Plate IX); and 14, the Prayer of Hezakiah.

Five different hands can be distinguished. The most capable of them was an artist of real ability; he did scenes 1, 2, 9, 10, 13, and 14. In the Prayer of Isaiah (Plate IX) the Prophet himself is painted with great feeling and skill. Behind him is the allegory of night, before him a cherub with a torch, signifying dawn. The second artist, who tried to follow the first but had less skill, did scenes 3 and 4. The third, who did scenes 7 and 8, liked rather static poses and his modelling was schematic, while the fourth, who did 5 and 6, was definitely incompetent. The fifth artist worked in a distinct, more oriental style, and the faces in his work are less carefully modelled than those of the other artists. He did scenes 11 and 12. The colouring throughout is, however, of very great beauty, regardless of the identity of the painter.

The miniatures must have been done in the court workshops at Constantinople, but their date has been much disputed. On the one hand they are so classical that a date before Iconoclasm has been suggested; on the other the style is so close to that of the Homilies of Gregory Nazianzus (Plates VI, VII, 84, 85) that a date in the ninth century seemed more probable. The latter supposition has now been generally accepted.

C. R. Morey, 'Notes on early Christian Manuscripts', Art Bulletin, XI, 1929, p. 28; H. Buchthal, The Miniatures of the Paris Psalter, London, 1938. See also K. Weitzmann, Illustrations in Roll and Codex, Princeton, 1947; Byzance, Plate 10.

88, 89 SANCTA SOPHIA: MOSAICS IN THE APSE. 9th century. Constantinople.

In the conch of the apse is the Virgin enthroned, with the Child on her knee; on the archivolt to the west there were originally two archangels full length, one on either side, but only one has survived. There are also fragments of a commemorative inscription in the names of Michael II (847–867) and Basil I (867–886), which suggests that part of the mosaic must date from 867. A suggestion put forward on technical grounds that the Virgin and the archangel are to be assigned to the same date is hard to accept, for the style is quite distinct both with regard to the way in which the tesserae are set, and as regard the character of the faces and the treatment of the costumes. The angel is much severer, sterner, and more transcendent, the Virgin, her face at least, more tender, delicate, and human.

The date of the apse mosaic has given rise to considerable discussion. In a sermon preached in Sancta Sophia in 868 Photios referred to a recently set-up mosaic of the Virgin; for a time it was held that it was this very composition that was concerned, but Mango objected that Photios speaks of a standing Hodegetria, whereas the Virgin here is seated, so that this association is impossible. He also suggested that the Virgin we see is a later restoration which replaced the standing one seen by Photios. Grabar on the other hand thinks that there is no reason to suppose that Photios was speaking of the Virgin in the apse at all; he discards Mango's proviso as to date and assigns the mosaic to between 843 and 855. He thinks that the archangel and the Virgin are contemporary. Jenkins sees no reason why the text should not be interpreted as referring to a seated figure.

Whittemore assigned the work to a painter called Lazarus, on the basis of an attribution made by an early Russian pilgrim, Anthony of Novgorod. Lazarus died before 867, so that if he is correct in his assumption the inscription must be a later addition. Gelassi suggests the seventh century, though he regards part of the mosaics as due to later restoration; he compares the archangel to those at Nicaea (Plates 76, 77), which he also assigns to the seventh or early eighth century. Lazarev favours the mid-ninth century, just after Iconoclasm. Morey regarded the Virgin as a later replica of a ninth-century original. Dates as late as the fourteenth century have been suggested verbally for the Virgin, though not for the archangel.

The archangel at Sancta Sophia is certainly closely akin to those at Nicaea, but even if these are pre-Iconoclast, it is inconceivable that a mosaic could have survived in Sancta Sophia in so prominent a place throughout the Iconoclast period. More important is the close similarity that it bears to certain works of post-Iconoclast date, notably an archangel in Sancta Sophia at Salonica, which dates in all probability from between 812 and 880 (*Lazarev*, 42), and an archangel in a medallion which appears beside Christ in the lunette over the narthex door in Sancta Sophia itself (Plate 93); this mosaic probably belongs to the time of Leo the Wise (886–912). The similarity of the way in which the nostrils are indicated and the way in which the eyebrows are depicted as high arches is especially striking.

On the basis of this evidence the archangel in the apse could date from any time between 812 and 912, though its style would favour a date earlier rather than later in this period; a date corresponding with that of the inscription, namely, 867, seems most likely. The refined, tender face of the Virgin, on the other hand, tends to suggest a later date for that figure, even one as late as the twelfth century, though it would not be impossible to date it earlier. It may well be —indeed it is even likely—that the face is a later restoration. Thus, unless further evidence is forthcoming, it is tempting to assign the angel to before 867, and to regard it as a part of the mosaic referred to by Photios in his sermon of 868, while the Virgin should, in part at least, be regarded as a later

restoration, done not earlier than about 900, and more probably a good deal later.

These mosaics were cleaned shortly before and during the war by the Byzantine Institute of America, but they have not yet been fully published, though a brief note with four plates by T. Whittemore appeared in 1942. See *American Journal of Archaeology*, 1942, p. 169; also *Metropolitan Museum of Art Bulletin*, 1946, p. 44. See also C. A. Mango, 'Documentary evidence on the apse mosaics of St Sophia', *B.Z.*, 47, 1954, p. 395; Gelassi, *Felix Ravenna*, No. 5, 1951, p. 32; also his *Bizanzio o Roma*, II, p. 307; *Lazarev*, 84 and Plate XVI; C. R. Morey, *Mediaeval Art*, 1942, p. 107; A. Grabar, *Byzantine Painting*, 1953, p. 94, and *L'Iconoclasme Byzantin*, Paris, 1947, p. 190.

90 ENAMEL: THE BERESFORD HOPE CROSS. *9th century. London. The Victoria and Albert Museum. Ht. 8·5 cm.*

The cross is hinged at the top and opens to provide a repository for relics. It is decorated on both sides with cloisonné enamels, on the front the Crucifixion, and on the back the Virgin Orans, together with half-length busts at the extremities.

The very light partitions, the wide expanses of enamel, and the nature of the colours all support an early date. Kondakov proposed a wide margin between the eighth and the twelfth century; Schlumberger favoured the twelfth, Rosenberg the ninth century. He suggested that the cross was of Roman workmanship, done under Syrian influence. It is hard to see for certain whether Christ wears a short collobium, the costume usual in Syrian work, or a loincloth, which was normal in Constantinople and the Byzantine world, but it seems to be a loincloth. Nor is there anything that is very Syrian about the work as a whole. Moreover, if the cross is to be dated later than about 700, it is unlikely that it could be Syrian, for the cultured cities of the area, where such work could have been done, were by then wholly assimilated to Islam. Opinion today is against a pre-Iconoclast date, so that on this argument a Constantinopolitan provenance seems much more likely than a Syrian one. To that may be added the fact that the capital was the obvious centre for such work. There is nothing to support the late date suggested by Schlumberger; one in the late ninth century seems most probable.

A. W. Franks, 'On certain ancient enamels', *Arch. Journal*, VIII, 1851, p. 58; Rosenberg, *Zellenschmels*, II, 1921, p. 56.

91 ENAMEL AND JEWELLED GOSPEL COVER. *9th century. Venice. The Marcian Library; Ms. Lat. Cl. 1, No. 101. Ht. 26 cm. W. 17·5 cm.*

The upper cover has a wide margin of stones or pastes inlaid in cells (*orfèvrerie cloisonnée*) and bordered on each side by pearls. At the centre is an enamel bearing the Crucifixion, Christ wearing the long robe or collobium; around it are a number of circular enamel plaques; all, including the Cruci-fixion, are bordered with pearls. The three plaques at the top show St Peter, St John the Baptist and St Andrew; the three at the bottom bear an ornamental composition, St Matthew and St James; above the arms of the cross are two arch-angels; below them are St Mark on one side, an archangel on the other. The back cover is of similar type, but has the Virgin Orans at the centre.

The decorative medallion in the bottom row is probably a later substitution. No doubt the St Mark originally took its place, and there was probably a fourth archangel where the St Mark is now placed.

The wide partitions, the rather summary drawing, the translucent colours and the green backgrounds are all characteristic of an early date, and the cover is close to the Beresford Hope cross (Plate 90) and is to be assigned to the ninth century or perhaps slightly later. These early works may be contrasted with the book-cover illustrated as Plate 141, where the harder line, the more precise drawing and the profusion of small partitions all attest a date in the twelfth century.

B.A. and A., p. 515; *Pasini*, Plates VI and VII and p. 115.

92 IVORY PLAQUE: CHRIST PANTOCRATOR. *9th century. London. The Victoria and Albert Museum; No. A.4. 1910.*

Christ is shown half length with one hand raised in blessing and in the other a scroll; the position is that associated with the Pantocrator. The background is plain. The ivory is said to have come from Aleppo.

The head is unusually free and full of character; far more so than those on several rather similar ivories of which there are examples in the same museum (No. 273—1867), in the Louvre, at Leningrad, in the Fitzwilliam Museum at Cambridge, and in the Bodleian Library at Oxford (Plate 107). These are to be assigned to the tenth century or later, whereas the example under discussion is more monu-mental in style and is probably to be dated to the ninth century. It may well be the prototype from which the other examples were copied. Goldschmidt and Weitzmann (No. 149) suggests that a very battered ivory of the Virgin and Child in the Victoria and Albert Museum (No. A.1. 1912) originally formed a pair to the Christ. An ivory of the Archangel Gabriel in the Tyler Collection (Plate 83) may also be compared; it too should be assigned to the ninth rather than the tenth century, but is perhaps rather earlier than the Christ.

G. and W., II, No. 149; *Longhurst*, p. 40; *Edinburgh*, No. 60.

93 SANCTA SOPHIA: MOSAIC OVER THE EN-TRANCE FROM THE NARTHEX. *886–912. Constantinople. Greatest height 2·30 m. Width 4·70 m.*

Christ is enthroned in the centre with an emperor prostrated at His feet. On either side above are medallions; that to Christ's right represents a female figure probably the Virgin, that to His left an archangel, probably Gabriel.

This panel was the first to be cleaned by the expedition sponsored by the Byzantine Institute of America; work was completed in 1932. There are fragmentary remains of the mosaics of Justinian's day in the narthex, but this panel, in the lunette over the main door into the church, is of later date. The emperor was identified by Whittemore as Leo VI (886–912), primarily on the basis of his appearance on coins, but also because the figure closely resembles an ivory of the emperor at Berlin, where he is shown between the Virgin and Gabriel. This identification was questioned by Schneider, who suggested that the emperor represented Basil I (867–886): Constantine VII Porphyrogenitus is also possible. But Whittemore's identification is supported by Lazarev, though he suggests that the influence of a local style which flooded Constantinople after the end of Icono-clasm (843) was to the fore when the work was done. The style certainly lacks the delicacy that is usually to be associated with the capital.

There has been a good deal of discussion as to the subject of this scene. The angel was no doubt intended to recall the legend of divine assistance offered to Justinian in the con-struction of the church. Stefanescu, however, probably provided the correct explanation when he stated that the scene illustrates a little-known prayer for the dedication of a church, the text of which implores Christ to send His angel, armed with a lance, to protect the church offered by the emperor and to hear the intercession of the Virgin on his behalf.

Whittemore, vol. I; A. M. Schneider, *Oriens Christianus*, série 3, No. 10, p. 75; Lazarev, 'Mosaics of Cefalu', *Art Bulletin*, XVI, 1933, p. 215; Stefanescu, 'Sur la mosaïque de la Porte Imperiale à Sainte Sophie de Constantinople', *Byzantion*, IX, 1934, p. 517; Mirković, 'Das Mosaik über der Kaisertur im Narthex der Kirche der Hl. Sophia in Konstantinopel', *Atti dell' VIII Congresso di Studi bizantini*, Rome, 1957, vol. II, p. 206; C. Oziechzhowska, 'La mosaïque de la Porte Royale à Sainte Sophie de Constantinople', *Byzantion* IX, p. 934, p. 41; Dölger, 'Justinian's Engel an der Kaisertier der Hl. Sophia', *Byzantion*, X, 1935, p. 1.

94, 95 MANUSCRIPT: THE BIBLE OF LEO THE PATRICIAN. *10th century. Rome. The Vatican Library; Cod. Vat. Reg. Gr. 1. Ht. 41 cm. W. 27 cm.*

Originally there must have been two volumes, containing the whole Bible, but only one now survives. It contains 565 leaves, the text being in two columns. There are eighteen miniatures, each occupying a whole page, and two distinct hands are to be distinguished, one artist working in a rather linear style, the other favouring a more colourful approach and including very elaborate backgrounds. But both must have been trained in a school where classical models were available. The miniatures are thus all broadly similar to those of the Paris Psalter (Plates VIII, IX, 86, 87), though the work is on the whole rather less accomplished.

A miniature on f. 2 v. depicts the donor, Leo the Patrician, presenting a copy of the book to the Virgin. The other illustrations comprise leaved crosses on f. 2 and f. 3 v., the Veneration of St Nicholas (f. 3), and scenes from the lives of Moses, David, and the Prophets. The two pages reproduced here show Moses on Mount Sinai (f. 155 v.) and the Anointing of David as King (f. 263). In the former a number of distinct scenes connected with the event are shown, the nature of each indicated in an inscription. To the left, above, Moses removes his sandals; the inscription reads, 'Moses lays down his sandals'. To the right he reaches out to receive the book of the law; the inscription reads, 'Moses takes the tables of the law from the hand of God'. Below, Hebrews are grouped in terror; in the centre is the inscription, 'The people stand astounded under the mountain of Sinai and wait for Moses'. To the right, below, is the personification of the landscape, identified by the inscription, 'The desert of Mount Sinai'. Around the margin is a longer inscription, reading 'The painter shows us Moses, inspired, taking the tables from the mountain, and the commandments of God written by the Holy Word with an alien hand.'

In the second scene Samuel stands to the right, David bowed before him. Behind David stands his father, Jesse, and his brothers, indicated as 'The brothers of King David'. Behind David is a woman in a chiton, symbolizing Meekness. Between David and Samuel is the inscription, 'The prophet anoints David and crowns him as King with the due measure of olive oil'. Around the margin is a longer inscription, which may be interpreted, 'He who is small in stature is not small in degree. David glorifies his tens of thousands, Saul his thousands. For David crowned tens of thousands for the increase of his line. He is the forerunner of our Lord Christ and remitted their decrees.' The 'thousands and ten thousands' is a reference to I Samuel xviii. 7.

A date in the tenth century seems certain, but there has been some discussion as to whether the manuscript should be assigned to the end or the beginning of the century. The inclusion of two leaved crosses, and other general similarities to the miniatures of the Homilies of Gregory Nazianzus in the Bibliothèque Nationale (Plates I, VI, VII, 84, 85), which is firmly dated to between 867 and 886, however, would definitely support a dating very early in the tenth century.

'Miniature della Bibbia, Cod. Vat. Reg. Gr. 1, e della Salterio Cod. Vat. Palat. Gr. 381', *Collezione Palaeografica Vaticana*, fasc. 1, Milan, 1905.

96 IVORY: THE CROWNING OF CONSTANTINE VII PORPHYROGENITUS. *c. 944. Moscow. The Museum of Fine Art. Ht. 18·6 cm. W. above 9·5 cm.*

Christ and the emperor stand below an arched canopy. The emperor is in imperial costume but without sceptre or orb. Christ, who is raised above him on a dais, places the crown

on his head. Above the emperor, and again between him and Our Lord, is an inscription which reads 'Constantine, through God, Autocrator, King of the Romans'.

Though the ivory is broken, a portion of the capital supporting the canopy survives behind Christ, thus indicating that there were never more than two figures on this ivory, not three as on the related Romanos panel (Plate 97). The theme was one of very great significance in Byzantine thought, symbolizing the almost divine character of the imperial office. The emperor was crowned as sole 'autocrator' in 944, and the ivory must date from about that year.

Goldschmidt and Weitzmann call attention to the eastern style of the work, but it is not very marked and the nature of the subject leads to the belief that the ivory was carved in Constantinople; even if the sculptor was an oriental, the similarities that this work show to the Romanos ivory suggest that he exercised a considerable influence on subsequent developments in the capital, more especially on those of what is usually called the 'Court' school.

G. and W., II, No. 35; G. Ostrogorsky, 'The Byzantine Emperor and World Order', *Slavonic and East European Review*, XXXV, 1956, p. 1; *Edinburgh*, No. 63.

97 IVORY: THE CORONATION OF ROMANOS AND EUDOXIA. *c. 950. Paris. Cabinet des Médailles. Ht. 24·5 cm. W. 15·5 cm.*

Christ is shown in the centre, standing on a dais, crowning the emperor and empress on either side of him with either hand. Their names are indicated by inscriptions.

Some doubt has been expressed as to whether the emperor is to be identified as Romanos II, or Romanos IV, who was crowned in 1068. The close similarity of this ivory to that in the Hermitage showing the crowning of Constantine Porphyrogenitus (Plate 96) supports the association with Romanos II, and this identification is accepted by most authorities. There remains the problem as to whether the ivory dates from 945, the year of Romanos II's crowning as co-emperor, or 959, the year when he finally came to the throne. Bréhier favours the former date, and there is no reason to contradict his assumption.

The work is of very high quality, as is that of several other closely related ivories, notably the Harbaville triptych (Plates 100–102) and leaves with saints at Vienna, Venice, and Dresden (Plate 103). All are to be assigned to the 'Court' school and to the period of its greatest ascendancy.

G. and W., I, No. 34; *Bréhier*, p. 28 and Plate XXX; Volbach, 'Les Ivoires sculptés', *Cahiers de Civilization Mediévale*, I, Poitiers, 1958, p. 23. He says 'Romanos II, not Romanos I', but he gives the date of Romanos IV, namely, 1068–1071.

98, 99 IVORY TRIPTYCH. *10th century. Rome. Palazzo Venezia. Ht. 24 cm. W. of central leaf 14·5 cm.*

The Deesis occupies the central panel, with Christ standing; below are St James, St John, St Peter, St Paul, and

313

St Andrew. On the broad band separating the two scenes is a metrical inscription asking the help of Christ, the Virgin and the saints for Constantine. On each of the wings are two pairs of saints, one above the other; to the left St Theodore the Tyro, St Eustathios, St Procopios, and St Arethas; to the right St Theodore Stratelates, St George, St Demetrios, and St Eustratios. The inscriptions on the central bands refer to saints and martyrs. On the back of the left wing are St Basil, St Gregory the Theologian, St Gregory the Wonder-worker, and St Severian, and on the right wing St John Chrysostom, St Clement of Ancyra, St Agathonikos, and St Nicholas. The panels have been wrongly assembled in the present mounting. On the back of the central panel is a cross.

There is a similar triptych in the Vatican and the disposition is close to that of the Harbaville triptych (Plates 100–102), but the figures are shorter and the relief rather higher. Opinions have been much divided as to whether this should be regarded as a decadent feature or one indicating a rather earlier date. Goldschmidt and Weitzmann thus suggest the first half of the tenth century as the date of the Palazzo Venezia triptych and identify the Constantine mentioned in the inscriptions as Constantine VII (913–959). Bréhier, on the other hand, thinks that the ivory is a late copy of the Harbaville triptych, and associates the Constantine with Constantine Dragases (1449–1453). This seems most improbable, for the style is quite unlike that of fifteenth-century work, which is either more humanist, or is cold, dry, and stereotyped. Constantine VIII (1025–1028), IX (1042–1055) and X (1059–1067) are all of course possible, but as the triptych would on stylistic grounds appear to be earlier than the Harbaville, an association with Constantine VII seems the most likely. If stylistic evidence is to be relied on, the most probable sequence for the three triptychs is that in the Palazzo Venezio (c. 950), the Harbaville triptych, late tenth century, and that in the Vatican, early eleventh century.

Catalogo, No. 103; *G. and W.*, II, No. 31; *Bréhier*, p. 31; *Edinburgh*, No. 68.

100–2 IVORY: THE HARBAVILLE TRIPTYCH. *Later 10th century. Paris. Musée du Louvre. Ht. 24·2 cm. Width of central panel 14·2 cm.*

On the central panel Christ is shown enthroned between the Virgin and St John the Baptist. Below are St James, St John the Theologian, St Peter, St Paul, and St Andrew; in the upper border are busts of the prophets Jeremiah, Elias, and Isaiah. On the left wing are St Theodore the Tyro, St Theodore Stratelates, St Eustratios, and St Arethas, and in the roundels St Mercurios, and St Thomas; on the right are St George, St Eustathios, St Demetrios, and St Procopios and in the roundels St Philip and St Pantaleimon. On the back of the central panel is a cross in the Garden of Paradise, with rosettes at the centre of the cross and at the terminals of

each arm; on either side are the letters IC XC / NI KA, signifying 'Jesus Christ conquers'. On the back of the left wing are St John Chrysostom, St Clement of Ancyra, St James the Persian, and St Gregory the Wonder-worker, and in the roundels St Cosmas and St Damian. On the right wing are St Basil, St Gregory the Theologian, St Nicholas, and St Severian, and in the roundels St Phocas and St Blaise.

There are similar triptychs in the Palazzo Venezia (Plates 98, 99) and the Vatican; the former is probably rather earlier in date, and the latter rather later. Goldschmidt and Weitzmann compare the Harbaville triptych to the Romanos ivory, which is to be dated to around 950 (Plate 97), and assign it to the tenth century. The very elegant figures and delicate faces of the triptych suggest that it is to be dated rather later than the Romanos ivory; the third quarter of the century seems most likely. The flowers below the cross on the reverse are particularly fine and show a close observation of nature; but the whole triptych is of outstanding quality and delicacy; and it is to be counted as one of the finest Byzantine ivories that have come down to us.

G. and W., II, No. 33; *Bréhier*, Plate XXXI; *Edinburgh*, No. 75.

103 IVORY: ST JOHN THE APOSTLE AND ST PAUL. *10th century. Venice. Museo Archaeologico. Ht. 24·5 cm. W. 13 cm.*

The saints are shown standing on a dais. Above their heads is an inscription reading 'The instrument of God [St Paul] holds colloquy with the chaste man [St John] to preserve the Emperor Constantine from harm.'

The ivory must have gone to form a pair with one at Vienna, bearing St Andrew and St Peter, the inscription on which reads 'Your blood brother [according to Matthew iv. 18, Peter and Andrew were brothers], the proclaimer of Divine Mystery, absolves the Emperor Constantine from sin.'

There is also a closely similar ivory at Dresden, bearing the same saints and inscription as that at Venice, but with a rather more elaborate border. All are to be attributed to the same carver. The inscriptions no doubt refer to Constantine VII (913–959), but Constantine VIII (1025–1028) would also be possible, though less likely. All three plaques represent the finest work of the court school. They may be compared with the Harbaville triptych.

G. and W., II, No. 43; *Trésors*, No. 54; *Edinburgh*, No. 73.

104, IVORY TRIPTYCH. *c. 988. London. The British*
105 *Museum; 1923–12–5. Ht. 27·5 cm. Width of central panel 16·3 cm.*

In the centre is Christ on the Cross, with the Virgin and St John, and half-figures of the Archangels Michael and Gabriel. On the left wing are: St Cyrus, St George, St Theodore, St Menas, St Procopios; on the right, St John,

St Eustathios, St Clement of Ancyra, St Stephen, St Cyprion. On the back of the left wing is a cross with medallions containing busts of St Basil, St Joachim, and St Barbara, and on the right a cross with medallions containing busts of St James the Persian, St Anna and St Thecla.

Stylistically the ivory is related to the panel showing Christ crowning the Emperor Romanos and the Empress Eudoxia (Plate 97). Goldschmidt suggests that the presence of female saints, and in particular the prominent position of the busts of St Joachim and St Anna in the centre of the crosses on the backs of the wings, makes it probable that the triptych was carved for the Princess Anna, daughter of the Emperor Romanos II, who married Vladimir the Great, Grand Duke of Russia, in 988.

G. and W., II, No. 38; Kitzinger, *Early Mediaeval Art*, 1955, p. 32, and pp. 57, 108; *Edinburgh*, No. 124.

106 IVORY STATUETTE: THE VIRGIN AND CHILD. *10th century. London. The Victoria and Albert Museum; No. 702. 1884. Ht. 32·5 cm.*

The Virgin stands with the Child on her left arm; the position is that of the Hodegetria. The folds of the costume are carefully sculptured at the back, and the statuette was originally carved as a free-standing sculpture. The head of the Child is a restoration, probably done in the west.

The ivory is assigned by Goldschmidt and Weitzmann to the Romanos group, and the work is of the highest quality. There are similar ivories at Hamburg and New York, but these have been turned into statuettes by cutting away the ground of the relief, whereas the London example was carved in the round; the back is as beautiful as the front. The face of the Hamburg ivory is perhaps the most expressive and delicate of the three, but on the other hand the drapery of the London example is more subtle and flowing, so that on balance it is certainly the finest. It is one of the very few pieces of Byzantine ivory designed and worked in the round.

G. and W., II, No. 51; *Longhurst*, p. 42; *Edinburgh*, No. 156.

107 IVORY: CHRIST. *10th century. Oxford. The Bodleian Library; Auct. T. Inf. 1.10. Ht. 15 cm.*

Christ is shown enthroned; the background of the ivory has been entirely cut away, so that only Christ and His throne remain. The ivory is now attached to a more recent metal back, and serves as binding to a manuscript of the New Testament.

The face is expressive and the work good; Goldschmidt and Weitzmann assign it to the 'Romanos' group, and date it to the tenth century. A date fairly late in the century would seem likely, especially if the earlier ivory of Christ in the Victoria and Albert Museum is compared (Plate 92); this,

it is suggested, should be assigned to the ninth century. There are several rather similar ivories of Christ in the Victoria and Albert Museum (No. 273. 1867) and elsewhere, but this is the finest of them.

G. and W., II, No. 62; *Edinburgh*, No. 159.

108, THE VEROLI CASKET. *10th century. London. The*
109 *Victoria and Albert Museum; No. 216. 1865. Ht. 11·5 cm. L. 40·5 cm. W. 15·5 cm.*

The casket is rectangular, with sliding top. On the top is a single long panel, bearing the rape of Europa and numerous figures with stones in their hands, inspired by the stoning of Acham as it is represented in the Joshua Roll. On the front are two panels showing Bellerophon and Iphigenia; on the back two panels with children and a second appearance of Europa with Mars and Venus; at one end is Bacchus in a chariot borne by panthers; at the other a nymph riding a sea-horse. All these scenes are enclosed in rosette borders; on the lid rosettes alternate with heads. On the top there is a scroll outside the rosette border; it is a rather oriental rendering of a classical prototype. Gilding remains in places.

The casket is the finest example we have of a very large group, of which over forty complete and as many incomplete examples survive. Most of them are decorated with classical scenes. They are usually known collectively as the 'rosette' caskets. Most authorities had come to believe in a post-Iconoclast date, when the matter was finally decided on the strength of a detailed comparative study by Weitzmann (*Greek Mythology in Byzantine Art*, Princeton, 1951). Goldschmidt and Weitzmann suggest the end of the tenth or the early eleventh century for the Veroli casket, but this would seem to be rather too late; a date in the tenth century seems more likely.

G. and W., I, No. 21; *Longhurst*, p. 34; *Edinburgh*, No. 122.

110, IVORY CASKET. *11th century. Paris. Musée de*
111 *Cluny. Ht. 11·5 cm. L. 41·5 cm. W. 17·5 cm.*

The casket is rectangular with a flat sliding top. This is made up of a 'rosette' border and a long panel with a series of battle scenes, in which two mounted warriors and two *bigae* (two-horse chariots) are taking part; there are also lancers charging out from behind a city wall. The sides and ends are made up of small rectangular plaques bearing warriors and figures of a mythological character; they are by a different hand from the frieze on the top, which is in higher relief and is more accomplished. On the 'rosette' bands, heads alternate with the usual rosettes.

The 'rosette' bands are very sharply and effectively carved. The frieze on the top may be compared with the Veroli casket in the Victoria and Albert Museum (Plates 108, 109). Goldschmidt and Weitzmann date the Cluny casket to the eleven or twelfth century. The similarity of the top to the Veroli casket suggests that it is certainly not to be dated later than the early eleventh and even the late tenth century is possible so far as that panel is concerned, though the small plaques on the sides may be later.

G. and W., I, No. 41.

112 CASKET: WITH WARRIORS. *10th–11th century.* (above) *New York. The Metropolitan Museum; No. 17. 190. 237. Ht. 11·1 cm. L. 43·5 cm. W. 17·5 cm.*

The casket is rectangular, with a sliding top. It is made up of small rectangular panels enclosed by the characteristic bands of rosettes. On the panels are warriors, some mounted, some on foot.

The warriors resemble some of the figures of the Joshua Rotulus or those on the ivory with scenes from Joshua's life, in the Victoria and Albert Museum (Plate 112 *below*). Goldschmidt and Weitzmann distinguish two hands, one better than the other; but both were masters of great accomplishment, and the casket is one of the most outstanding of the group. They date it to the late tenth or early eleventh century, and there seems no reason to question their conclusion.

G. and W., I, No. 12.

112 PANEL FROM CASKET: SCENES FROM (below) **THE LIFE OF JOSHUA.** *10th century. London. The Victoria and Albert Museum; No. 265. 1867. Ht. 7·5 cm. L. 27 cm.*

Two scenes are shown; to the left Joshua enthroned receives the envoys of Gideon; to the right he sits full face, with warriors behind him and the envoys in front.

The scenes are close to the Joshua Roll in the Vatican (Cod. Vat. Palat. Gr. 431), but there are certain minor differences, which suggest that the ivory was copied from a prototype rather than from the roll itself. There are caskets with similar scenes from Joshua's life at New York (*G. and W.*, I, Nos. 1, 2, and 3). The date of the panel has been disputed, attributions having varied between the eighth and twelfth centuries. The ivory is, however, not likely to be earlier than the roll. Even if Weitzmann's attribution of the roll to the tenth century is not accepted (*The Joshua Roll*, Princeton, 1948), a comparison of the plaque with other caskets supports a dating in the tenth century.

Longhurst, p. 39; *Edinburgh*, No. 91.

113 ILLUMINATION FROM THE THERIACA OF NICANDOR. *10th century. Paris. Bibliothèque Nationale; Ms. Suppl. gr. 247. Ht. 14·8 cm. W. 11·8 cm.*

The manuscript is a very small octavo. It was designed to be decorated with illustrations of figures and animals on practically every page, but in many cases these were never completed. The most interesting of the illustrations are reproduced here; they cover a double page and are by a different hand from the others, working on a more elaborate scale (f. 47v. and 48); they show figures in a picturesque landscape, of very Hellenistic character. It is one of the few illustrated secular manuscripts that have come down to us, and is to be counted a work of the capital.

Omont, *Miniatures des Manuscrits grecs de la Bibliothèque Nationale*, Paris, 1929; *Byzance*, No. 3.

114 IVORY: THE ASCENSION. *10th century. Florence. Museo Nazionale. Ht. 15 cm. W. 12 cm.*

Christ, seated on a star-studded mandorla, is borne upwards by two angels. Two more angels flying below address the Virgin and the Apostles standing in a row in front of two stylized trees: 'Men of Galilee, why do you stand gazing at the sky?' The inscription recording these words is in the centre of the panel.

The composition is balanced and very beautiful. The ivory is to be assigned to the 'Romanos' group.

G. and W., II, No. 58; *Edinburgh*, No. 130.

115 IVORY: THE ENTRY INTO JERUSALEM. *10th century. Berlin, Dahlem. Ehemals Staatliche Museen; Skulpturabteilung Nr. 1590. Ht. 18·4 cm. W. 14·7 cm.*

Beneath a pierced dome decorated with acanthus-shaped acroteria and raised on pierced columns is set the scene of Christ's Entry into Jerusalem. Christ sits sideways on the donkey, in front of which boys lay their cloaks, and is followed by seven disciples. From the Gate of Jerusalem appear men, a woman, and children, and in the tree beside the Gate are two more children. A mountain is shown behind Christ and a slight slope of foreground to the bottom left of the panel. The inscription reads 'The bearing of Palms'.

The ivory is assigned by Goldschmidt and Weitzmann to their 'pictorial' group. The relief is, however, unusually high.

Wulff and Volbach, p. 36, Plate XIII; *G. and W.*, II, No. 3; *Katalog, Europäische Bildwerke von der Spätantike bis zum Rokoko*, 1957, No. 26; *Edinburgh*, No. 88.

116, IVORY: THE FORTY MARTYRS. *11th century.* **117** *Berlin, Dahlem. Ehemals Staatliche Museen; Skulpturabteilung Nr. 574. Ht. 17·6 cm. W. 12·8 cm.*

Above is Christ enthroned in glory, with three angels on either side in attitudes of adoration and with veils over their hands as a sign of reverence. The martyrs appear below, with a considerable open space in the centre, on which is written to the left of the panel the title of the scene, while on the right is a domed building, the bath from which the martyrs come.

The relief is high and the work shows considerable feeling and expression; it is far freer and finer than that on a very similar ivory in the Hermitage, which Goldschmidt and Weitzmann regard as the prototype from which the Berlin example was copied. The Hermitage ivory is perhaps to be dated to the tenth century; the Berlin one is later; it even seems to herald the art of the Palaeologue revival, so vivid and humanist is the work. It is included by Goldschmidt and Weitzmann in their 'pictorial' group.

G. and W., II, No. 10; *Edinburgh*, No. 132.

118 IVORY TRIPTYCH. *10th or 11th century. Paris. Musée du Louvre. Ht. 12·2 cm. Width of central leaf 10 cm.*

The Nativity is shown on the central panel, enclosed in an open-work arcade. On one leaf, in two registers, are the Entry into Jerusalem and the Anastasis, on the other the Ascension.

The relief is high, especially on the wings, and the style close to that of the miniature paintings. The ivory clearly falls into the group distinguished by Goldschmidt and Weitzmann as the 'pictorial'. They date it to the tenth century; it may perhaps be rather later. The ivory must have been carved in a workshop quite distinct from that where ivories of the 'Court' school like the Harbaville triptych (Plates 100–102) were produced. The panel with the Dormition of the Virgin at Munich (Plate 119) is closely similar and must come from the same workshop.

G. and W., II, No. 4.

119 IVORY: DORMITION OF THE VIRGIN. *10th–11th century. Munich. Staatsbibliothek; Cod. Lat. 4453. Ht. 14·5 cm. W. 11 cm.*

The bier extends across the whole width of the ivory but for the figure of Paul at the foot; other figures are grouped behind. Christ is in the centre behind the bier, with two angels above, their hands hidden under veils. The whole composition is enclosed in an ornamental open-work frame. Originally the plaque formed the central leaf of a triptych; today it occupies the centre of a book-cover, mounted in a border of gems and cameos.

The relief is high and the work expressive, but the style rather exaggerated; it is very far removed from the delicacy of the later ivories of the Romanos group. Goldschmidt and Weitzmann assign it to the 'pictorial' group on the grounds of the architectural frame. It is likely that elaborate work of this sort was done in the capital and this ivory should be attributed there. It serves to show the diversity of styles prevalent there in the tenth and eleventh centuries. A triptych

in the Louvre (Plate 118) and an ivory with the Entry into Jerusalem at Berlin (Plate 115) are both akin, and Goldschmidt and Weitzmann also compare a steatite at Vienna which was shown in Paris in 1931 (*V.S.D.*, Plate 39B); they suggest that it may even be by the same hand, though this seems hardly likely; the steatite is probably later in date.

G. and W., II, No. 1.

120, IVORY RELIQUARY. *963–969. Cortona. Church* **121** *of St Francis. Ht. of panel 31 cm. W. 17·4 cm.*

The ivory is enclosed in a baroque mount; on the front there are three medallions above, showing Christ between the Archangels Michael and Gabriel, and three below, in the middle the Emperor Constantine, with St Helena to his right and St Longinus to his left. The central part of the plaque is hollowed out in the form of a cross, now covered with an open-work metal cover of western workmanship; in the four spaces above and below the transverse arm are figures of the Virgin and St John the Baptist above and St Stephen and St John the Evangelist below. On the back are inscriptions, one around the margin, the other forming a cross; the former reads 'Stephen the keeper of the Treasury of the great church of the Wisdom of God, to the monastery which nurtured him'; the latter reads 'Formerly Christ gave to the mighty ruler Constantine the cross of salvation, which is now in the possession of the Emperor of God, Nicephoras, who with its aid puts the barbarians to flight'.

The church referred to in the first inscription is undoubtedly Sancta Sophia at Constantinople; the Nicephoras in the second is to be identified with Nicephoras Phocas (963–969) rather than Nicephoras Botaniates (1078–1081).

Goldschmidt and Weitzmann selected this ivory as the 'type example' of a large group, which they term the Nicephoras group. A triptych at Luton Hoo (Plate 123) may be noted as a related example. The style is rather heavier and more expressive than that of the ivories of the true 'Court' school like the Romanos ivory (Plate 97) or the Harbaville triptych (Plates 100–102).

G. and W., II, No. 77.

122 MARBLE: HEAD OF THE ARCHANGEL MICHAEL. *10th century. Istanbul. The Archaeological Museum; No. 3930. Ht. 30 cm.*

A portion of a flat slab with slightly raised border, bearing a head in high relief surrounded by a halo; the incisions in this were probably originally filled by coloured stones or pastes representing jewelling. Above on the margin are the letters MIX — —.

The head is expressive and characterful; its identity is established as the Archangel Michael by the fragmentary inscription above. The work is of high quality and is

317

probably to be assigned to the tenth century; the archangels in mosaic on the vault before the apse of Sancta Sophia may be compared (Plate 88), but the style is even closer to that of the Cortona ivory (Plate 121), and the sculpture may be assigned to the same workshop, perhaps even to the same hand.

123 IVORY TRIPYTCH. *Late 10th century. Luton Hoo. The Wernher Collection. Ht. 18·5 cm. Width of central leaf 11·5 cm.*

On the central panel stands the Virgin, below an open-work baldachino supported on columns; on each of the side leaves are three medallions bearing archangels above, two saints below. To the left are St Nicholas and St Theodore, to the right St John Chrysostom and St George. In no case are the usual inscriptions with the initial letters or names of the saints present. The outsides of the side leaves bear crosses and the back of the central panel an arcade, lightly engraved with a crown suspended from its centre.

The quality of the work is very high, but the faces are full and round and the style is distinct from that of ivories of the Romanos group. The triptych is assigned by Goldschmidt and Weitzmann to the Nicephoras group and dated to the third quarter of the tenth century. There seems no reason to question this suggestion.

G. and W., II, No. 78; Molinier, *Ivoires*, p. 110; *Edinburgh*, No. 128

X, RELIQUARY FOR THE TRUE CROSS. *c. 960.*
124-6 *Limburg on the Lahn. Cathedral Treasury. Greatest height 48 cm. Greatest width 35 cm.*

The reliquary itself is in the form of a double armed cross framed in gold; on the front the wood is visible except at the junction points of the arms, where there are jewelled bosses; the gold mount extends over the back; there is a long inscription upon it, in upstanding letters. This relic fits into a gold case with sliding lid, and the inscription is continued around its margin. The framing of the relic is made up of enamels, and above the main cross are four cherubin and four seraphim, together with four archangels; below are eight seraphim, four cherubin and six archangels; each series has an ornamental border. The back of the actual case is entirely occupied by a design in repoussé work of a very ornate cross framed below in foliage. The lid is richly adorned at the ends with inlaid jewels and at the centre with nine enamels; the central one shows the Deesis, that is, Christ enthroned, with on either side the Virgin and St John the Baptist; behind each of the two latter figures is an archangel. Each of the plaques bear two Apostles above and below, so completing the twelve.

The work is throughout of the very best; this reliquary is indeed probably the most important and complete example of the Byzantine jeweller's art that has come down to us. The inscription states that the Emperors Constantine and Romanos were responsible for the manufacture of the reliquary; the first must be Constantine VII Porphyrogenitus (913–959), the second could be either Romanos I (920–944) or Romanos II (945–963), both of whom ruled with Constantine as joint emperors. The inscription could, however, hardly refer to Romanos I, for he was the more important of the dual emperors and his name would therefore have come first in the inscription, not second as it actually does. The date is therefore narrowed to the years between 945 and either 959, the year when Constantine died, or 963, the year of Romanos II's death. Constantine was himself not only a keen patron of the arts, but also a practising goldsmith, and it is possible that he actually worked on the frame of the cruciform relic itself. There is also a reference in the inscription to Basil the Proedros, and this title only came to him in 963; a paten and a chalice in St Mark's at Venice also bear his name. It would therefore seem that the relic itself was framed about 959, and that the case was completed about 963. Romanos was responsible for several pious foundations, and would have been keen to see his father's name perpetuated.

When completed the reliquary formed part of the imperial treasury at Constantinople until the attack of the fourth Crusade in 1204. It was then taken to Europe by Heinrich von Uelmen and in 1208 presented to a nunnery at Stuben on the Mosel. On the dissolution of the nunnery in 1789 the relic was taken to the Carmelite monastery at Koblenz, and from there it eventually reached Limburg in 1827. In 1951 it was cleaned and restored.

J. Rauch, Schenk zu Schweinsberg and J. M. Wilm, 'Die Limburger Stuarothek', *Das Münster*, Munich, 1955; M. Ross, 'Basil the Proedros', *Archaeology*, II, No. 4, 1958, p. 271.

XI, 127 PSALTER OF BASIL II. *976–1025. Venice. The Marcian Library; Cod. Gr. 17. Ht. 39·5 cm. W. 30·5 cm.*

This large volume of 430 leaves contains two illuminated pages only, at the beginning. The first bears a portrait of the emperor standing in the centre in armour, a spear in his right hand. Above is a bust of Christ and at the sides are the Archangels Michael and Gabriel. Below the former are busts of St Theodore the Tyro, St Demetrios and apparently St Theodore Stratelates; below the latter are St George, St Procopios and St Mercurios. The inscription on the right reads 'Basil trusting in Christ' and that on the left 'King of the Romans the new (second)'. Below are eight figures grovelling in attitudes of submission. The other leaf is divided into six compartments in which are shown the Anointing of David, David defending his flock against a bear, David and the lion, David and Goliath, David and Saul, and the Penitence of David.

The work is close to that of Basil's Menologion in the Vatican (Plate 128), some of the David scenes being especially similar. The drawing is at times rather clumsy, but the colour is brilliant and effective. The illuminations were probably done about 1020.

K. Weitzmann, *Die Byzantinische Buchmalerei des IX. und X. Jahrhunderts*, Berlin, 1935, p. 29; S. der Nercessian, 'Remarks on the date of the Menologion and Psalter written for Basil II', *Byzantion*, XV, 1940-41, p. 115.

128 THE MENOLOGION OF BASIL II. *979-984. Rome. The Vatican Library; Cod. Vat. Gr. 1613. Ht. 36·4 cm. W. 28·4 cm.*

The manuscript contains an ecclesiastical calendar from the beginning of September till the end of February; the last few pages bear illustrations but no text, and this suggests that the manuscript was never finished. If that is so, it is likely that the second volume was never actually written. The text consists of brief notes on the saints depicted; there is one illustration on each page, each extending across the page and occupying half of it. Each is horizontal, about 18 × 12 cm., and as the main subject is the portrait of a saint, there is a considerable space beside each figure, which is occupied either by landscape or architecture. Eight painters were engaged on the work, their names being written in the margins. Two came from the Blachernae, so it is probable that the miniatures were done in the imperial workshops at Constantinople.

The pages illustrated represent, above, the Martyrdom of Hermione (f. 12) and, below, the story of Moses (f. 13). In the former the body of the martyr is extended full length across the middle of the picture, as if levitated; the severed head is separated from it, with a halo behind it. In the centre is the executioner, at either side are conventional mountains, and behind one of them an arcaded structure. In the margin is the name of the painter, Georgios. In the second picture Pharaoh's daughter appears to the left, bending over the cradle, which floats in the waters of the Nile; to the right the Archangel Michael bends over the body of Moses, which is extended at full length, a naturalistic landscape behind it. In the margin is the name of the painter, Pantoleontes; the style of his work is quite distinct from that of Georgios.

Miss der Nersessian has put forward evidence to show that the manuscript was produced between 979 and 984; her conclusion is based on two facts: firstly, though an earthquake of 740 is recorded, there is no mention of one in 989, when Sancta Sophia was damaged; it is therefore likely that the manuscript was written before that year. Secondly, one of the miniatures at the end, which lacks a text, is shown to represent St Luke the Stylite, who was commemorated on Thursday, December 11. It is certain that this man died in or shortly before 984; in these years the 11th December fell on a Thursday only in 979 and 984; he must therefore

have died in one or other of these years, so that the date of the manuscript is fixed between the two dates.

'Il Menologio di Basilio II', *Codices e Vaticanis selecti*, vol. VIII, Turin, 1907; S. der Nersessian, 'Remarks on the date of the Menologion and Psalter written for Basil II', *Byzantion*, XV, 1940-41, p. 104.

129 SANCTA SOPHIA. MOSAIC OVER THE SOUTH DOOR. *986-994. Constantinople. W. 4·935 m. Greatest height 3·02 m.*

The Virgin is enthroned between Constantine and Justinian, who present models; that of Constantine represents the city of Constantinople, that of Justinian the Church of Sancta Sophia.

The mosaic occupies a position of importance and is to be taken as emblematic of the Virgin's role as protectress of the city and guardian of its greatest church. The technique is accomplished and elaborate, the tesserae being inclined at angles calculated to give the best effect from below; when seen close to, the spaces between them seem unduly wide. The colours are subtle, the faces characterful, and the composition dignified. The date of the mosaic is not easy to determine for certain; there seems, however, no serious reason to contradict Whittemore's suggestion that it should be assigned to the reign of Basil II and to a date between 986 and 994, when Sancta Sophia was closed for repairs.

Whittemore, vol. II.

130 SILK WITH ELEPHANTS IN MEDALLIONS. *c. 1000. Aachen. The Cathedral Treasury. Total length 162 cm. Ht. 136 cm.*

The silk bears a design of large circles, each of which encloses a stylized elephant with an ornamental tree ('hom' or tree of life) behind it; the spaces left vacant by the medallions are filled by rosettes. On the border is an inscription which reads 'Under Michael, chief chamberlain and keeper of the privy-purse, Peter being archon of the Zeuxippos; in the second indiction'. The silk was found in the tomb of Charlemagne.

The title of Keeper of the Privy-purse does not appear before the end of the ninth century, so that the stuff must be later in date than Charlemagne; the style suggests that it may well have been introduced into the tomb when it was opened by Otto III in the year 1000. The inscription is important, for it shows that this silk was woven in the imperial workshops at Constantinople. A number of other stuffs can be classed with it on the grounds of their technical and stylistic similarity. Of these a textile bearing confronted lions which was at Siegburg but which is now destroyed is specially important, for it bore an inscription in the names of the Emperors Romanos and Christopher (921-931). There is a closely similar stuff at Düsseldorf in the names of Constantine and Basil (976–1025), and a similar but smaller fragment at Maastricht. A textile at Ravenna with lions in medallions is to be assigned to the same group, rather than to Persia, as has sometimes been suggested (*Edinburgh*, No. 72).

Seidenweberei, abb. 241, 242; *Silks*, Fig. 185.

131 SILK DAMASK: THE SHROUD OF ST SIVIARD. *11th century. Sens. The Cathedral Treasury. Total height 135 cm. W. 85 cm.*

The design shows winged gryphons in circles, alternate ones facing in opposite directions; in the corners between the medallions are eight pointed rosettes. The heads, feet, tails, and a few details on each animal are in purple; the rest is of a lovely cream colour, and the design is made apparent by the damask weave, not by difference of colour.

This is one of the most outstanding productions of the imperial workshops at Constantinople, and shows their absolute mastery of a technique which was also practised in the Islamic world.

V.S.D., Plate 97; *Seidenweberei*, abb. 244; *Silks*, Fig. 193.

132 SILK: THE SHROUD OF ST GERMAIN L'AUXERROIS. *Late 10th century. Auxerre. Church of St Eusebius. Ht. 170 cm. W. 115 cm.*

The textile is of silk and its design is made up of great spread eagles and small rosettes in gold, against a purple ground.

It is one of the grandest stuffs that have come down to us, for each eagle is more than half a metre in height, and the quality both of design and of workmanship is outstanding. The work is undoubtedly Constantinopolitan, and the textile is to be assigned to the end of the tenth century. A silk at Bressanone (Plate XII) bears a similar design though the proportions are less grand; smaller related fragments survive in other collections. A later variant of the same eagle theme appears on an embroidery known as the Cope of Charlemagne now at Metz; it was probably made in Germany in the twelfth century (*Edinburgh*, No. 226).

V.S.D., Plates 91–92.

XII SILK: THE CHASUBLE OF ST ALBUIN. C. 1000. *Bressanone. The Cathedral Treasury. Ht. 1·50 m. Total width 3·40 m.*

The design of spread eagles is in black on a purple ground; between the eagles are rosettes, also black. The eyes and claws are golden and the eagles hold golden rings in their mouths.

The association of this magnificent textile with Bishop Albuin (975–1006) is of long standing and is in accordance

with the evidence of style, for the late tenth century is the most probable date. The eagles are not quite as elegant or as finely proportioned as those on the Auxerre stuff (Plate 132), but the general effect is most impressive, and the textile is undoubtedly to be regarded as an outstanding product of the imperial workshops at Constantinople.

Sakrale Gewänder des Mittelalters, Munich, Austellung, 1955, No. 17; *Seidenweberei*, abb. 251; *Silks*, Fig. 188.

XIII, SANCTA SOPHIA. MOSAIC: THE ZOE PANEL.
133 *1028–1042. Constantinople. Original height 2·44 m. W. 2·40 m.*

The panel is situated on the east wall of the south gallery and shows Christ enthroned, between the standing figures of Constantine IX Monomachos (1042–1055) and the Empress Zoe (1028–1050). The figures are identified by inscriptions, and parts of these and of the heads have at some time or another been re-done.

The inscription associated with Zoe is part of the original mosaic, and it would therefore appear that the mosaic was in the first instance set up by her. She had three husbands, firstly Romanos III Argyros (1028–1034), secondly Michael IV the Paphlagonian (1034–1041), and thirdly Constantine Monomachos. A careful examination of the inscription associated with the emperor suggested to Whittemore that it originally referred to the first of these, for the letters of his name would exactly fill the available space. It was, he thinks, subsequently altered, somewhat clumsily, to refer to Constantine Monomachos, and it was necessary for part of this emperor's name to be added at the end. At the same time, the head of this emperor was substituted for that of his predecessor. Zoe's head was perhaps to some extent re-done at the same time, either for aesthetic reasons or because the previous portrait had been damaged during Zoe's exile in 1042. The main portion of the mosaic is thus probably to be dated between 1028 and 1034, while the heads were re-done soon after 1042.

Whittemore, III, 1942.

134 ENAMELS FROM THE CROWN OF CONSTANTINE MONOMACHOS. *1042–1055. Budapest. The National Museum. Average height of the rectangular plaques 9 cm. Average width 4·5 cm.*

There are ten plaques, bearing designs as follows:

1. The Emperor Constantine, with an inscription reading: 'Constantine, Emperor of the Romans, Monomachos'.
2. The Empress Zoe with an inscription reading: 'Zoe, the most excellent Empress'.
3. Her sister, the Empress Theodora, with a similar inscription.
4, 5 and 6. Dancers in blue and white.

7 and 8. Female personifications of Humility and Truth, between formal trees.

9 and 10. Round gold plaques of St Peter and St Andrew.

There were also precious stones forming part of the crown.

The enamels of this crown are of great importance, not only because they are of very high quality, but also because they are exactly dated. Zoe was Constantine's wife; Theodora was the sister of Zoe and was also crowned empress, for the two ruled jointly before Constantine came to the throne. Zoe died in 1050, so that the enamels must date from between 1042 and 1050. They were originally arranged together to form a crown akin in shape to the famous crown of St Stephen of Hungary. The enamels were certainly made in Constantinople; the crown probably came to Hungary as a present to the Byzantophile Hungarian King Andrew I (1046–1060). The dancing girls are of very oriental character. There is a plaque with a very similar one in the Victoria and Albert Museum, but it is probably a forgery.

V.S.D., Plate 60; M. Barani Oberschall, 'The Crown of the Emperor Constantinos Monomachos', *Arch. Hungarica*, XXII, 1937.

135 RELIQUARY OF THE TRUE CROSS. *11th century. Esztergom. The Cathedral Treasury. Ht. 35 cm. W. 25 cm.*

The relic itself, in the form of a cross with double traverse, is in the centre, and is framed in a silver gilt mount, to which are attached four enamels, showing Constantine and Helena at the centre, two angels at the top, and the Road to the Cross and the Crucifixion below. The enamels are of very high quality and are to be dated to the eleventh century; they are akin to those of the Monomachos crown (Plate 134). The border, in repoussé work, is a later addition of the early fifteenth century.

V.S.D., Plates 65 and 66; E. Vavju, 'La staurothèque de Gran', *Magyar Müveszet*, VII, 1931, p. 433 (in Hungarian); *B.Z.*, XXXII, 1932, p. 230.

136 SILVER PATEN. *11th century. Halberstadt. The Cathedral Treasury. Diam. 38.8 cm.*

The paten is of silver, with a design in repoussé work. At the centre of the base, which is flat, is the Crucifixion. There is an angel on either side above the arms of the cross; below, the Virgin stands on one side, St John on the other; between them and the cross are the words 'Behold thy son' and 'Behold thy Mother'. The scene is surrounded by the normal consecration formula 'Take, eat . . .' (F. E. Brightman, *Liturgies Eastern and Western*, Oxford, 1896, p. 328) in fine upstanding letters. Beyond this the margin rises at a sharp angle. It is divided into eight lobes, in each of which is the bust of a saint; above is a flat margin, with a similar bust

corresponding to the projection of each lobe. Rim and margin are also adorned with an elaborate scroll pattern in very low relief.

The lobed form seems to have been usual for patens; a superb one of alabaster in St Mark's Treasury, Venice, may be compared (Plate 137).

B.A. and A., p. 554 and Fig. 318.

137 ALABASTER PATEN. *11th century. Venice. The Treasury of St Mark's. Diam. 34 cm.*

The paten is of the finest white alabaster with six lobes. It stands on a silver-gilt base and at the centre of the interior is an enamel of Christ, surrounded by the usual consecration formula, 'Take, eat ye all; this is my Body'. The rim is adorned with jewels in cabochon mounts.

The paten is to be dated to the eleventh century. The silver paten at Halberstadt is similarly lobed and may be compared (Plate 136). The patens in St Mark's are not as numerous as the chalices, but they are all fine; this is one of the most important and stands out because of the simplicity and purity of its design.

Pasini, No. 106, Plate XLVIII and p. 63.

138 GOLD AND ENAMEL BOOK-COVER. *11th century. Venice. The Treasury of St Mark's. Total height 45 cm. W. 30 cm. The central panel: Ht. 26 cm. W. 16 cm.*

The central panel is of gold, to which are attached eleven enamels, representing Christ on the Cross, St John and the Virgin, two angels, the sun and the moon, two inscriptions reading 'Mother of God, behold thy son', and 'Behold thy Mother', and the initials of the Virgin MP ΘΥ, curiously placed on either side of the cross. This central panel is enclosed by an inclined border, with an engraved design and fourteen precious stones, and a flat outer border decorated with stylized acanthus scrolls in repoussé, ten jewels in ornate mounts, and two enamels of the Archangels Michael and Gabriel. At the top is an inscription in niello, reading: 'O mighty cross, powerful against evil spirits; thou guardian of life, thou divine wood.'

The central panel, the enamels and the inscriptions are Byzantine. The wide partitions of the former and their rich colours suggest a date in the early eleventh century; the border is perhaps to be assigned to the Venetian craftsmen who restored the Byzantine objects in the treasury after a fire in the thirteenth century.

The binding is a fine and characteristic example of a group of which there are several other examples in St Mark's Treasury and in the Marcian Library. The Nicephoras Phocas (963–969) Bible cover in the Lavra on Mount

321

Athos may also be compared, though it is of slightly earlier date (see D. Talbot Rice, *Byzantine Art*, Oxford, 1930, Plate 37B; also Pelican edition, Plate 57A).

Pasini, No. 3, Plate III and p. 73.

139 CHALICE. *11th century. Venice. The Treasury of St Mark's. Ht. 23·5 cm. Diam. 18 cm.*

The body of the chalice is of sardonyx, the stem and ornamentation of silver gilt, on which pearls and enamels are mounted. Around the rim is the consecration formula, 'Drink ye all of this . . .'. Below this are four vertical bands with busts in enamel representing St Demetrios, St Procopios, St Theodore, and St Acindinos. On the base are four more busts of St Gregory Nazianzus, St Theophilattos of Nicomedia, St John Boccadoros, and St Ignatius of Antioch. At the centre of the interior is a gold medallion with a bust of the Saviour in enamel.

The work is of the finest and the nature of the enamel suggests a date in the early eleventh century.

There are no less than thirty-two chalices in the Treasury of St Mark's, all of great richness. All are of the tenth or eleventh century; a few even bear names, on the basis of which they can be exactly dated, one to the second half of the tenth century, another to the time of Romanos IV (1067–1071); some show signs of restoration, and a good deal was done in this way by Venetian craftsmen after a fire in the thirteenth century. All must, however, have been made in Constantinople, whence they were brought as part of the booty gathered after the sack of Constantinople in 1204. The chalices are of two principal types, one with high, wide spreading foot, the other on a lower foot, and with two wide-spreading handles; one of those with two handles, however, has the tall foot of the first group.

Pasini, No. 61, Plate XXXV and p. 55.

140 SILVER GILT AND ENAMEL BOOK-COVER. *12th century. Venice. The Marcian Library; Ms. Lat. Cl. 3, No. 111. Ht. 35 cm. W. 25·5 cm.*

This is the reverse of the cover with Christ (Plate XIV below). At the centre is the Virgin in the orans position; above are three plaques: St John the Evangelist, St Eugenios, and St Mark; below are St Matthew, St Simon, and St Luke; to the Virgin's right are St Madarios and St Mark, to the left St Orestes and St Ausenios. The enamels are separated by metal bands, with settings for jewels in cabochon mounts; the jewels have mostly disappeared.

The enamels are of different types and dates. The tall proportions of the figure and the profuse narrow partitions in the enamel of the Virgin attest a date in the late twelfth or early thirteenth century. The four plaques of evangelists in

the corners have Latin inscriptions and are western work of the thirteenth century. The style of the others suggests an earlier date, perhaps in the eleventh century, more probably in the twelfth century. Unlike many of the objects in St Mark's Treasury, this book-cover has not been subsequently restored.

Pasini, Plate XI and p. 116.

141 SILVER GILT AND ENAMEL BOOK-COVER. *12th century. Venice. The Marcian Library; Ms. Lat. Cl. 1, No. 100. Ht. 30 cm. W. 21·5 cm.*

In the centre is Christ full length, holding a book in His left hand and blessing with his right. The plaque is surrounded by twelve circular medallions; above are St Andrew, an archangel, and St Paul; below are St Matthew, the Prophet Elias, and St Simon the Zealot; on Christ's right are St Luke, St Mark, and St Thomas; on His left are St James, St Mark, and St Philip. The enamels are set in mounts of pearls and other small stones; the whole is surrounded by a border of large jewels in cabochon mounts. The reverse bears a figure of the Virgin and smaller enamels of the Archangel Michael, St John the Baptist, St John Chrysostom, St Peter, St Bartholomew, St Gregory, St Nicholas, St Basil, St Accasias, St Joseph, St Elizabeth, and St Anne.

The enamels are Byzantine, but the cover itself has been considerably restored. It is now used for a Latin manuscript.

Pasini, Plates X, XI and p. 117.

XIV GOLD AND ENAMEL BOOK-COVER. *12th century. Venice. The Marcian Library; Ms. Lat. Cl. 3, No. 111. Ht. 35 cm. W. 25·5 cm.*

The cover is bordered and also divided vertically into three sections, by bands of jewels in cabochon mounts; that at the top is missing. In the upper register are three rectangular enamels of St Peter, St Andrew, and St Paul; at the centre is a tall plaque of Christ, the right hand blessing, the left holding an open book; on either side are two small plaques, to Christ's right St Matthew and St Luke, to His left St James and St Proclos; at the bottom are St John, St Theodore, and St Bartholomew—not Thomas, as stated by Pasini. For the reverse, see Plate 140. The cover is now used for a Latin missal of the fourteenth century.

The rather pale flesh tints, the opaque colouring and the very linear character of the work attests its fairly late date; the twelfth century is likely, though it has sometimes been proposed that the cover is of the same date as the manuscript within. It is far more likely that the work was done before 1204 and was brought home as loot from the sack of Constantinople by a member of the Fourth Crusade.

Though late, the front cover remains unrestored, and in this may be contrasted with some of those in the Treasury of St Marks, like the book-cover shown in Plate 141.

B.A. and A., p. 518; *Pasini*, Plate IX and p. 116.

XV GOLD AND ENAMEL BOOK-COVER: THE ARCHANGEL MICHAEL. *11th century. Venice. The Treasury of St Mark's. Ht. 48 cm. W. 36 cm.*

At the centre is the Archangel Michael, partly in relief, his rich costume and wings of enamel, the halo and background of minute filigree work; on either side are circular enamel plaques, two small ones with the letters $\frac{X}{MI}$ and $\frac{A}{HA}$ respectively, and two large with the busts of St Simeon and Our Lord. This central panel has an enamel border, outside which are six more enamel plaques, four circular and two rectangular; those above represent St Mark, the Archangel Uriel and St Luke, those below the Baptist, the Archangel Gabriel and St Bartholomew. The raised border is adorned with appliqué scroll-work and with fourteen enamel plaques; at the top are St Procopios, St Matthew, St John the Evangelist, and St Thomas; at the bottom are St George, the Virgin, St Demetrios, and St Philip; on the archangel's right are St Eustathios, St Mercurios, and St Paul, on his left St Matthew again, St Theodore Stratelates and St James. The figures are not in their original order. The back is adorned with a very rich embossed decoration of scrolls and busts of saints, with a cross at the centre.

The work is exceptionally rich, and the technique, enamel on a highly embossed surface, virtually unique.

B.A. and A., p. 513; *Pasini*, Plate IV and p. 73.

142 MARBLE RELIEF: THE VIRGIN ORANS. *11th century. Istanbul. The Archaeological Museum; No. 3914. Ht. 2·01 m. W. 99 cm.*

The plaque is of very fine marble, the carving in low relief, little higher than the border. The halo and two rectangular plaques on either side of the head have been left rough; they must originally have been covered with metal, and the holes for attaching this remain. The footstool on the other hand was elaborately finished off and polished by the sculptor. The relief was found in the area of the Mangana Palace at Constantinople shortly after the 1914–1918 war.

In spite of the low relief and the very battered state of the slab, the very high quality of the work is at once apparent. The style is perhaps more that of ivory carving than stone sculpture, but it is none the less most effective; though the folds of the costume are formal and severe, they are also subtle and beautiful; though the attitude is frontal and rhythmical, it is also profoundly expressive. This is, in fact, a very beautiful work, and serves to show the high quality of the best large-scale Constantinopolitan sculpture in the

eleventh century. There are several slabs bearing the same subject elsewhere, notably at Athens, Ravenna, Venice, and Berlin, but none is as fine as the Mangana Virgin. There are also other renderings in the Istanbul Museum, but they are crude and coarse in comparison.

R. Demangel and E. Mamboury, *Le Quartier des Manganes*, Paris, 1939, Plate XIV and pp. 155 ff.; *Firatli*, Plate IX.

143 IVORY: THE VIRGIN AND CHILD. *11th century. Utrecht. The Archiepiscopal Museum. Ht. 26 cm. W. 13·6 cm.*

The Virgin is shown standing against a plain background, and is of the type known as 'Hodegetria'.

The work is exceptionally fine and detailed, and is typical of the 'Court' school of Constantinople at its best; it was the same workshop that produced the Harbaville triptych (Plates 100–102) and most of the other fine ivories of the Second Golden Age. Goldschmidt and Weitzmann date this ivory to the tenth century, but it seems more probable that it should be assigned to the eleventh, when, on the evidence of the miniatures and other paintings, it would seem that this refined elegant style was more to the fore. There is a similar, but not quite so fine, ivory at Liège; several others, where the backgrounds have been cut away so that they form free-standing statuettes, may also be compared; those at Hamburg and New York are the most important.

G. and W., II, No. 46; *V.S.D.*, Plate 32; *Edinburgh*, No. 102.

144 IVORY: ST JOHN THE BAPTIST. *11th century. Liverpool. The Archaeological Museum; No. M. 8014. Ht. 24·2 cm. W. 10·1 cm.*

St John the Baptist is shown full length, holding a scroll inscribed in Greek: 'Behold the Lamb of God, who taketh away the sins of the world.' Only the figure and the scroll are original, the background is modern.

Perhaps this ivory once formed the left wing of a devotional triptych. The style of the figure is similar to the panel showing Christ crowning the Emperor Romanos II and the Empress Eudoxia, in the Cabinet des Médailles at Paris (Plate 97), but the conception is more tender and humanistic. The ivory is certainly a work of the 'Court' school at its best, but is to be regarded as later in date than the Romanos panel.

G. and W., II, No. 52; *Liverpool*, No. 21; *Edinburgh*, No. 76.

145 IVORY: ST JOHN THE BAPTIST AND APOSTLES. *11th century. London. The Victoria and Albert Museum; No. 215. 1866. Ht. 23·5 cm. W. 13·5 cm.*

In the centre is St John the Baptist, and at the corners St Philip, St Stephen, St Andrew, and St Thomas, all in medallions. Traces of colour and gilding remain. The heads are finely carved and the faces expressive.

Goldschmidt and Weitzmann compare this with early ivories of the Romanos group and suggest that it may have been part of a casket. The ivory is certainly to be assigned to the 'Court' school at Constantinople, but the rather effeminate style suggests a later date than the tenth century. It is probably to be assigned to much the same date as the Liverpool St John (Plate 144). A date towards the latter part of the eleventh century seems most likely.

G. and W., II, No. 63; *Longhurst*, p. 40.

XVI, 146 PAINTING ON SILK: ST JUST. *11th century. Trieste. Cathedral of St Just. Ht. 128 cm. W. 45 cm.*

The saint is shown full face and full length, his left hand raised, his right in his garment. He has a halo, and his name is written in Latin characters on either side of the head.

The Latin script suggests that the work was done in Italy, but the style is wholly Byzantine; indeed, the painting is in the elegant, refined manner of the 'Court' school, as we see it in the ivories and there is every reason to agree with Demus and to assign the painting to a master who had been trained in Constantinople, even if he was working for a Latin patron.

V.S.D., Plate 100; *Edinburgh*, No. 112; O. Demus, *Die Mosaiken von S. Marco in Venedig*, Baden bei Wien, 1935, p. 96.

XVII PSALTER: THE CROWNING OF DAVID. *1066. London. The British Museum; Add. Ms. 19352. Ht. 22·4 cm. W. 19·6 cm.*

The leaf reproduced (f. 106 r.) shows Solomon holding a horn of oil above David's head; both have haloes. Below is David's flock, of six sheep and a dog, amidst foliage. Above is a bust of the Virgin and Child before a stylized building. The Psalter was written by Theodore of Caesarea for Michael, Abbot of the Monastery of St John of Studion, and was completed in 1066. It is adorned with numerous marginal illustrations, many of them concerned with the life of the Psalmist. Most are vivid and expressive.

Marginal psalters of this sort were generally associated with monastic institutions and with Asia Minor, and the illustrations are usually somewhat crude, though expressive. In this manuscript, the monastic conception of marginal illustrations has been adhered to, but the work is more sophisticated, and the illustrations of the British Museum Psalter take a place from the stylistic point of view half-way between the crude monastic manner and the sophisticated style of the 'Court' school of Constantinople.

British Museum: Reproductions from Illuminated Manuscripts, Series II, 1907, Plates 2 and 3.

147 IVORY: TOP OF A CASKET. *11th century. Stuttgart. Württembergisches Landesmuseum. L. 16·5 cm. W. 9 cm. Ht. 5·5 cm.*

On the top of the casket is depicted the Ascension; above is Christ against an oval mandorla, upheld by two angels and accompanied by two more. In the centre is a delicately cut inscription in relief from John xiv. 27: 'Peace I leave with you; my peace I give unto you.' Below is a group of figures watching the manifestation from amongst trees. The ends of the casket bear roughly cut inscriptions drawn from Matthew xxviii. 5, 6; originally plaques with scenes must have been attached above these. There is a long dedicatory inscription in relief around the sides of the lid. The front shows in the centre Christ descending to Hell; on either side the graves give up their dead. On the back are six isolated figures; in the centre is David, between the Prophets Jeremiah and Ezekiel, Daniel, and probably Isaiah.

The whole composition was apparently designed by the owner as indicating the way to the future life as exemplified finally by Christ. The work is throughout of the very highest quality and combines a curiously archaic approach on the sides, where the inclusion of formal trees and the disposition of the figures is reminiscent of the sixth-century sarcophagi, with a delicacy and humanism on the lid, which herald the art of Kariye and Mistra. Goldschmidt and Weitzmann suggested a date in the eleventh century, but noted that the work was unusual. The top would seem to be by a different hand from the sides but is not likely to be later in date than the eleventh century.

G. and W., II, No. 24; *Edinburgh*, No. 151.

148 MARBLE: STATUE OF AN EMPEROR. *11th century. Istanbul. The Archaeological Museum; No. 4207. Ht. 73 cm.*

The figure is clothed in the conventional imperial costume with richly embroidered and bejewelled loros. The head and portions of the feet are missing.

The conventional pose, with the left hand in front of the chest, is paralleled on ivories like that of the crowning of Constantine Porphyrogenitus in Moscow (Plate 96), and that of Romanos and Eudoxia in the Cabinet des Médailles (Plate 97). The indications of bejewelling on the sculpture are, however, rather more restrained, and there is a more marked feeling for naturalism in the treatment of the robe, especially the sleeve; the hand is especially well carved. It is a great pity that the head has perished, but enough has survived to show that this was originally a very fine piece of work of the 'Court' school, akin to the ivories mentioned above or to the stone carvings of rather later date, like the Mangana Virgin (Plate 142). The figure is probably to be dated to the middle of the eleventh century; by the twelfth century the relief would have been flatter; a stone figure of

the Archangel Michael at Berlin may be compared (Staatliche Museen zu Berlin, No. J.2429; see *Frühchristlich-
Byzantinische Sammlung*, 1938, Plate 25). There is a stone
relief of rather later date, bearing an emperor similarly
clothed, at Dumbarton Oaks (*Handbook of the Collection*,
No. 42).

Arif Mufit, 'Erwerbungsbericht des Antikenmuseums zu Istanbul
seit 1914', *Archäologischer Anzeiger*, 1931, p. 187, abb. 12.

149 PLAQUE OF INCRUSTATION WORK: ST EUDOXIA. CONSTANTINOPLE. *11th century. Istanbul. The Archaeological Museum; No. 4309. Ht. 67 cm. W. 28 cm.*

St Eudoxia is shown full length, her hands raised in prayer,
in imperial costume, richly bejewelled. There is a decorative
border, part of which is missing on the figure's right side.
The face is of ivory, the costume and bejewelling of coloured
stones.

The plaque was found face downwards on the floor of
one of two small chapels on the roof of the northernmost of
the two buildings that compose the Church of St Mary
Panachrantos in 1928 (Plate 63). A number of fragments
in the same technique were found in the filling of the floor
inside the church itself; they comprised incised pieces of
marble, fragments of faces in bone or ivory, and pieces of
coloured marble, as well as a few more complete pieces on
a smaller scale than the St Eudoxia panel; one of them bears
a very expressive duck. A marble plaque in the Byzantine
Museum at Athens, bearing three saints, is cut out in the
same way, but the filling is there of coloured pastes. Work
in a similar technique was also common in Italy from the
eleventh or twelfth century onwards, but the motifs there are
all geometric. Inlaid floors like that in the Church of
St John of Studion or St Saviour Pantocrator may also be
compared, though there the work is a 'mosaic' of coloured
stones shaped to fit side by side; they do not fit into a single
slab, hollowed out to receive them, as is the case here.

Firatli, Plate IX; see also Casson, *Burlington Magazine*, LIX, 1930,
p. 212, and D. Talbot Rice, *Burlington Magazine*, LXII, 1933;
V.S.D., Plate 72.

150 CIRCULAR RELIEF OF GREEN PORPHYRY. *1078–1081. London. The Victoria and Albert Museum; No. A.1. 1927. Diam. 17·9 cm.*

The bust of the Virgin is shown in the centre, full face,
her arms raised in prayer. Around the edge is an inscription
in Greek, invoking the help of the Mother of God for
Nicephoras Botaniates (1078–1081). It was at one time in
the Abbey of Heiligenkreuz in Austria, and was published
in an engraving of 1661.

The rendering of the face, fat and round and in a realist

style, is unusually developed for Byzantine art of the period.
The style is allied to that of the group of ivories distinguished
by Goldschmidt and Weitzmann as the Nicephoras group
(Plates 120, 121, 123). It is of special importance, being one
of the very few dated examples of eleventh-century art that
are known.

F. de Mely, 'Le camée byzantin de Nicéphore Botaniatés',
Monuments Piot, VI; *Longhurst*, p. 49; *Burlington Magazine*, 1927,
p. 107; *Bréhier*, Plate XVII; *Edinburgh*, No. 100.

151 MARBLE RELIEF: THE VIRGIN AND CHILD. *Late 11th century. Istanbul. The Archaeological Museum; No. 4730. Ht. 78 cm. W. 74 cm.*

The type is that of the Hodegetria, the Virgin holding the
Child on her left arm. The usual initials appear within
circles on either side of the head. The haloes, borders of the
costume and other details are marked with incisions, which
probably served originally for the attachment of precious
stones or metal adornments, like those on a sculpture in
Santa Maria in Porto at Ravenna (Diehl, *L'Art chrétien
primitif et l'art Byzantin*, Paris, 1928, Plate XLVIII). The
border of the slab is left in relief and an inscription appears
at the top and on the left side. The opposite side has been
broken off and the raised border here is a restoration. The
slab is also broken below, and it is probable that the figure
of the Virgin originally stood full length. The inscription is
fragmentary and is indecipherable as it stands.

The relief was found near the Sokollu Mehmet Pasa
mosque not far from the Church of SS. Sergius and Bacchus
in Constantinople.

The modelling is full and rich, the faces and hands rather
plump. A comparison with the circular relief of green
serpentine in the Victoria and Albert Museum (Plate 150)
at once comes to mind, and the relief is probably to be
assigned to much the same date, even perhaps to the same
workshop.

Firatli, Plate VII; Mango, *Am. Journ. of Arch.*, 54, 1951, p. 66,
mentions the inscription, but does not give a copy.

152, 153 IVORY: CASKET WITH HUNTING SCENES AND RIDERS. *11th century. Troyes. The Cathedral Treasury. Ht. 14 cm. W. 13 cm. L. 26 cm.*

On the front are two mounted hunters, attacking a lion with
bow and sword; on the back a hunter with three dogs is
spearing a wild boar; on the top are two mounted figures in
imperial costume with a fortified city between them, from the
gate of which a woman bearing the city's crown, emerges; at
the ends are birds amid foliage. The casket is said to have
been brought back from Constantinople after the sack of
1204 by Jean Langlois, chaplain to Garnier de Traisnel,
Bishop of Troyes.

The riders on the top are akin to figures that appear on textiles like the famous 'rider' stuff at Lyons. The scene on the lid almost certainly refers to the capture of a city by an emperor, and may be compared in a general way to the silk tapestry found in the tomb of Bishop Gunther (d. 1065) now in the Cathedral Treasury at Bamberg, where a female figure offers a crown to a mounted emperor. The hunting scenes, particularly the lion-hunt, have been compared to Sasanid silver dishes, but there seems little need to go to Persia for iconographic parallels; such scenes were part of the heritage left to Byzantium out of the Graeco-Roman ornamental repertory, being very usual on mosaic floors. The phoenix is another matter. It appears in a Byzantine manuscript, dating from the middle of the tenth century (Berlin, Phillips, 1538; cf. Weitzmann, *Die Byzantinische Buchmalerei des IX. und X. Jahrb.*, Berlin, 1935, Plate XXI). Grabar suggests that the bird may have come to Byzantium with the assistance of Turkish art and quotes the gold vessels from Kopeny (Altai) dating from the seventh and eighth centuries (*Münchner Jahrbücher*, II, 1951, p. 54). A more probable explanation is that imported Chinese silks were used as models (cf. *Seidenweberei*, I, abb. 118, 119; *Silks*, 87, 88).

Peirce and Tyler, followed by Goldschmidt and Weitzmann, have compared the emperors to the Coronation panel of Romanos II, and a date in the tenth century has been advocated for the Troyes casket, but its style seems a great deal coarser and freer than that of ivories of the 'Romanos' group, and it would seem probable that a date in the middle of the eleventh century is more likely. Grabar assigns the casket to an even later date.

Peirce and Tyler, *Arethuse*, July 1927; *V.S.D.*, Plates 26–29; *G. and W.*, I, No. 122; A. Grabar, 'La Soie byzantine de l'évêque Gunther à Bamberg', *Münchner Jahrbuch*, VII, 1956, pp. 7ff.; *Edinburgh*, No. 135.

154 TWO IVORY PANELS: THE VIRGIN AND CHRIST. *11th century. Bamberg. Staatliche Bibliothek; Cod. A.11. 54 and 55. Ht. 27·9 cm. Width of each 11·3 cm.*

Christ is shown full length, frontally; the Virgin is in three-quarter face. There are two other plaques on the binding of the same book, bearing St Peter and St Paul, both in a three-quarter position.

On all the plaques the relief is very low and the details are much simplified. Goldschmidt and Weitzmann assign the ivories to the Romanos group. They certainly savour of the capital, but the manner is distinct, and they are not only to be assigned to a master who was a good deal less skilled than the men who carved such ivories as the Romanos plaque or the Harbaville triptych, but are also to be dated a good deal later, especially because of the three-quarter pose. Goldschmidt and Weitzmann suggest *c.* 1000, but a date nearer the middle of the eleventh century is more likely. A rather

similar style characterizes the mosaics of the Zoe panel in Sancta Sophia, which are firmly dated to the second quarter of the eleventh century (Plates XIII, 133).

G. and W., II, Nos. 65 and 66.

155 PORTATIVE MOSAIC: THE VIRGIN AND CHILD. *c. 1065. Istanbul. The Church of the Patriarchate. Ht. 2·67 cm. W. 1·65 m.*

The iconographic type is that of the Hodegetria. The Virgin is shown half-length, holding the Child on her left arm, and pointing to it with her right hand.

The rendering is severe and formal, and contrasts markedly with that to be seen on later paintings or mosaics, for example the famous 'Our Lady of Vladimir' (Plate 171). It is typical of the majestic manner of mid-Byzantine art. The early date suggested by the style is borne out by what is known of the history of the icon, for it was brought to the Patriarchate from the Church of St Mary Pammakaristos when the church became a mosque in 1586, and Sotiriou shows that there is good reason to believe that it was made for that church as part of a re-endowment by John Comnenos and Anna Delassena; she died in 1067, so that the mosaic would date from around 1060. It is the earliest example of a portative mosaic that we know.

G. Sotiriou, 'L'Icone de la Pammakaristos trouvée dans l'église du Patriarcat', *Praktika* of the Academy of Athens, VIII, 1933, p. 359 (in Greek).

156 TWO SCULPTURED SLABS WITH GEOMETRIC ORNAMENT. *12th century. Istanbul. The Archaeological Museum.*
(above) No. 2250. Ht. 93 cm. L. 195 cm.

A triple band of the border turns to connect with and form the outline of the main design, a series of octafoils. The spaces between the border and the octafoils are filled with stylized acanthus leaves, and the octafoils themselves with geometric interlacing of differing types. One complete and one incomplete octafoil survive, but the slab was originally longer. The ornament has a distinctly Islamic flavour and the slab can hardly be earlier than the twelfth century. The provenance of the slab is not known, but it may well have been carved in either Asia Minor under Seljuk influence, or even Constantinople itself.

Mendel, II, No. 732.

(below) No. 2922. Ht. 71 cm. W. 73 cm.

The ground has been cut away to leave a basically geometric pattern in very low relief. The triple band of the border interlaces to form the principal design, a circle within a square disposed diagonally; inside the circle is a pattern like a catherine-wheel, and in the four corners are fan patterns, all similar in shape, though the number of the leaves varies. Slabs with geometric patterns of this sort were usual from the sixth century onwards; the low relief and the nature of the design suggest a fairly late date in this case, probably the twelfth century.

157 PAIR OF SCULPTURED SLABS WITH PEA-COCKS. *12th century. Istanbul. The Archaeological Museum; Nos. 3978 and 3979. Ht. 78 cm. L. 119 cm.*

The two slabs bear peacocks in very low relief and are identical except that the peacocks face in opposite directions. The reverse sides of both slabs are sculptured with geometric motives, but are very severely eroded. The slabs were found in Constantinople at Yenikapı.

Closure slabs decorated with low relief work of this type appear from the sixth century onwards, but the extreme degree of stylization here suggests a late date; the geometric motif on the back is probably earlier, and the peacocks no doubt belong to a re-carving. They fall into the group classed as 'embroidery' sculpture by Bréhier (L. Bréhier, 'Récherches sur la sculpture byzantine', *Nouvelles Archives des Missions scientifiques*, nouvelle série, fasc. 3, Paris, 1911). The peacock was a very popular motif and slabs with pea-cocks treated more naturalistically or in higher relief which are to be assigned to the sixth century survive at Ravenna and elsewhere; there is a particularly fine slab at Berlin of the seventh century (S. Bettini, *La Scultura Bizantina*, Florence, II, p. 4; also L. Bréhier, *La Sculpture et les Arts mineurs byzantins*, Paris, 1936, Plate VIII). In spite of the stylization, however, the Constantinople slabs are not without distinction.

Arif Mufit, 'Erwerbungsbericht des Antikenmuseums zu Istanbul', *Archäologischer Anzeiger*, 1931, abb. 26 and p. 208.

158 CAST BRONZE TRIPTYCH. *12th century. London. The Victoria and Albert Museum; No. 1615. 1855. Ht. 15·4 cm. Total width 20·1 cm.*

The Virgin is enthroned on the central panel, with the Child on her knee. On one side is St John Chrysostom, on the other St Gregory Nazianzus. On the outside of each leaf is a cross and the letters IC XC NI KA, 'Jesus Christ conquers'. The Virgin's pose, with the left hand hanging down, is that distinguished by Kondakov as the 'Cyprus' icono-graphical type. It is an unusual one in mid-Byzantine iconography, where the 'Hodegetria' was more popular, but it was common in the sixth and seventh centuries.

The throne is of a form similar to those on later paintings, and suggests a date in the twelfth century. Few Byzantine works in cast metal are known, but whether this is because

few were made or because solid metal objects proved profit-able to melt down during the subsequent periods it is impossible to say. The general appearance here is close to that of an ivory, and it is possible that an ivory was used for the matrix.

Peirce and Tyler, *Byzantine Art*, Plate 72; *V.S.D.*, Plate 58; *Edinburgh*, No. 175.

159 COPPER GILT PLAQUE: THE VIRGIN AND CHILD. *12th century. London. The Victoria and Albert Museum; No. 818. 1891. Ht. 22·4 cm. W. 14 cm.*

The Virgin is standing full length, in the pose known as the Hodegetria. On either side of the head are the usual initials, MP ΘΥ, and below an inscription which reads 'Mother of God, strengthen thy servant Philip the Bishop'. The bishop has not been identified.

The plaque came from Torcello, but the style is metro-politan, and it is more likely to have been made in Constantinople. It is to be assigned to the twelfth century. It has, unfortunately, been re-gilt comparatively recently. There is a similar plaque not perhaps quite so fine, in the museum at Plovdiv in Bulgaria, but the Virgin is turned to the left instead of to the right.

See K. Miatev, 'A bronze relief of the Virgin in Plovdiv Museum', *Seminarium Kondakovianum*, v, 1932, p. 39 (in Russian with short summary in French); *Edinburgh*, No. 189.

160, IVORY CASKET. *12th century. Florence. Museo*
161 *Nazionale. Ht. 12 cm. L. 49 cm. W. 15·2 cm.*

The casket is rectangular, with a flat sliding top. It is made up of eighteen large rectangular panels, bearing below arcades the figures of Christ, the Virgin, and saints; the plaques are bordered by the usual rosette bands. On the lid are half-figures of Christ, the Virgin, St John Chrysostom, and St John the Baptist. On the front, St Thomas, St Philip, St Simon the Zealot, St James the son of Zebedee, and St Andrew. On the back are St John, St Matthew, St Luke, St Mark, and St Bartholomew, while at the sides are St Peter and St Paul, St Sergius and St Bacchus.

The figures on the lid appear to have been rearranged at some later date; the present order is unorthodox and presum-ably the bust of Christ should be between those of the Virgin and St John the Baptist. The style of the head of Christ has been compared to that in mosaic at Monreale, where Christ is shown crowning King William II (1181), and the saints have also been compared in a general way to mosaics in the same church dating from the late twelfth century. On these grounds attempts have been made to assign the casket to a Sicilian workshop, but the style is so refined that a Constan-tinopolitan origin seems much more likely. It should also be borne in mind that there is every reason to accept Demus's conclusion that much of the best work in the Sicilian mosaics was done by Greeks who were brought from Constantinople for the purpose.

G. and W., I, No. 99; V.S.D., Plate 36; Edinburgh, No. 82.

XVIII–XXI MINIATURES FROM THE OCTATEUCH. *12th century. Istanbul. Topkapu Saray Library; Codex 8. Ht. 42·6 cm. W. 32 cm.*

The manuscript contains 570 leaves of parchment and 352 miniatures, as well as 70 smaller illustrations in the text.

Plate XVIII (f. 471 v.) shows two miniatures; the upper one shows Moses led by an angel to his last encounter with the Almighty; on the lower his death is depicted; Plate XIX (f. 43 v.) the Garden of Eden. Plate XX (f. 257) shows Moses on Sinai; Plate XXI (f. 197 v.), the Israelites crossing the Red Sea, led by the pillar of fire; the grey figure is the personification of night and the naked one that of the sea.

The Octateuchs constituted one of the most common forms of Bible manuscript in the Byzantine world; they contained the first eight books of the Old Testament. That in Topkapu Saray at Istanbul was copied early in the twelfth century in the imperial scriptorium. Isaac, youngest son of Alexios Comnenos (1081–1118), actually collaborated in the work. Several different hands can be distinguished, but it is not possible to identify the miniatures for which the young prince was responsible. The illustrations reproduced on our first plate are clearly by a different painter from those on the second.

A number of other copies of Octateuchs survive; the closest in date and style is one in the Vatican (Gr. 747), but it varies both in the way the scenes are done and in the selection of the scenes to be illustrated. Other examples which are less closely related are in the Vatican (Gr. 746), in the Laurentian Library at Florence (V. 38), and in the monastery of Vatopedi on Mount Athos. A particularly rich copy done in the time of Alexios I Comnenos (1081–1118) was unfortunately destroyed in the great fire of Smyrna in 1920.

A. Deichmann, *Forschungen und Funde im Serai*, Berlin, 1933, p. 46; K. Weitzmann, 'The Octateuch of the Seraglio and the History of its Pictures' Recension', *Actes du xième Congrès International d'Etudes byzantins à Istanbul*, 1955, Istanbul, 1957, p. 183. The fullest publication remains that of T. Uspensky, 'The Octateuch of the Saray Library at Constantinople', *Transactions of the Russian Archaeological Institute at Constantinople*, XII, Sofia, 1907 (in Russian).

162 STEATITE: THE ARCHANGEL GABRIEL. *12th century. Fiesole. Museo Bandini. Ht. 15·2 cm. W. 10·9 cm.*

The archangel stands full length and almost full face within an arcade, holding a medallion of Christ in one hand and

a staff in the other. The top of the plaque is rounded. The steatite was originally gilt, and a good deal of the original gilding remains.

The carving is precise and delicate, and the style follows that of the 'Court' school of ivory carving in the tenth century, though the relief is lower and the touch rather more effeminate. The steatite is probably to be dated to the twelfth century when, perhaps for economic reasons, this material to some extent replaced ivory. Rather similar, but rather drier, works continued to be produced in this material right down to the fifteenth century.

V.S.D., Plate 39A; Edinburgh, No. 142.

XXII, 163 MANUSCRIPT OF THE HOMILIES OF ST JOHN CHRYSOSTOM. *c. 1078. Paris. Bibliothèque Nationale; Ms. Coislin 79. Ht. 41·5 cm. W. 31·5 cm.*

There are four pages of portraits at the beginning; otherwise the manuscript only contains decorative chapter heads. The first portrait (f. 1) shows the Emperor Nicephoras Botaniates (1078–1081); the second shows the emperor and his empress, Mary, with a small figure of Christ blessing them above (f. 1 v.); the third shows the emperor enthroned, with his courtiers below and two personifications above (f. 2); the fourth, illustrated here, shows the emperor between St John Chrysostom and the Archangel Michael (f. 2 v.). At the emperor's feet is prostrated a diminutive figure which no doubt represents the artist.

The work is of outstandingly high quality, especially the picture of the emperor between St. John Chrysostom and the archangel.

Omont, *Miniatures*, Plates LXI–LXIV; *Byzance*, No. 29.

XXIII, 164–5 SANCTA SOPHIA. MOSAIC: THE JOHN AND ALEXIOS PANELS. *1118–1122. Constantinople. Ht. 2·47 m. W. 4·45 m.*

The mosaic is in the south gallery on the east wall; the Virgin is shown between the Emperor John II Comnenos (1118–1143) and the Empress Irene; at right angles on an adjoining pilaster is a portrait of Alexios Comnenos.

The figure of the Virgin is hieratic and the pose follows an old iconographic tradition. The portraits are rigid, but characterful; most outstanding of them is that of Alexios, which is not only obviously a striking likeness of a young man but also clearly a very spontaneous work. It also heralds the style of the future, for the marked white highlights that we see here as a series of thin lines on the face were later to become characteristic of painting as a whole. Whittemore believed that the same man was responsible for both sections of the mosaic, but the Alexios portrait is so much fresher than the rest of the mosaic that it seems more likely that it should be attributed to a different hand, though the dates of the two sections must be close. The John panel was probably done soon after the emperor's accession in 1118; the Alexios portrait was probably added in 1122 when he was proclaimed co-emperor.

Whittemore, vol. III.

166, SILVER GILT RELIQUARY. *12th century. Paris.*
167 *Musée du Louvre. Ht. 42 cm. W. 29·8.*

The two plaques, both in the embossed technique, belong to the same reliquary, the smaller one being the inside. It bears a cross, flanked below by acanthus leaves and above by the letters IC XC and a series of stars. The larger one shows the two Marys at the sepulchre, with an angel indicating the rejected grave wrappings. Below the mummy the plaque is damaged, but the figures of the soldiers, on a much reduced scale, can be distinguished. Above them is an inscription which is a paraphrase of Matthew xxviii. 4, 'and for fear of him the guards did shake and became as dead men'. The inscription above the angel reads, 'Come, see the place where the Lord lay' (Matthew xxviii. 6). Above the Marys, the inscription reads 'For they trembled and were amazed' (Mark xvi. 8). On the opposite side is the title 'The Tomb of the Lord'. Around the margin is a longer inscription which describes the scene. It reads 'With what glory the angel appears to the women. From afar shine the signs of her innate quality, of her immaterial purity. By his beauty he reveals the splendour of the Resurrection, crying aloud, "The Lord is risen"'. The text is taken from the *Paraklitike*, 8th tone, Canon for Sunday, Ode 1. On the reverse of the smaller plaque is a quotation from Mark xvi. 6, 'Behold the place where they laid him.' The reliquary was formerly in the Treasury of the Sainte-Chapelle.

The proportions are strange and the aesthetic effect is perhaps somewhat marred by the profusion of inscriptions, but the reliquary is nevertheless striking. It has been variously dated to the tenth, eleventh, and twelfth centuries; a date in the twelfth century is on the whole most probable.

V.S.D., Plate 57; *Monuments Piot*, XXXII, 1932, p. 89.

168 PORTATIVE MOSAIC: CHRIST. C. *1100. Berlin, Dahlem. Ehemals Staatliche Museen; Nr. 1989. Ht. 74·5 cm. W. 52·5 cm.*

Christ is shown as the Pantocrator, and the conception is close to that of the wall mosaics, where He appears in the dome or, in default of a dome, in the eastern apse; the renderings in the dome at Daphni near Athens (*c.* 1100) and in the apses of Cefalù (1148) or the cathedral at Monreale (*c.* 1190) may be compared.

The portative mosaic at Berlin, and another in the Museo Nazionale at Florence, which is not dissimilar (Plate 169),

are to be dated to before the middle of the twelfth century; a date around 1100 seems most likely in the case of the former and one around 1150 in that of the latter.

Wulff, *Altchristliche and Mittelalterliche, Byzantinische und Italienische Bildwerke*, III, Pt. II, Berlin, 1909, p. 95; Felicetti-Liebenfels, *Geschichte der Byzantinischen Ikonenmalerei*, Lausanne, 1956, Taf. 70, p. 63.

169 MINIATURE MOSAIC: CHRIST. c.1150. *Florence. Museo Nazionale. Ht. 54 cm. W. 41 cm.*

Christ is shown as the Pantocrator, half-length; His right hand is raised in blessing, His left holds an open book with the words 'I am the light of the world' upon it.

The conception is still austere; though it is more emotional than in work of the eleventh century, like the similar icon in Berlin (Plate 168); yet it lacks the tenderness that characterizes works of the Byzantine revival, for example, in the wall mosaics of Kariye Cami at Constantinople (Plate 182). So far as expression is concerned, the rendering is not far removed from that of the dome mosaic at Daphni (*c.* 1100) for it has something of the same unworldly glory and transcendental beauty. It is, however, certainly later in date, and is probably to be assigned to much the same period as the Christ in the apse at Cefalù (1148). Both Myslević and Muratov are wrong when they assign it respectively to the thirteenth or fourteenth and to the tenth centuries.

Felecetti-Liebenfels, *Geschichte der Byzantinischen Ikonenmalerei*, Lausanne, 1956, p. 63 and Plate 71; J. Myslević, *Ikona*, Prague, 1947, Plate 5; P. Muratov, *La Peinture byzantine*, Paris, 1928, Plate LXXXIV; L. Marcucci, *Catalogi dei Musei e Gallerie d'Italia: Gallerie Nazionale di Firenze, Dipinti Toscani, Scuole Bizantine*, 1958, Plate 25; *Edinburgh*, No. 218.

XXIV, ENAMEL CROSS. *12th century. Cosenza. The*
170 *Cathedral Treasury. Ht. 26 cm. W. 21 cm.*

The cross is of silver gilt and is adorned with enamels. On one face is the Crucifixion, with circular medallions at the extremities of the arms, the Archangel Michael above, the Virgin and the Baptist on the traverse, and the 'Hetoimasia' ('Preparation of the Throne') below; on the other face is Christ in a medallion at the centre, with the four evangelists at the extremities.

The partitions of the enamels are small and the work delicate; on stylistic grounds alone it should be assigned to the twelfth century. Concrete evidence supports this dating, for the cross was presented to the cathedral by Frederic II in 1222; it was probably made towards the end of the preceding century. It may be accepted as of Byzantine workmanship, for a suggestion that it is to be regarded as Italian is at once discounted if it is compared with typical Italian work, like the large enamel of Christ in the Palazzo Venezia at Rome.

V.S.D., Plates 60–63.

PANEL PAINTING: OUR LADY OF VLADI-
MIR. C. 1130. *Moscow. The Tretiakov Gallery. Original
height 78 cm. Original width 54·6 cm. Present dimensions:
Ht. 105·6 cm. W. 68·5 cm.*

The icon shows the Virgin and Child; the type is that
known as the 'Eleousa' or 'Virgin of Tenderness', where the
Child's face is pressed against the Virgin's cheek in affection.
The Child is supported by the Virgin's right arm; her left
hand just touches the Child, but the position of the hand is
still close to that usual in pictures of the more austere iconographical rendering known as the 'Hodegetria' or 'Indicator
of the Way'. The back of the icon bears a rendering of a
mystical composition, showing a cross and an altar with
a Bible upon it; it is a Russian work dating from soon after
1500, when the front also underwent an extensive restoration.
The panel has been repainted but a very careful cleaning
undertaken in 1919 indicated that both faces and part of the
Child's shoulder belonged to the original painting.

Documentary evidence shows that the original icon was
taken from Constantinople to Russia in the twelfth century,
probably in 1131. The icon must thus have been painted in
Constantinople. It may be assumed that it was done for the
occasion, so that we may conclude that it was painted in the
first years of the second quarter of the twelfth century; stylistic
evidence makes it most unlikely that it could have been done
in the eleventh century as some authorities have suggested.
Whenever it went, however, we know that in 1155 it was
taken from Kiev to Vladimir. From that time onwards
it became famous for its miracle-working properties. Soon
after that it was adorned with a frame of precious stones. It
was apparently saved in the fire of 1185, but the frame was
stripped off when the Tartars sacked Vladimir in 1237. The
icon itself was, however, preserved and remained at Vladimir
till 1395, when it was taken to Moscow.

It has usually been agreed that the icon as we see it today
is, apart from the restorations, the original that was brought
to Russia from Constantinople. Recently, however, Dr
Konrad Onasch has questioned this, suggesting that the
original icon was burnt in the fire of 1185, and that the one
that survives is a copy of it done in the first half of the
thirteenth century. He bases his argument to some extent on
the fact that the evolution of the 'Eleousa' type could hardly
have advanced so far by about 1130. This has important
implications, for the icon constitutes one of the principal
pieces of evidence that the new, more personal and tender
style which characterized the Palaeologue 'Revival' was
actually born quite early in the twelfth century. The wall-
paintings at Nerez in Yugoslavia of 1164 constitute further
evidence.

In the 'Hodegetria' type the Virgin points to the Child as
a symbol of the Christian faith; there is no hint of human
tenderness or affection. In later variants of the 'Virgin of
Tenderness' on the contrary, the Virgin clasps the Child
firmly and looks at it with affection and not at the spectator,
as is the case here. Our Lady of Vladimir thus represents an
embryonic version of the new iconographic theme. Recent
discoveries, however, tend to suggest that the introduction of
'humanism' into Byzantine art was already in full swing
quite early in the twelfth century, and this being so, the
half-developed version of the 'Eleousa' type that is constituted by the Vladimir Virgin does not seem unduly
precocious for the time. It must also be remembered that we
have to do with a Constantinopolitan work, and that the
adoption of new ideas might be expected to have progressed
further in the capital than in the provinces. In view of this,
there seems no real reason to query the traditional dating,
and we may regard the icon as a Constantinopolitan work
done between 1125 and 1130.

A. J. Anisimov, *Our Lady of Vladimir*, Prague, 1928; Konrad
Onasch, 'Die Ikone der Gottesmutter von Vladimir in der
Staatlichen Tretjakov-Galerie zu Moscau', *Wissenschaftliche Zeitschrift der Martin Luther Universität*, Halle-Wittenberg, V, Heft 1,
1955, p. 51.

XXV– SANCTA SOPHIA. MOSAIC: DEESIS PANEL
XXVII, IN THE SOUTH GALLERY. *12th or 13th century.*
172 *Constantinople. Average height 5·95 m. Average width
4·08 m.*

Christ stands in the centre; to His right is the Virgin and
to His left the Baptist, who intercede for the sins of the world.
Only the upper portions now survive.

The panel was uncovered in 1933 and published in
1952, in a posthumous work by Thomas Whittemore. He
proposed a date at the end of the eleventh or early in the
twelfth century, on the evidence of the palaeography of the
inscriptions. A comparison with the icon of Our Lady of
Vladimir (Plate 171) appeared to him to support his conclusions on stylistic grounds, in any case so far as the figure of
the Virgin was concerned. Nothing in the iconography or
style of the other heads seemed to Whittemore to contradict
this deduction. The Vladimir icon must date from before
1130. Others have questioned Whittemore's conclusion,
calling attention to the similarity of the technique and style
to the mosaics of Kariye Cami, especially to the large panel
of Christ and the Virgin in the inner narthex (Plate XXXI).
Bettini ('I mosaici dell' Atrio di San Marco e il lore seguito',
Arte Veneta, VIII, 1954, p. 38) even goes so far as to suggest
a date even later than Kariye.

Though the Kariye panel of Christ and the Virgin is now
firmly dated to around 1305 (P. Underwood, 'The Deesis
Mosaic in Kariye Cami at Istanbul', *Late Classical and
Mediaeval Studies in Honor of A. M. Friend*, 1955, p. 254),
its style seems somewhat archaic in comparison with the
other Kariye mosaics, and alone would not have precluded
an earlier date. Nor do other comparisons of the Sancta
Sophia panel necessarily all point to the early fourteenth
century. The date around 1100 proposed by Whittemore is

no doubt too early. But one at the very end of the twelfth century is possible, and if the trend towards delicacy and humanism that we see here seems precocious before about 1270, it must be remembered that Constantinople was the capital and that it was there that the most experimental and progressive work would have been done. If the mosaic was not done before the Latin conquest, a date around 1270 is likely.

As a work of art this mosaic is outstanding; it is perhaps the most outstanding of all the mosaics in the church.

Whittemore, vol. IV, 1952.

173 MINIATURE MOSAIC: THE CRUCIFIXION.
Late 12th century. Berlin. Staatliche Museen; Nr. I. 6431. Ht. 36·5 cm. W. 30 cm.

Christ is shown on the cross, between the Virgin and St John. Below, the walls of Jerusalem appear in the background; the sky is silver. The mosaic is of glass and silvered cubes, on a wax ground.

Christ's body is severely bent in agony, and the arms are greatly elongated; the Virgin and St John on the other hand are calm and collected and evince no great emotion. The stylistic evidence as to dating is thus somewhat contradictory and has led different authorities to assign the mosaic to as early as the eleventh century and to as late as the fourteenth century. A date at the very end of the twelfth century seems most likely. The silver background is an unusual feature. The technique is extremely accomplished.

The mosaic came from Sicily and it has sometimes been held that it was made there; this, however, is unlikely, for both the quality and the character of the work suggest the capital and the style is distinct from that of the Sicilian wall mosaics.

O. Wulff, *Altchristliche und Mittelalterliche, Byzantinische und Italienische Bildwerke*, Berlin, 1909, III, Ht. 2, Taf. XVII, who suggests the thirteenth–fourteenth century; P. Orsi, 'Quadretto bizantino a mosaico della Sicilia', *Studi Bizantini*, Naples, 1924, p. 221, who assigns it to the eleventh or twelfth century; see also *Exposition*, No. 639, where it is assigned to the thirteenth century. There is an excellent coloured plate in Wulff-Alpator, *Denkmäler der Ikonenmalerei*, Leipzig, 1925, abb. 39; *Edinburgh*, No. 220.

174 SILVER-GILT BOOK-COVER. 13th century.
Venice. The Marcian Library; A.1, No. 55. Ht. 33 cm. W. 20 cm.

The ornament is in repoussé; at the centre is the Anastasis; twelve other larger and four smaller plaques with figures, and a number of smaller ones with scroll or interlacing patterns, surround the main one. The larger plaques depict at the top the Prophet David, the Hetoimasia ('Preparation of the Throne') and the Prophet Solomon; at the bottom are St Gregory the Theologian, the Prophet David, and St Nicholas. On Christ's right are the Prophets Jonah and Isaiah and St John Chrysostom; on His left are the Prophets Elias and Jeremiah and St Gregory the Theologian. The smaller plaques above represent archangels; below they show St George and St Demetrios.

Work of a rather similar type was done in Italy from the fourteenth century onwards, but this example is certainly to be assigned to a Greek craftsman. The scroll work suggests a fairly late date; the fourteenth or early fifteenth century are likely.

It forms the reverse of a binding on the front of which the main scene is the Crucifixion. Pasini dates it to the twelfth century, but it can hardly be so early.

Pasini, Plate XII and p. 118.

175 IVORY: SCENES FROM THE LIFE OF CHRIST
13th century. London. The Victoria and Albert Museum; No. 295. 1867. Ht. 25 cm. W. 12 cm.

The ivory is divided into three registers. In the upper one are the Annunciation and the Nativity; in the centre the Transfiguration and the Raising of Lazarus; below are the Marys at the Sepulchre and Christ with the Marys in the Garden.

The panel was dated to the eleventh century and assigned to their 'border' group by Goldschmidt and Weitzmann; others, especially Keck, regard the whole group as provincial and date the ivories that belong to it to the twelfth and early thirteenth centuries. The style is rather coarse and a thirteenth-century date seems likely; it is possible that the ivory was carved in Constantinople during the Latin domination.

Longhurst, p. 45; *G. and W.*, II, No. 198; A. S. Keck, *Art Bulletin*, XII, 1939, pp. 147 ff.; *Edinburgh*, No. 90.

176, MANUSCRIPT: PSALTER. 13th century. Rome.
177 *The Vatican Library. Cod. Vat. Palat. Gr. 381. Ht. 33·5 cm. W. 23·1 cm.*

The manuscript has 386 leaves and four full-page miniatures, showing David composing the Psalms (f. 1v.), David between Wisdom and Prophecy (f. 2), Moses receiving the Law on Mount Sinai (f. 169v.) and Moses presenting the Law to the people (f. 170).

The pages reproduced here show Moses on Mount Sinai (Plate 176) and David between Wisdom and Prophecy (Plate 177). Both are enclosed in decorative borders; that of the second subject is suggestive of the decorative bands that separate the figures of angels in the dome frescoes of the Pareccleseion at Kariye Cami, of about 1305. The rendering of the Almighty in the Sinai scene is close to depictions in the later manuscripts. The other scene is more conservative as to disposition, but the delicate treatment of the figures is typical of the 'Revival' period. The book held by David bears part of the text of Psalm 70.

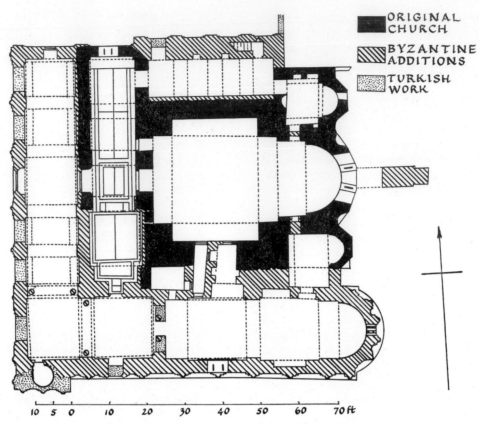

Fig. 4 Plan of the Church of St Saviour in Chora [Kariye Cami] (after Van Millingen)

The manuscript is said to have come from a monastery in Asia Minor or on Mount Athos, but the style of the work is Constantinopolitan, and the miniatures are in a grand, refined manner, akin to that of the psalters of the 'aristocratic' group, but obviously of later date. They have been dated both to the twelfth and the thirteenth century; recent opinion, put forward by Demus, tends to favour the thirteenth, and regards the manuscript as typical of the Palaeologan style. It may, however, have been done during the Latin interregnum, for Weitzmann has shown that the production of work, in any case of that on a small scale, no doubt continued in spite of the Latin domination.

'Miniature della Bibbia, Cod. Vat. Reg. gr. 1, e della Salterio, Cod. Vat. Palat. gr. 381', *Collezione Palaeografica Vaticano*, Fasc. 1, Milan, 1905; O. Demus, 'Die Entstehung des Palaologenstils in der Malerei', *Berichte zum XI. Internationalen Byzantinischen Kongres*, Munich, 1958; K. Weitzmann, 'Constantinopolitan Book Illumination in the period of the Latin Conquest', *Gazette des Beaux Arts*, April 1944.

178, THE PALACE OF CONSTANTINE PORPHY-
179 ROGENITUS. *12th or 13th century. Constantinople.*

This is the only secular building in Constantinople that survives above ground-level. Originally it formed an annex to the Blachernae palace, standing on the hill above the meeting of the land walls and the Golden Horn. It is variously known as the Palace of Constantine Porphyrogenitus or by its Turkish name of Tekfur Saray.

There has been some dispute as to its date, for some have assigned it to Constantine VII Porphyrogenitus (913–959), some to Manuel I Comnenos (1143–1180), and others to the Palaeologue period. The presence on the walls of plaques bearing the Palaeologue monograms ΠΑ and the four B's, standing for βασιλεὺς βασιλέων βασιλεύων βασιλευόντων, supports a Palaeologan date. The brickwork is of the decorative type which came into great popularity in later Byzantine times, and the building itself is ornate and spacious. It probably gives a good idea of what the later imperial and princely palaces of the Byzantine world were like. On stylistic grounds an assignation to as early as the tenth century is most unlikely.

K. Wulzinger, *Byzantinische Baudenkmäler zu Konstantinopel*, Hannover, 1925, pp. 64–89. For other interpretations of the monogram see S. Casson, *Preliminary Report upon Excavations in the Hippodrome of Constantinople in 1927*, Oxford, 1928, p. 41.

180 THE CHURCH OF ST THEODORE (KILISSE
CAMI). *10th–13th century. Constantinople.*

The identity of the present mosque of Kilisse Cami has been debated, but its association with the Church of St Theodore is now generally accepted, though it remains uncertain whether it is to be regarded as the Church of St Theodore τὰ καρβουνάρια or that of St Theodore πλησίον τοῦ χαλκοῦ τετραπύλου. The building is in two parts, a three-aisled domed church of the 'obscured cross' plan, with a transverse narthex, and an outer narthex of five bays, each roofed with a dome. The end bays of this are actually extended beyond the church; they originally probably communicated with subsidiary structures which have since disappeared. The exterior of this exo-narthex is one of the most attractive in Constantinople. Above are triple windows in semicircular openings; below there are arcades supported on two brick piers at the centre and on four marble columns, two at each side; those to the north have elegant lobed capitals; those to the south have Corinthian ones. Between the columns there are marble closure slabs with varying geometric motifs. Capitals and closure slabs alike are of sixth-century type, and represent re-used material, for the exo-narthex is itself an addition; it must date from the late thirteenth or early fourteenth century, while the church itself —the inner narthex and the church date from the same period —is to be assigned to the tenth century, though some, notably Diehl, have dated it to the eleventh.

In 1937 mosaics were discovered in the drums of two of the domes of the outer narthex; in the southern dome is the Virgin and Child, surrounded by Prophets, and in the central one, two palace functionaries and other Prophets; in both the gold cubes that formed the background have been robbed. The style is a characteristic of the fourteenth century, but the technique is not nearly as fine as at Kariye and the cubes are larger and coarser.

R. Janin, *La Géographie Ecclésiastique de l'Empire Byzantin*, III, Paris, 1953, pp. 155 and 161; A. Van Millingen, *Byzantine Churches in Constantinople*, London, 1912, Ch. XVI; J. Ebersolt and A. Thiers, *Les Eglises de Constantinople*, Paris, 1913, p. 147.

181 THE CHURCH OF ST SAVIOUR IN CHORA
Fig. 4 (KARIYE CAMI). *12th–14th century. Constantinople.*

There has been some dispute as to the meaning of the term 'Chora', one school of thought supporting the practical explanation that it is to be interpreted as meaning 'in the fields', the other that the term has a spiritual significance and should be interpreted as denoting the attributes of Christ as the sphere of man's highest aspirations. It is in this latter sense that the word is used in inscriptions in the mosaics, where the word appears in association with the representations of Christ as ἡ χώρα τῶν ζώντων and with that of the Virgin as ἡ χώρα τοῦ ἀχωρήτου. But this connotation is of late date and the name originally no doubt implied 'in the fields' or 'outside the walls'. The first building must thus have antedated the construction of the land walls by Theodosios II early in the fifth century. The church is supposed to have been rebuilt by Justinian, as the earliest

one was destroyed by an earthquake in 558. It was again rebuilt in the seventh century, thanks to an extensive endow-ment made by Priscus, who had ended his days as a monk there; a number of important persons were buried there in the eighth century; in the Iconoclast period the monastery attached to it was suppressed and the church apparently suffered severely. It was restored in the ninth century, but by the reign of Alexios Comnenos (1081–1118) it was again in ruins. It was then rebuilt more or less on the plan that exists today, that is, a square, domed 'bema' preceded by a transverse narthex, thanks to the munificence of Alexios's mother-in-law, Maria, wife of Andronicos Ducas. It is probable that the superb marble revetment of the bema, as well as the dedication to the Saviour, also dates from this period. The marbles have recently been cleaned and now present a clearer picture of a Byzantine interior than does any other structure. The building was further embellished by Isaac II, who intended that he should be buried there; for long the 'Deesis' mosaic (Plate XXXI) was associated with him.

The church and buildings of the monastery suffered again during the Latin inter-regnum, but were restored by Theodore Metochites during his years of prosperity as Grand Logothete of the Treasury; he ended his days there as a monk in 1331. He probably built the outer narthex and the 'pareccleseion' or side aisle on the north, and certainly set up the mosaics that now decorate the two narthices, as well as those of the church itself. The wall-paintings of the pareccleseion are also to be assigned to his day. Metochites's work was finished before 1321, for Nicephoras Gregoras, writing in that year, notes that the church had been reopened. Work had been begun before 1303, for one of the mosaic panels bears that date in Arabic numerals. The building was converted into a mosque between 1495 and 1511, and the minaret was added at that time; the central dome is in the main a restoration of Turkish date. Apart from these wide generalities, the architectural history of the building presents numerous problems which will only be solved when the very full examination that the church is now undergoing by members of the staff of the Byzantine Institute of America has been completed.

R. Janin, 'Eglises et Monastères', *La Géographie Ecclésiastique de l'Empire Byzantin*, III, Paris, 1953, p. 545; A. Van Millingen, *Byzantine Churches in Constantinople*, London, 1912, p. 288.

XXVIII THE MOSAICS OF ST SAVIOUR IN CHORA
–XXXI (KARIYE CAMI). *1300–1320. Constantinople.*
182–4

The church itself (Plate 181, Fig. 4) dates from various periods, but a recent examination conducted on behalf of the Byzantine Institute of America shows that the mosaic decoration is all of one date; it was set up under the patronage of Theodore Metochites between about 1303 and 1320, during the time that he was a prosperous court official; he later fell into disgrace and ended his days as a monk in the monastery he had formerly so richly endowed.

The mosaics decorated the church itself and the two narthices that precede it. Only three panels now survive in the church; on the eastern wall are Christ on one side, the Virgin on the other, below sculptured arcades; over the west door is the Dormition of the Virgin. The greater part of the decoration of the narthices is on the other hand preserved. The mosaics of the roof and upper parts of the walls comprise two cycles, illustrating the life of the Virgin and the life of Christ. The scenes of the former follow the Protoevangelion of St James; those concerned with Christ deal with His life only; the Passion scenes were perhaps shown in the church itself. Of the main scenes the Flight into Egypt (Plate XXIX) and the Nativity (Plate XXVIII) are especially well preserved. Both are shown in great detail and the colouring is through-out of unusual brilliance. The Numbering of the People is especially effective as a composition (Plate 184); the Annunciation to Elizabeth at the well shows the intimacy and tenderness of the work (Plate 183). The Pantocrator over the door of the inner narthex is more conservative in style (Plate 182).

In addition to the scenes, one or two other compositions are included, the most important of which are a panel with Christ and the Virgin on the eastern wall at the south end of the inner narthex, usually known as the 'Deesis' panel (Plate XXXI), and a panel over the door from the inner narthex into the church, where Metochites is depicted, presenting a model of the church to Christ (Plate XXX). He wears a high head-dress, very like those worn by Turkish courtiers in early prints, and an elaborate mantle made, no doubt, from one of the silks woven on the Constantinopolitan looms. It is a fine decorative work, and may be compared with the portrait of the High Admiral Apocaucos in a fourteenth-century copy of Hippocrates in the Bibliothèque Nationale, Paris (Ms. gr. 2144; see Plate XXXIV).

Though less decorative, the panel with Christ and the Virgin is in some ways perhaps more important, for the work is outstandingly fine and delicate. At one time it was thought that this panel was of earlier date than the other mosaics in the church, and it was, by Kondakov and others, assigned to the twelfth century and to the period of the church's reconstruction by Isaac II. Recent cleaning conducted on behalf of the Byzantine Institute of America has, however, disclosed two additional figures on a smaller scale than those of Christ and the Virgin; one is a commemorative portrait of Isaac Porphyrogenitus, son of Alexios Comnenos, and the other depicts a nun named Melane. They are accompanied by inscriptions; that associated with Melane shows that she was none other than the Princess Maria Palaeologina, daughter of Michael VIII Palaeologos and sister of the Emperor Andronicos II (1282–1328); she was married to the Mongol Khan Abagu in 1265, and on his death in 1281 she returned to Constantinople and founded the Church of St Mary of the Mongols. She became a nun some time after 1307, for in that year her remarriage was contemplated. The portrait must therefore be later in date than 1307, and as a technical examination shows that the mosaic is undoubtedly all of one date, the fact that it is of the same period as the other mosaics in the church can no longer be doubted.

The scenes as a whole are particularly lively; they are full of detail and the figures are expressive as well as elegant. The palette is particularly varied, and the decorative effect of these mosaics is unsurpassed. The church is, in fact, a jewel in itself—one of the most, if not the most, precious example of later Byzantine art that has come down to us. The admirable work of cleaning, conducted by the Byzantine Institute over the last five or six years, has served to enhance its richness, and to prove, if proof were indeed needed, the outstanding quality of the art of the so-called Byzantine Revival in the fourteenth century.

H. E. del Medico, 'La mosaique de la Dormition à Kahrie Djami', *Byzantion*, VII, 1932, Plate 123; P. A. Underwood, 'The Deesis Mosaic in the Kariye Cami at Istanbul' in K. Weitzmann, *Late Classical and Mediaeval Studies in Honor of A. M. Friend*, Princeton, 1955, p. 254. The standard work still remains that of Th. Schmidt, 'Kahrie Djami', *Transactions of the Russian Institute at Constantinople*, XI, Sofia, 1906 (in Russian, with album of plates).

XXXII, 185 THE WALL-PAINTINGS OF ST SAVIOUR IN CHORA (KARIYE CAMI). c. 1310. *Constantinople.*

Beside the main church, and extending as far west as the exo-narthex, stands a side-chapel or pareccleseion. It is rectangular in plan, with an apse at the east end and a dome at the centre. There are elaborately sculptured tomb niches in the north and south walls below the dome. Otherwise the interior was formerly entirely decorated with wall-paintings. The greater part of the painted area survives intact, in remarkably good condition; the task of cleaning off defacement and overpainting done during the Turkish period which has been in progress for some years is now complete. Like that of cleaning the mosaics, it has been undertaken by the Byzantine Institute of America, but in this case work which was completely obscured has been brought to light, whereas the beauty of the mosaics was already known, though it has been considerably enhanced by the cleaning. The paintings are of outstanding quality, and the decoration of the chapel constitutes a unity which can be justly compared so far as quality is concerned with the almost exactly contemporary decoration of Giotto's Arena Chapel at Padua.

The scenes that are shown at Kariye are somewhat un-usual, though well suited to a mortuary chapel. In the apse is the Anastasis—the scene where Christ descends to Hell and raises up Adam from the dead; it was the scene usually chosen by the Byzantines to depict the Resurrection. In the

334

bema are the Raising of Jairus's daughter and the Raising of the Widow's son; in the dome are the Virgin and Child at the centre and below, above the windows, the Twelve Angels of the Lord, separated one from the other by decorative bands of great beauty; in the pendentives are four Old Testament scenes, all having some reference to the theme of death and resurrection; the same is true of the scenes on the walls below.

The work is of great excellence, and is to be attributed to the hand of a master of outstanding ability, but he remains anonymous. Underwood has, however, suggested that it is possible that he is to be identified as the very man who designed the mosaics, though he would of course have been aided by assistants in the actual setting of the latter. But whether or not the master is the same, the frescoes are to be attributed to the same date, the early years of the fourteenth century.

Their discovery is particularly fortunate, for evidence has been gradually accumulating since Gabriel Millet first went to Greece in the nineties of the last century, to prove the high quality of later Byzantine painting. But until the cleaning of the Kariye paintings nothing was known from the capital itself. The style of the work is finished, accomplished and decorative. It lacks the greater realism of contemporary work at Salonica, and it is from this point that it now becomes possible to trace the separation of the two main schools or trends in later Byzantine painting, the 'First Revival' or 'Macedonian' school, with its centre at Salonica, and the 'Second Revival' or 'Cretan' school, which we know best, from the wall-paintings of Mistra. This school descended in a direct line from that developed around 1300 at Constantinople, and exemplified in the Kariye frescoes.

P. A. Underwood, 'First preliminary report on the restoration of the frescoes in the Kariye Cami at Istanbul by the Byzantine Institute', *Dumbarton Oaks Papers*, Nos. 9 and 10, 1955-56, p. 255, and No. 11, 1957, p. 175.

XXXIII MOSAIC: CHRIST. CHURCH OF ST MARY PAMMAKARISTOS (FETIYE CAMI). *14th century. Constantinople.*

Mosaics in the dome of a side-chapel have for long been visible; others, in the apse and on the walls of the same chapel, are now being cleaned by the Byzantine Institute of America. At the centre of the dome is a bust of our Lord as the Pantocrator—the usual subject for the dome of a mid or later Byzantine church. He is surrounded below by the Twelve Apostles; here they are actually on the vault of the dome; a century or so earlier they would probably have been on the drum, so that a larger area would have been available for the medallion of the Pantocrator.

The colours are rich, the attitudes of the Apostles alive and varied, and our Lord's expression gentle and tender.

The work is, however, rather less brilliant than that at Kariye. It is, none the less, typical of the revival style and is to be assigned to the first half of the fourteenth century.

186-7 ST MARY PAMMAKARISTOS (FETIYE CAMI). *13th century. Constantinople.*

Originally there was a monastery on the site; Michael Tarchaniotes Glabas was its benefactor some time before 1293, but there was probably an older church there before that. At a subsequent date the building appears to have been transformed into a nunnery, for there were nuns in it in 1455, when it was taken over by the Patriarchate; in 1586 it became a mosque.

Nothing of the monastery remains above ground except for the church, and that has been considerably altered since it became a mosque, though the original plan of a three-aisled, three-apsed church with central dome and extensive narthex is apparent inside. The date of the building is uncertain, but it is probably not later than the tenth century. While it was still a church, perhaps when Glabas endowed it towards the end of the thirteenth century, it was enlarged by the addition of an exo-narthex and outer aisles. The aisle to the south terminated in a side-chapel or pareccleseion. At the eastern end this is now the most attractive part of the building. Inside, it has important mosaics (Plate XXXIII) and good capitals decorated with acanthus leaves in low relief. Outside, it is adorned with niches and blank arcading of unusual elaboration. It is one of the best examples of a later Byzantine exterior that survive in the capital.

R. Janin, *La Géographie Ecclésiastique de l'Empire Byzantin*, III, Paris, 1953, p. 217; A. Van Millingen, *Byzantine Churches in Constantinople*, London, 1912, Ch. VII; J. Ebersolt and A. Thiers, *Les Eglises de Constantinople*, Paris, 1913, p. 225.

XXXIV, MANUSCRIPT OF HIPPOCRATES. C. 1342.
188 *Paris. Bibliothèque Nationale; Ms. gr. 2144. Ht. 41.5 cm. W. 35 cm.*

There are only two illustrations in this manuscript; one, on f. 10v., depicts Hippocrates in a bright red cloak, seated on a brown throne, with a greyish curtain behind. The other (f. 11) shows the High Admiral Apocaucos seated on a large wooden throne; there are red curtains in the corners, and the head of a small figure, perhaps his page, appears over the back of the throne. The costume is greyish-blue in colour, and must have been modelled on one of the finest figured silks of the Constantinopolitan looms, similar to actual examples of earlier date that survive. His name and title, 'Great Duke Apocaucos', is written between the curtains over his head.

The manuscript was done for Apocaucos who was High Admiral and prefect of Constantinople during the minority of John V Palaeologos (1341–1347); he was murdered in 1345, so that the manuscript must date from about 1342. The style may be compared to that of panels of the second half of the fourteenth century, like the Christ Pantocrator in the Hermitage of 1363 (*Lazarev*, Plate 318), or an icon at Nicosia in Cyprus with Christ above and the portrait of a princess below, dating from 1356 (D. Talbot Rice, *The Icons of Cyprus*, 1937, No. 6). The style in all of these is rather drier than that of the early fourteenth century, for example, in the Kariye mosaics.

Omont, *Miniatures*, Plates CXXVIII–CXXXIX; *Byzance*, No. 64.

XXXV ICON: THE TWELVE APOSTLES. *14th century. Moscow. The Museum of Fine Art. Ht. 38 cm. W. 34 cm.*

The Apostles are arranged in two rows, the four Evangelists in front, with haloes, the eight others behind. The background is gold, with an inscription above giving the title of the scene, 'The Assembly of the Twelve Apostles' and the names. The panel is hollowed out, with a broad margin.

The highlights, in narrow lines on the faces and broad splashes on the costumes, are in a manner characteristic of the first half of the fourteenth century. The style is in general close to that of Kariye and the work is to be regarded as typical of what was being done in Constantinople round about 1325.

Lazarev, I, Plate XLVI and II, Plate 305; *Burlington Magazine*, LXXI; for a coloured plate, see J. Myslevic, *Ikona*, Prague, 1947, Plate 1; *Edinburgh*, No. 208.

XXXVI, MINIATURE MOSAIC. DIPTYCH: THE
XXXVII TWELVE FEASTS. *14th century. Florence. Opera del Duomo. Height without frame 27 cm. Width of each panel 8 cm.*

The mosaics are mounted in a silver-gilt frame, adorned with enamels, all of later date. Six scenes are shown on each leaf, on one the Annunciation, the Nativity, the Presentation, the Baptism, the Transfiguration, and the Raising of Lazarus; on the other, the Entry into Jerusalem, the Crucifixion, the Anastasis, the Ascension, Pentecost, and the Dormition of the Virgin.

The work is fine and delicate; the flesh tones are carefully modelled, highlights being very sparingly used. The ground is gold. The mosaic is certainly to be assigned to Constantinople, for similarities to the wall mosaics of Kariye are marked. A comparison with the mosaic of the Crucifixion at Berlin (Plate 173) and that of the Annunciation in the Victoria and Albert Museum (Plate XXXVIII) suggests that it is perhaps rather later than the former and rather earlier than the latter. A date early in the fourteenth century is most likely, though the work might perhaps date from before the re-establishment of Byzantine rule in the capital; there is no reason to suppose that the production of works of art on a small scale entirely ceased as a result of the Latin conquest, even if large-scale mosaics were not done in Constantinople between 1204 and 1261.

V.S.D., Plates 73, 74. See also V. Lazarev, 'Byzantine Icons of the fourteenth and fifteenth centuries', *Burlington Magazine*, LXXI, 1937, p. 250.

XXXVIII MINIATURE MOSAIC: THE ANNUNCIATION. *14th century. London. Victoria and Albert Museum. Ht. 13·3 cm. W. 8·4 cm.*

The angel approaches from the Virgin's right. Both figures are tall, the Virgin especially so; they stand before an elaborate architectural background. The sky is gold.

The cubes are small, the work extremely delicate, and the colours unusually rich. The tall, elongated figures and the elaborate architectural background are both characteristic of the fourteenth century, and on the basis of style the mosaic may be assigned to a date around 1340; it is certainly rather later than the decoration of Kariye Cami. The work is, however, obviously Constantinopolitan.

Lazarev, Plate 303.

189 ICON: THE ARCHANGEL MICHAEL. *14th century. Pisa. Museo Civico. Ht. 32·8 cm. W. 24·5 cm.*

The panel is hollowed so that the archangel stands below a semicircular arch. His wings are spread behind; he holds a spear in his right hand with which a minute figure of the devil is being transfixed. From his left hand the scales of justice are suspended. The colours are particularly brilliant, and the icon is in unusually fresh condition.

The scales and the devil have apparently been repainted at a later date; they are not usually present in the Byzantine world; see for instance a somewhat similar icon in the Tretiakov Gallery at Moscow (Weidlé, Plate 20). The greater sobriety of this panel suggests that it should be assigned to a rather earlier date than the miniature mosaics of the Annunciation (Plate XXXVIII) or the Twelve Feasts (Plates XXXVI, XXXVII).

V. Weidlé, *Le Icone Bizantine e Russe*, Florence, 1950, Plate 21; *Lazarev*, p. 352, Notes 127 and 128, Plate 274; *Edinburgh*, No. 170.

XXXIX, MANUSCRIPT OF JOHN CANTACUZENOS.
190 *1370–1375. Paris. Bibliothèque Nationale; Ms. gr. 1242. Ht. 33·5 cm. W. 25 cm.*

The manuscript contains four full-page illustrations. On f. 5v. the emperor is shown enthroned between bishops and monks; he is presiding at the council summoned by him at Constantinople in 1351; on f. 92v. is shown the Transfiguration; on f. 93 is St Gregory Nazianzus enthroned; on

f. 123 v. is a second portrait of the emperor showing him standing full length with a monk after his abdication, with the Old Testament Trinity above.

The Transfiguration is closely similar to panel paintings of the second half of the fourteenth century and is in the very effective manner characteristic of the period. The colouring is especially brilliant, and the work of high quality.

Omont, *Miniatures*, Plates CXXVI–CXXVII; *Byzance*, No. 50.

XL, MANUSCRIPT: LINCOLN COLLEGE TYPI-
191–2 CON. c. *1400. Oxford. The Bodleian Library. Ht. 25 cm. W. 18 cm.*

The manuscript contains the monastic rule of the Nunnery of Our Lady of Good Hope at Constantinople, preceded by a preface of the foundress, Euphrosyne Comnena Ducaena Palaeologina, who was grand-niece of the Emperor Michael VIII Palaeologos. The text is preceded by nine double portraits of the foundress, her parents and other members of her family (Plate XL), as well as by a picture of the Virgin of Good Hope (Plate 192) and one of the whole monastic community (Plate 191). Three distinct hands apparently worked on it. The book must have been produced in Constantinople between 1399 and 1400. The manuscript is on loan to the Bodleian Library (No. Gr. 35).

G. Mathew, *Byzantine Painting*, London, Plate 9; O. Pächt, *Bodleian Picture Books: Byzantine Illuminations*, Figs. 21, 22; *Edinburgh*, No. 195.

XLI– ICON: THE ANNUNCIATION. *14th century.*
XLIII *Skopolje. Macedonian State Collections. Ht. 92 cm. W. 68 cm.*

The Virgin is seated below a canopy in the form of a stone structure on four columns. The angel approaches from her right, while she shrinks back with a gesture of modesty. Behind the figures is an architectural composition; the sky above is gold. The painting is on a hollowed panel with margin of medium breadth. On the opposite face is a magnificent rendering of the Virgin and Child, with the special designation, 'The Saviour of Souls' (*Edinburgh*, No. 232). The icon was originally a processional one, and the places where a staff for carrying was mounted at the bottom are clearly discernible, though the staff has dis-appeared. The icon comes from the Church of St Clement at Ochrida.

Milković-Pepek suggests that this icon is by the same hand as several smaller ones from the same church showing Doubting Thomas (*Edinburgh*, No. 215), The Baptism (*Edinburgh*, No. 219) and other subjects, and he attributes all of them to the painter Michael, who signed the wall-paintings in the same church along with Eutychios. He

attributes a large icon of St Matthew which was also shown at Edinburgh (No. 227) to the latter painter. He wrote before the icons had been cleaned; now that they have been, the colouring and style of the Annunciation are seen to be quite distinct and the painter was obviously a different man from the one who did the other icons. The rather mono-chrome tones of the small panels and their very full composi-tions are typical of the Macedonian school; the brighter colours and the greater restraint of the Annunciation savour much more of Constantinople. Aesthetically it is far superior to the others, and its superb quality marks it out as a work of world-wide significance.

Michael and Eutychios, who did the wall-paintings in St Clement's, were working there around 1295, but the nature of the highlights and the general style of the Annun-ciation suggest a rather later date, and the first half of the fourteenth century seems more likely.

M. Corović-Ljubinković, *The Icons of Ochrid*, Belgrade, 1953, Plate 2 (before cleaning); P. Milković-Pepek, 'Les auteurs de quelques Ikones d'Ochrid du XIII–XIVs.; Mihailo ou Eutihie?', *Glasnik*, 1, No. 3, Skopolje, 1954 (in Serbo-Croat, with short summary in French); *Edinburgh*, No. 228.

XLIV, ICON: VIRGIN AND CHILD. *14th century.*
193 *Moscow. The Tretiakov Gallery. Ht. 76·5 cm. W. 62·5 cm.*

The Virgin holds the Child on her left arm; the type is that of the Hodegetria. She bears the special title, 'the Virgin of Pimen'. The panel is slightly hollowed, with a wide margin. A green undercoat was used and now shows through the superimposed colours to a far greater degree than was originally the case.

Lazarev assigns the icon to Constantinople and to the fourteenth century. He regards it as a metropolitan example of the style which was developed all over Greece and the Balkans from the fourteenth century onwards and which is usually termed the Italo-Cretan. He compares the richness of the painting to work of the Flemish school in the fifteenth century. The icon is certainly of outstanding importance from the artistic point of view, and is also undoubtedly to be regarded as a Constantinopolitan product.

Lazarev, Plate 322 and pp. 228–229; *Edinburgh*, No. 223.

194 EMBROIDERED EPITAPHIOS. *1407. London. The Victoria and Albert Museum; No. 8278. 1863. Ht. 86 cm. L. 1·38 m.*

The dead body of Our Lord is shown full length in the centre, with an angel at head and foot holding a liturgical fan. This is surrounded by a scroll pattern; in each corner is an Apostle, and around the margin runs an inscription—the text of a Good Friday hymn which reads 'Noble Joseph, when he had taken Thy pure Body from the tree, did wrap it in fine linen and spices, and sorrowing did lay it in a new sepulchre. An Angel stood between the Myrrh-bearing Women at the Tomb crying: – Spices are meet for the dead, but Christ hath revealed Himself as a stranger to corruption.' Above there is also a dedication, reading 'The prayer of the servant of God, Nicholas, son of the blessed John with his wife, and children. Amen. In the year 8915 [1407].'

The man is probably to be identified with a fourteenth-century notable of Serres in Macedonia. Epitaphioi of this type were used on Good Friday in the Orthodox world. The design is entirely embroidered, and such embroideries became very popular after about 1400. This is one of the earliest dated pieces.

G. Millet, *Broderies religieuses de style byzantin*, Paris, 1947, p. 89 and Plate CLXXXI.

195 EMBROIDERY: THE SO-CALLED 'DALMATIC OF CHARLEMAGNE'. *15th century. Rome. Museo Sacro Vaticano. Ht. 162 cm. Width at shoulders 144 cm.*

The decoration is embroidered in gold on a blue silk ground, with scenes from the New Testament. On the back is represented the Transfiguration, together with two subsidiary scenes; on the shoulders is shown the Communion of the Apostles; on the front is the Glorification of Christ between the Virgin and the Baptist, each heading an angelic procession. The background is filled in with a mass of stars, scrolls, etc.

This is actually a late orthodox vestment, and has no connexion with Charlemagne; it is first mentioned in an inventory of 1489, and is probably to be dated to the early fifteenth century. It is, however, an exceptionally fine example of a type of embroidery which became very popular in the late fourteenth century and remained so for another four hundred years. Embroideries of the same type are preserved in numerous museums and treasuries; many must have been done all over Greece and the Balkans, but few are as fine as the Vatican example, which is probably to be regarded as a Constantinopolitan work.

G. Millet, *Broderies religieuses de style byzantin*, Paris, 1947, p. 67 and Plates CXXXV-CLI.

196 GOLD RELIQUARY. *15th century. Istanbul. Topkapu Saray. L. 49 cm.*

The reliquary takes the form of an arm and hand, the latter naturalistically treated. At the back of the hand is an opening through which the relic itself is visible. At the wrist are inscriptions reading 'Prayer of the servant of God, Daniel, the monk. This is the hand of John the Baptist. Behold the lamb of God.' The last words are those normally associated with the Baptist on icons. The gold arm is covered with a lightly engraved design of stylized foliage.

The style of this ornament, as well as that of the lettering, suggests a date in the fifteenth century. The hand is supposedly that of St John the Baptist. It was no doubt taken over at the time of the Turkish Conquest.

It was at one time supposed that objects of great richness were replaced in the last phase of Byzantine culture in the fourteenth and fifteenth centuries by ones of a less precious type; the empire was admittedly much reduced and the court impoverished, but precious objects were still produced, and a number of examples may be cited, such as the reliquary at Quenca, or the Chalice of the Despot Manuel (1348-1380) in the monastery of Vatopedi on Mount Athos. The Saray reliquary is to be numbered among these. It was perhaps made in the capital as one of the last treasures produced there before the Turkish Conquest. A mark at the cuff would appear to be superimposed and later. It is not very clear and may be either a Turkish stamp or the mark of the Famagusta silversmiths, the arms of Jerusalem in a circle.

ACKNOWLEDGEMENTS

In addition to those mentioned in the Preface thanks are due to the following individuals and institutions for their assistance and kind permission to photograph objects and monuments in their charge:

Their Graces the Bishops of Cosenza and Rossano; the Priory of San Francesco, Cortona; the Trustees, Opera del Duomo, Florence; Dr Jean Babelon, Director, Cabinet des Médailles, Bibliothèque Nationale, Paris; Dr. P. Verlet, Director, and Dr M. Sallet, Conservator, Musée de Cluny, Paris; Dr Wolfgang Hörmann, Director, Department of Manuscripts; Bayerischen Staatsbibliothek, Munich; the Trustees, Library and Treasury of Topkapu Saray, Istanbul.

The photographs specially taken for this book by Professor Hirmer with the assistance of Miss Julia Asen were supplemented by illustrations from the undermentioned sources; the references are to the plate numbers:

XII; Verlag Bruckmann, Munich—XVII; British Museum, London—24, 25; Österreichische Nationalbibliothek, Vienna—36, 42; The Hermitage, Leningrad—40, 41, 53, 183, 184; Josephine Powell, Rome—70 (*above*); G. W. Allan, London—70 (*below*), 147, 168; H. Schmidt-Glassner, Stuttgart—71, 195; Alinari, Rome—76, 77; Th. Schmidt, *Koimesis-kirche*—79; W. F. Volbach, *Tessuti*—88, 89, 93, 165, 185; Byzantine Institute of America, Boston—94, 95, 128 (*above and below*), 176, 177; Dr Enzo Crea, Studio di Consulenza grafica editoriale, Rome—106, 108, 109, 112 (*below*), 145, 175, 194; Victoria and Albert Museum, London—112 (*above*); Metropolitan Museum of Art, New York—130; O. von Falke, *Seidenweberei*—131; Volbach, Salles, Duthuit, *L'Art Byzantin*—132, 139, 135; Giraudon, Paris—136; Bissinger, Erfurt—155; The Patriarchate, Istanbul—171; A. J. Anisimov, *Our Lady of Vladimir*—181; Atlantis-Verlag, Zürich.

GENERAL INDEX

AND ICONOGRAPHICAL INDEX

GENERAL INDEX